THE RAVENOUS EYE

It is Milton Shulman's belief that hitherto a child's development has been conditioned primarily by four major factors — the home, the neighbourhood, the school and the Church. Now, he suggests, television has reared its often misused and potentially ugly head as the fifth factor in this chain of influences.

No one who cares for the importance of the media in our modern lives can afford to ignore this book. It deserves to be taken seriously by all those interested in modern cultural and social forces — a book that is unlikely to be supplanted for many years to come as to its essential arguments and its sowing of seminal ideas.

MILTON SHULMAN is well known as a columnist on both the *Daily Express* and the *London Evening Standard*, writing on a host of subjects that includes politics, theatre and television. He is the author of a previously successful Coronet title on the collapse of the German armies in the Second World War — DEFEAT IN THE WEST.

The Ravenous Eye

Milton Shulman

CORONET BOOKS
Hodder and Stoughton

Copyright © by Milton Shulman 1971, 1973, 1975

First published in Great Britain 1973 by
Cassell and Company Limited

Coronet edition (revised) 1975

Printed and bound in Great Britain for
Coronet Books, Hodder and Stoughton,
St. Paul's House, Warwick Lane,
London, EC4P 4AH
By Cox & Wyman Ltd, London, Reading and Fakenham

ISBN 0 340 19855 9

CONTENTS

ISBN 0 340 19855 0

To Charles Wintour

Introduction

In December 1972 David Attenborough, a former head of BBC-2 and Director of BBC-TV programmes, gave up his administrative post to return to filming animals. Asked during a TV interview what he liked least about television, he replied, 'One of the things that worries me, which you can't very well say if you are a Director of Programmes, is that people watch television too much. The average man spends more time watching TV than any other activity except his work and sleeping.'

'What's wrong with that?' asked Michael Dean, one of his interviewers. 'What would you rather he did? Aren't you in Milton Shulman country? He'd rather we all gathered on village greens and danced around Maypoles and did handicraft.'

No doubt Mr. Dean would admit on reflection that most people lived reasonably fulfilled lives before television. Nor were Maypole dancing and handicrafts the only alternative means of recreation. But his remark indicates the views of some professional broadcasters that, for most people, watching the small screen is the most exalting and enhancing activity they are ever likely to experience.

This book takes a more sceptical view of the influence of the small screen. Six years of working in television and eight years of writing about it have convinced me that in its present primitive phase in countries like Britain and America it does, on balance, more harm than good. I certainly share David Attenborough's anxiety not only about the indiscriminate way in which people experience television but about the manner in which it is now taking over the hours of our lives. Even overriding the question of quality is the question of purpose and pervasiveness. There is much talk about access and participation. But there is too little thought given to the consequences for any society that encourages its citizens to become creatures of the box. Is there not a danger that more access to the box will merely produce *vicarious* participation rather than *real* participation?

It is only in recent years that evidence of the addictive nature of the medium has become available. The argument that no institution can adequately exercise its function — Parliament, the Church, the Law, the trade unions, the universities, the Monarchy — unless it is properly reflected on the small screen, indicates the trend, particularly in Britain, towards a telly society.

One might assume that if we are, indeed, facing the prospect of a television takeover, governments would display more awareness of the significance of the box. Although Britain is presumed to have one of the more responsible systems of broadcasting, the way in which television has retreated from any role of moral and cultural leadership has been the most characteristic feature of its post-war development. The casual manner in which British television has succumbed to the notion that the supply of entertainment is its primary and dominant function has been more fully described in my book, *The Least Worst Television in The World*.* Until it has been proved that television can have serious repercussions, some of which are undesirable, upon society, it is likely that governments will prefer drift to positive action about the medium.

This book, I hope, makes some contribution to the argument. I am resigned to the fact that some critics will claim that I have gone too far. Others will no doubt assert that I am blaming all the world's ills on television. Should they do so, I will console myself with the view that they have no more factual evidence than I have or that they have not understood the meaning of the book's half-title.

Many of the thoughts in *The Ravenous Eye* first occurred to me whilst writing a weekly TV column for the London *Evening Standard*. For giving me complete independence to express them over eight years — perverse and provocative as some of them may have sounded at the time — I must thank Sir Max Aitken, Chairman of Beaverbrook Newspapers, and Charles Wintour, editor of the *Evening Standard*. Since it was Charles Wintour's idea that I write on television in the first place, I am

* Barrie and Jenkins, London, 1973.

particularly grateful for the steadfast support he has given me and for the equanimity with which he has borne the abuse that has often been showered on him as on me because of something I had written.

I would also like to thank Ann Armitage for her research and for patiently typing this book over and over again through its many manifestations. Finally, a word for my wife, Drusilla, who has not only encouraged me to write this book but has been always ready to discuss and argue about most of the things in it.

CHAPTER ONE

Who Cares?

Of all the inventions of our time it is likely to prove the most destructive. Whereas nuclear power can only reduce us and our world to a cinder, the camera grinds us down to spiritual dust so fine that a puff of wind scatters it, leaving nothing behind.
Malcolm Muggeridge, *New Statesman*, June 21st, 1968

TV's power for good or evil is roughly equivalent to that of the hula-hoop.
Keith Waterhouse, *Punch*, July 20th, 1966

It sits there in the corner of the living-room relentlessly transmitting its mosaic of life. Image after image, incident after incident, emotion after emotion, juxtaposed with anarchic, confused and irresponsible logic. A man, doused in petrol, sets fire to himself outside the White House. A dentist discovers a gas to destroy mankind. Which is true? Which is false? A Biafran soldier is shot through the head by a Nigerian officer. An East European dictator is blown to smithereens by a devilish device set off by a man from UNCLE. Which demands our concern; which warrants our indifference? Does it matter?

Never before has man's mind been bombarded by so many facts, ideas, dreams, lies, fantasies in such rapid succession in so compressed a period of time. An ordinary evening's television viewing in Britain and America can be equivalent to seeing a one-act play in the theatre; skimming through a short story; going to the town hall to hear a political debate; being harangued or flattered or frightened by fifty salesmen trying to sell their wares; glancing through the main items in a newspaper; sitting in a stadium at a football game; watching a discussion about social or moral problems in a university lecture room.

Before television, some individuals might have experienced one or two of these activities perhaps once a week; some, once or twice a year; some hardly at all. Now it happens to most people almost every day of the year. The average Briton or American devotes to television more hours than any other average person before him devoted to radio, books, theatre, cinema and newspapers *combined*. Does the individual psyche remain immune to this unique battering of visual and aural stimuli? Can any society, deeply immersed in the telly environment, remain unaffected by its influences and pressures? Does it matter?

Anyone would concede that a child brought up from infancy in the Brazilian jungle would be different from a child reared in New York. Anyone would agree that a child who had lived its formative years in Tokyo would have different values and attitudes from a child raised and educated in London. Similarly, it must be evident that any child brought up in the television age, any child who spends 22,000 hours between the ages of 3 and 18 watching the small screen, who spends more hours under the influence of the box than under the influence of its parents, its teachers, its neighbours, or its priests, must be different from a child who was born and reared in a non-television age. Is that difference unimportant, minimal, illusory?

Until very recently the proposition that TV — the goggle box, the idiot screen, chewing gum for the eyes, moving wall-paper — could make any significant, durable, worthwhile or malevolent impact upon the nature or shape of a mature, industrial society would have been greeted by snorts of derision. Perhaps the most astonishing phenomenon in television since its rapid development has been the refusal of important people to take it seriously. 'Important' in this context means those persons who are theoretically in control of the social and political apparatus and who are conveniently labelled as Authority, the Establishment or the Government.

Is it possible to confine the most powerful medium of mass communication man has yet devised to the fringes of our national life? Can television be largely monopolised by the values of the advertiser and the entertainer without setting up attitudes and tensions and frustrations which might have profound effects — some dangerous, some revolutionary, some salutary, some welcome — on the nature of our society?

If the over-all image of our civilisation as reflected on the small screen is trivial, frivolous and violent will it not set up, particularly amongst the young, patterns of imitative acceptance, on the one hand, and spasms of violent rejection, on the other? Can the countervailing influences of formal education, home environment, parental control, religious teaching, conventional mores, reduce the conditioning power of television to negligible proportions? Lastly, is there any danger that the electronic jester in our midst is slowly becoming a beaming cyclops, devouring with its ravenous eye old attitudes, values and assumptions and leaving in their place little but an illusory euphoria and an increased demand for consumer goods?

Curiously enough, it is these root questions about television, these awkward queries digging back into the very foundations of the medium and its organisation and structure, that are so often dismissed as tendentious or pedantic or irrelevant.

Yet when it comes to the details of the small screen — the individual programme rather than the telly totality — there is a plethora of comment, protest, concern. Each separate interest-group in Britain is almost hyper-sensitive about how it is depicted and projected on the box. Whenever television dares to involve itself in a discussion or assessment of anything touching upon the commercial or political interests of any significant sector of the community, there is an almost paranoiac sifting of the minutiae of the programme to determine what beneficial or baleful influence it might have had.

Politicians, of course, have been intensely conscious of the impact of television upon their careers ever since John Kennedy's 1960 Presidential victory following the much-discussed Kennedy–Nixon television debates. But while they are aware of what television can do to political parties and parliamentary institutions, they display a curious complacency when they are asked to contemplate what it is doing to other aspects of our national life. If television has changed our attitudes to politicians, why should it not also change our intellectual attitudes, our behaviour patterns, our moral standards? Whether this change is for the better or for the worse is only part of the problem. The very speed at which society is changing and the ability of our institutions and leaders to adjust are also matters for urgent consideration. Delayed, ignorant or

15

apathetic governmental responses to this catalytic element in our midst could be costly and possibly dangerous.

Bedevilling the entire discussion about television is the abysmal absence of hard facts and convincing statistical evidence about its impact and influence. Comparatively little has been done in this significant field of research either in Britain or America, and the pros and cons in this debate are equally matched in ignorance. In this arena, opportunities for scaremongering, demagogic appeals for censorship, smug complacency, pseudo-sociology, academic hair-splitting are wide open.

'Television is thought by many as an extremely important agent of mass persuasion and mass change,' said Dr. William Belson, Director of the Survey Research Centre at the London School of Economics. 'For the great majority of programmes we know little or nothing about the extent of the changes they *actually* produce. This applies both to programme material which is *intended* to produce changes and to programmes which we may suspect are *incidentally* producing changes.'[1]

Stuart Hood, former BBC Controller of TV Programmes, confirms this assessment by an eminent social researcher in the TV field, from a TV executive's point of view. 'The fact is that we know far too little about the effects of television,' he wrote in the London *Spectator*, 'far too little about the role it plays in the lives of the viewers and in the life of their communities, far too little about what they take from it.'[2]

Like the printing press before it, television is altering society. But society has had 500 years to adjust to the changes that were taking place through the spread of the printed word. We will not be vouchsafed such a generous allotment of time to condition ourselves to the changes wrought by television. It is the very speed with which television can challenge, upset, modify and destroy our existing attitudes and conventions that can produce significant dislocations in our society if the men in charge of it have little idea about what is happening.

Television alone cannot change the entire structure of society. In some spheres it may merely reflect and not perceptibly influence shifts in the social structure; in other places its presence may act as the catalyst that hastens the fruition and frenzy of changes already bubbling to the surface; and in some cases television could be the dominant element bringing about changes that might never have occurred in the manner, in the style and at the time that they did take place were it not for its impact. Can we discern, then, in which areas of our society the TV factor is playing a minor or major part? If we acknowledge the existence of a TV factor, where does it play a *positive* role, where a *probable* role, and where a *peripheral* role?

Without any convincing data one can, at this stage, merely pose intuitive questions. By examining the manner in which television has evolved in Britain and America since the war, and by studying the programming trends and values that dominate television output in those countries, I hope to show that there are definite links between the medium and certain important aspects of social behaviour and certain changes in our social institutions.

Since it is obvious that the impact of television on behaviour patterns varies, it is necessary to attempt some sort of evaluation of the force of that impact and the likelihood of its operating in certain social areas. Where I believe the impact is profound and certain, it will be said a *positive* TV factor is at work. Where the impact is important but the logical link with television more speculative, it will be claimed that a *probable* TV factor is operating. Where the impact is indirect and oblique in the sense that other institutions have been forced to change or adjust purely because television exists, then it will be said a *peripheral* TV factor is functioning.

In examining the impact of television I am certainly not predicting a sudden, cataclysmic upheaval of our social structure caused by a malevolent electronic genie. Every social organism changes; in some of these cases television's only contribution will be to hasten that change. And many of these changes will probably be for the better. But, if unrecognised, the very speed of the changes can have dangerous consequences. Societies must inevitably adjust to every form of moral, economic, and technological pressure. But what extra disturbances will mankind have to suffer, what extra costs will have to be paid, what extra mistakes will have to be rectified, if the TV factor in our lives continues to be as neglected and ignored as it is today? When historians survey these decades of the 60s and 70s, I feel confident that they will be much more aware of the effects of television than those who now dismiss it as having about as much influence as the hula-hoop. The ravenous eye, subtly preying on values, surreptitiously absorbing institutions, steadily shifting foundations and traditions, can no longer be made to go away. Posterity will certainly shake its head and marvel that we cared and did so little about it.

CHAPTER TWO

The Medium With a Difference

> *Today, suddenly, because all the peoples of the world are part of one electronically based, intercommunicating network, young people everywhere share a kind of experience that none of their elders ever have had or will have.*
>
> Margaret Mead, *Culture and Commitment*

> *The man at home at his own fireside after a busy day at the office, desk or factory bench, or the woman marooned by her children in a multi-story block of flats, primarily does not want to be educated. They want to be entertained — and what is wrong with that?* (Cheers)
>
> Lord Denham, debate in the House of Lords, *The Times*, May 20th, 1971

'A social scientist at the Massachusetts Institute of Technology recently put up a scheme for research into "television tastes" that will take more than twenty years to complete. The intention is that 500 four-year-old children will be asked to keep a diary of their television viewing for one week a year for the next two decades. It is expected that a minimum of one hundred persons of each sex will complete the marathon, and that the diaries will then tell an interesting tale of the development of their likes and dislikes. What further conclusions might be drawn from such research remain to be seen — all one can say is that they will entirely depend on the intelligence and aptitude of the investigators. But research on some such massive scale is now clearly necessary if the impact of television on our lives is to be properly measured.'

This comment from a leader column in *The Times Literary Supplement* of February 18th, 1965 poses the dilemma facing anyone trying to assess the social consequences of television. Is it possible to debate intelligently the question of the impact of television without the evidence of long-term research? And even if the Massachusetts Institute of Technology acquires its twenty-year diaries meticulously kept by conscientious guinea-pigs, one can be reasonably sure that whatever interpretation is put on these case histories will be hotly contested by opposing factions of social scientists, pyschiatrists and other experts on human behaviour. That, at least, is the record of such short-term research as has been done on television and there is little reason to assume that long-term research will fare any better.

The only concrete, uncontested, generally admitted fact about the social consequences of television is that we know very little about it. In the words of Mr. James Halloran, one of the handful of social scientists in Britain studying the problem, the discussion about the effects of television has been 'a heated rather than an enlightened one'.[1]

The *cri de coeur* that rises from any governmental body or investigative committee charged with the task of trying to find a causal link between the small screen and some particular social phenomenon is that the facts at their disposal are both inadequate and contradictory. The Pilkington Committee, for example, boldly took the line that if no convincing evidence was available to the contrary, it must be assumed that television was a major factor in shaping our society.

'So far, there is little conclusive evidence of the effects of television on values and moral attitudes,' its Report noted. 'But those who work professionally in this sphere told us that what evidence there was, showed that there was an effect. We were told that this effect, good or bad, need not be sudden or spectacular. Rather it was compared with that of water dripping on a stone; persistent, apparently imperceptible, but in the end prevailing. It may be that in this sphere cause and effect can never be absolutely demonstrable ... Our own judgment, after weighing such evidence as is available to us, leads us to a clear conclusion. It is that unless and until there is unmistakable proof to the contrary, the presumption must be that television is and will be a *main* [my italics] factor in influencing the values and moral standards of our society.'[2]

More depressing than the lack of research is the inability of

20

governments or establishment bodies to agree about the relevance of such research that has been done and to use it to correct or ameliorate social ills.

'It is almost axiomatic that, when government investigations fail to lead to meaningful action, the same problems are investigated once again,' writes Mr. Arnold Arnold about the American situation in his book *Violence and Your Child*. 'This semblance of activity is a substitute for genuine solutions or an excuse for inaction. Those who have anything to gain by maintaining the status quo plead for "further study". Thus, violence in all its forms has been investigated eight times by government bodies in the past 15 years. Nothing has changed. In fact, the evidence indicates that the conditions have deteriorated steadily, the media have become more harmful and the effect on youth increasingly disastrous.'[3]

Although there is much talk about the imperative need for hard facts and interpretative research about the influence of television, it cannot be said that it is an issue about which many people feel very deeply. The public, politicians, broadcasters and intellectuals are united in this indifference. Indeed, the assumption that television, conveniently branded and dismissed as a national plaything, should be worth serious consideration as a significant social influence strikes the ordinary man and many an intellectual as derisory. The public as a whole in Britain and America like television just as it is. The average man thinks of it as an entertainment medium and wants it to remain that way.

In Britain a Government social survey published in 1969 showed that watching television was by far the most popular pastime in the country.[4] A survey published in the *Evening Standard* by the Opinion Research Centre in 1968 showed that 47 per cent of people listed television as the leisure activity to which they gave most of their time. By comparison 17 per cent said they gave most of their time to gardening, 16 per cent to reading papers and books, 10 per cent to going to a pub, 8 per cent to sport, 2 per cent to going to a cinema. Of the leisure activities most enjoyed, as opposed to being done, 32 per cent chose television. Only 4 per cent most enjoyed the cinema.[5] Similar surveys in America show that television is by far the most popular leisure activity and most people, although they may evince concern about certain of its effects, are not anxious to see it changed very much.

The British viewers have few articulate views about television. They accepted the Reithian concept of broadcasting without complaint. They displayed no passionate desire for commercial television but, when it came, accepted it gratefully. They were not, on the whole, over-concerned about the more liberal, controversial edge given to the BBC by its Director-General, Sir Hugh Greene, nor are there any signs of protest from them now that the BBC is retreating to a less involved, more orthodox posture. It seems that almost anything could be done with television, so long as it is changed subtly and not too abruptly and so long as it retains a reasonable entertainment element, without the general public evincing outrage, interest or concern. They like what they have and cannot see that it can possibly do them any harm. In their complacency and equanimity, the British television public resembles smokers before there was any evidence that cigarettes could be responsible for cancer and heart disease. There is, therefore, no pressure coming from the mass audience itself demanding any more knowledge about the impact of television.

The politicians, too, are well aware that there are no votes to be gathered worrying about the organisation, structure or philosophy of television. Government after government has been prepared to accept the idea that television should be treated primarily as an entertainment medium and that the more it is confined to this area the less of a nuisance it will be.

In America, too, the attacks by Spiro Agnew when he was Vice-President on the bias and integrity of current affairs commentators and broadcasters reveal this impulse on the part of politicians to neutralise the medium. As the broadcasters bow under this pressure, television becomes increasingly institutionalised, increasingly innocuous, increasingly a reflection of the status quo, increasingly a pliant aspect of the nation's power structure.

Politicians, like the public, prefer to rely upon their instincts rather than information when dealing with the medium. Their instincts tell them that the checks and balances they have instituted — the Governors of the BBC and the IBA* in Britain and

* Early in 1972 the Independent Television Authority changed its

the Federal Communications Commission in America — will provide the necessary supervision to safeguard the interests of parties and the people.

Nor are the broadcasters very keen on research about the medium since it is time-consuming, costly, and might bring into question their competence and sense of responsibility. In America broadcasters are perfectly prepared to boast about any research that reveals TV's great selling power, but they are not so keen to investigate its influence over other patterns of behaviour.

In a statement given to the National Commission on the Causes and Prevention of Violence in December, 1968, by Mr. Nicholas Johnson, a Federal Communications Commissioner, the don't-blame-me, we-have-no-influence argument of American broadcasters was demolished. 'Whenever the question arises of the impact of television programming upon the attitudes and behavior of the audience, industry spokesmen are likely to respond with variants of three big myths (1) We give the people what they want . . . (2) Entertainment programming doesn't have any "impact" upon people . . . (3) We report the news . . .'

Mr. Johnson then pointed out that television is sustained by advertising and that it attracts something like 2·5 billion dollars annually from advertisers on the assumption that it is the advertising medium with the greatest impact. Could it seriously be claimed that this influence only asserted itself upon buying habits and upon nothing else?

To show how television has changed living habits in America, Johnson cited the Brooklyn sociologist, Dr. Clara T. Appell whose research revealed that because of television 60 per cent of American families had changed their sleep patterns, 55 per cent had changed their eating schedules and 78 per cent used television as an 'electronic babysitter'. Could it seriously be contended that if television had these effects, it could not possibly influence the aggressive behaviour of children or play some part in other significant aspects of human activity?[6]

While one can understand British commercial executives

---

name to the Independent Broadcasting Authority. When dealing with events prior to 1972, the intitials ITA will be used for the Authority.

agreeing with their American counterparts that the influence of television is over-rated and that the system now prevailing is the best of all possible systems, it is odd that BBC broadcasters are also eager to deprecate and underplay the medium in which they operate as a serious social force. They are keen to emphasise the entertainment function of television and thereby imply that its impact is superficial and relatively harmless. They pour scorn on the possibility that British television could have any serious bearing on the increase in violence in Britain. They deny the suggestion that television creates attitudes and insist that television does nothing more than act as a mirror or a reflection of the society in which it operates. If anything is going wrong it is the fault not of television but of society. They resort to overworked theories and dubious research to prove that television is little more than a glittering pool in which society can see its image, ripples and all.

It should be added that the defensive posture constantly adopted by broadcasters when their role is questioned is not surprising. After all, they are where they are because they efficiently produce what is now demanded of the medium. If it were decided that television should have its entertainment-bias seriously curtailed or its function reformed, there would have to be significant personnel changes at all levels of the television hierarchy. No wonder there is little keenness amongst most broadcasters to investigate or disturb the existing nature of TV.

We have seen how the public, the politicians and the broadcasters — united in their belief that television's most commendable function is to entertain the masses — have formed an unconscious conspiracy to belittle the power of the medium. Another group that has remained largely indifferent to the argument about the impact of the medium and by their aloofness acquiesced in the assumption that television is unimportant, is, oddly enough, the academic and intellectual world. In Britain their emotions can be aroused when the structure and function of radio is challenged, as was clearly seen when dons protested vehemently about the BBC's decision to kill its cultural Third Programme. But they display an only intermittent interest in the small screen.

'Too many of the "intelligentsia" hate serious analysis of the media,' wrote Richard Hoggart in his book *Speaking To Each Other*. 'They prefer them to be kept in a compartment labelled "For Fun Only"; and they dismiss attempts to discuss them as "puritan", "over-earnest", "old-fashioned moralising".'

In America, where television is so deprived of serious content as to be a cultural wasteland, the intellectuals are even more contemptuous of the medium than in Britain. Occasionally someone like Arthur Schlesinger Jr. makes a speech or writes an article attempting to assess the contribution television makes to the ever-increasing atmosphere of violence in America. Or someone like the German philosopher Herbert Marcuse, teaching at the University of California, will identify television as a significant part of the indoctrinating apparatus which conditions the American people to accept the corrupting and repressive aspects of Western capitalism. But the more common view amongst the intellectual élite is that television is not a cause but an effect, not a concern but a frivolity.

There are, of course, a number of other reasons why intellectuals are patronising and detached from television. One can, for example, consider Marshall McLuhan's explanation. This controversial sage of our electronic age believes that it has something to do with the reluctance of a print-conditioned cultural establishment to face up to the implications of the potential power of the new non-verbal media. 'Our Western values, built on the written word, have already been considerably affected by the electric media of telephone, radio and television,' he writes. 'Perhaps that is the reason why many highly literate people in our own time find it difficult to examine the question without getting into a moral panic.'

Jonathan Miller, who has not only worked in television but has written a devastating attack on McLuhanism,[7] has articulated this resistance to crediting TV with any original or important qualities. 'Television is simply a hole through which you push various communications,' he said in an interview.[8] And in a television discussion in April 1971, he firmly insisted that television was not a medium at all but merely 'a letter box'.[9] The use of this metaphor, with its implication that television is merely a receptacle for written ideas, is a particularly apt illustration of McLuhan's analysis of the way many intellectuals react to the output of the small screen.

It is evident, too, that television has not yet indicated that it has any unique or distinctive qualities as an art form. Its handling of film — the way in which it is cut, edited, juxtaposed — is rarely, because of limited finances, as adroit, imaginative or subtle as that of the cinema. Videotape, although it is quicker and less expensive to use than celluloid, tends to make a clumsier visual statement than film. Again this is due more to restricted technical facilities than to any inherent inferiority of tape *vis-à-vis* celluloid. It is, indeed, well recognised that television is too often the art of the cheap budget.

Another reason the intellectuals and academics resist any serious examination of television is their natural fear of state control over ideas. In the mind of the liberal, control suggests rigid censorship. In America it is assumed that the dictatorship of Madison Avenue over broadcasting contents is preferable to the supervision of Congress or the President. In Britain, too, intellectuals feel that television run as entertainment is less likely to interfere with basic liberties than if it were part of some more integrated aspect of the educational, informational and recreational system. The choice, of course, is not so stark as that between unfettered show business and a restrictive state apparatus. The choice is really between varying degrees of social responsibility and ensuring that men with the proper priorities are placed in charge of the medium. The intellectual dilemma was faced by the famous political commentator, Walter Lippmann. 'A continual exposure of a generation to the commercial exploitation of the enjoyment of violence and cruelty is one way to corrode the foundations of a civilised society,' he wrote. 'For my own part, believing as I do in freedom of speech and thought, I see no objection in principle to censorship of the mass entertainment of the young. Until some more refined way is worked out of controlling this evil thing, the risks to our liberties are, I believe, decidedly less than the risks of unmanageable violence.'

Perhaps before going on to examine the influence of the television factor, one should review the barriers that stand in the way of any such examination. In the first place, although there is an instinctive presumption, as stated by the Pilkington Committee, when it investigated the impact of television in Britain, that TV is a *main* factor in the shaping of values and moral

26

standards, the research of social scientists has not yet been able to describe convincingly either the nature of that influence or how and in what areas of human behaviour it operates. This dearth of facts has resulted in the complacence of the vast majority of people concerning the manner in which the medium is structured and orientated. The public is happy about the use of television as primarily a relaxing and entertaining device; the politicians are content if television is neutralised and operates as a reassuring cement for the status quo; the broadcasters are eager to appease their masters — the politicians and the public — and go along with the view that the medium is not a message but a mirror, and that mirrors can do very little harm; and the intellectuals have been so alienated by the basic triviality of American and British television that they refuse to take its operation very seriously.

It is therefore with a certain amount of trepidation and humility that one puts forward the hypothesis that not only is television a major and significant factor in determining the values, morals and conduct of a society but that in any society where access to the television screen is substantial (let us say where over 60 per cent of the population regularly watches it) there is practically no aspect of human behaviour that is not affected by its presence. Sometimes such effects are substantial and important; often they are minimal and peripheral. But what is the case for such an hypothesis?

Now it is obvious that television like any other medium or any other environmental influence cannot *on its own* do anything. No individual comes to it as a physical blank devoid of an emotional or mental past; no individual leaves it without the prospect of coming into contact with environmental forces that will contradict, qualify, reinforce or intensify impressions he has received from the box. Even a two-year-old infant placed in front of the screen for the first time is already a product of conditioning influences that have aroused his five senses.

It is also obvious that each individual is an active battlefield in which environmental factors contend with hereditary ones and environmental pressures struggle against each other for influence over the psyche and the personality. Sometimes these factors reinforce each other (stable home and good school); sometimes they are at odds (unstable homes versus good

27

school). Some influences are weightier than others even if we cannot determine their exact relative importance. Television has been one of the consistently underestimated and ignored factors in the mysterious amalgam of forces that go into the making of a total human being.

It is generally accepted that the most dominant environmental factors in a child's life from birth to about ten years of age are the home and family, the neighbourhood, the school and the church. In countries where formal religion is discouraged the church is usually replaced by an alternative ideological absolute factor like Communism, Maoism or Fascism. Where television exists on a wide scale, I believe it ranks in children's lives as the fifth factor — alongside home, neighbourhood, school and church — in determining what values they will ultimately have and how they will eventually exercise them. Of course, it is a *contributing* factor, but a *major* contributing factor which demands as much attention and concern as we give to the quality of education a child receives, the impact of his neighbourhood, the influence of his parents and the inculcation of his spiritual or ideological beliefs.

As the child grows older into adolescence and maturity other factors like work, class, culture, status pressures, join the jostling regiment of influences on the human personality. But do these later value acquisitions and moral attitudes completely blot out or subdue or neutralise the values and attitudes received when the child was most receptive and vulnerable to fresh experiences? Of course not. That is why the Jesuits could confidently claim that if they had the child for his first seven years they would have the man for the rest of his life.

When assessing the influence of television at this stage in its development, one has to segregate by age the groups who have been exposed to the small screen. Someone brought up from infancy with the box as a sort of electronic nipple for three to four hours a day is likely to have been more affected by television than a man who started to watch it in middle-age when his views had acquired a tough shell of resistance to change.

'In assessing the generalisations about the effects of mass communication, it needs to be appreciated that very little work has been carried out on the role of television in the early stages of the child's development,' says the introduction to a study of

28

television and delinquency conducted at Leicester University. 'It may be true that television has relatively little influence when attitudes and values are well formed, but what about when they are not well formed, but are actually in the process of formation?'[10]

The most inhibiting aspect of any study of the consequences of television is the relatively tiny number of years in which we can say the medium existed at all as a social force. We are like the victims of an express train who have been hit and have only the sight of a fast, receding blur in the distance as evidence that anything really happened at all. Not only do we not know what has hit us but we haven't even had time to pick ourselves up from the ground to find out whether any serious damage has been done.

As a technical phenomenon, television only started practically to function in Britain in 1947; a couple of years earlier in America. By the 1970s it was little more than a quarter of a century old. By 1951 only 9 per cent of British homes possessed television sets. By 1956 half the country had sets. It was not until 1964 that 90 per cent of homes had sets and that we could think in terms of an entire nation in contact with the electronic box. In America the statistics reveal the same spectacular growth, each stage being about two years earlier. Thus by the end of 1949, television sets were owned by 9 per cent of American homes; by 1953, half the country's homes had sets; by 1962, America became a telly democracy with 91 per cent of homes equipped with sets.[11]

The pattern of television ownership thus leads us to the conclusion that at the beginning of the 1970s there were in Britain three separate age groups that had to be considered when contemplating the impact of television. If we accept the fact that the early formative years up to the age of six play a vital role in shaping the adult for the rest of his life, then we can calculate that practically no one *over the age of 28* in Britain in 1974 had been influenced in those significant character-forming years by the small screen. In America those over 28 who were in contact with television before they were six would be little more than 5 per cent of the population. On the other hand, practically everyone in 1974 *under the age of 14* had had those early years affected by television. Between those under 14 and those over

29

28, some had and some had not been affected in their most impressionable years by television. In this age group there were more who hadn't had television in their early years than those who had.

In other words, television as a medium is still in its swaddling clothes. By 1970 less than one-fifth of the population of Britain and America had been subjected to the small screen in their early childhood. In Britain a society in which almost every citizen under the age of 25 had grown up as a telly baby will not come into existence, significantly enough for George Orwell disciples, until 1984. It will not be until the year 2000 that we will have a society in which everyone under the age of 45 will have gone through the childhood television experience.

Thus when we try to assess the consequences of television, we must be careful to relate our observations to the relevant age group. Anyone over 28 in Western societies was brought up in a verbal, print-orientated society in which books, newspapers and magazines provided the basis for most ideas and values. The chances are that anyone in their adolescence or older who had been first taught the authority of the printed word, and had received most of his imaginative and indirect experiences from reading, would have acquired a built-in resistance to any television which came into his life after that mental barrier had been erected. It is probably this group, whose attitudes were strongly moulded by the printed page, who are affected least by the box and who use it primarily to reinforce fixed and pre-conceived views.

But what about children who have from their earliest moments been subjected to television? Since most children do not start reading until they are five or six, it is clear that before television existed the printed word was in touch with a child's mind when it was relatively uncluttered, when only its infant training and parental guidance had conditioned it. Now in those non-reading years, television takes over. It has become a first and primary environmental influence alongside parents, brothers and sisters, nurse or nannie. It speaks to the child before the teacher and the priest. It fills its mind with images, visions, emotions and experiences long before any printed word. Even where it is read to, the child will probably be receiving a ten times larger dose of telly than it ever gets of print.

30

This means that just as in the older age groups television's impact had to meet the competition of a print-orientated mind, so in the generation weaned on the electronic nipple, it is the printed word that has to meet the resistance of a television-orientated mind. It may be this conditioning by the visual image that accounts for the growing number of reports from teachers that they are finding it increasingly difficult to get children to start reading and to form a reading habit.

Now, of course, none of these facts about the differential quality of the impact of television on various age groups would matter very much if it could be decisively established that the influence of the box on young and old was so small that it could be at best but a marginal contributing factor in the formation of the conduct, attitudes and values of the individual. This question is still wide open. Those who insist that the medium is, on the whole, benign or neutral in its influence defend their position by pointing out that in the past other media — newspapers, films, radio, comic strips — have similarly been singled out as scapegoats for all or some of the social ills of society. Most research has in general tended to exonerate such obvious culprits as sadistic films, pornographic literature and brutal comic strips from having made any significant contribution to the violence, perversion and unrest in Western societies.

This lumping together of all media, as if they were all qualitatively alike in their impact, can be seen from the following contradictory statements. J. M. Martin and J. P. Fitzpatrick in 1966 in their book, *Delinquent Behaviour*, concluded that there was 'no acceptable evidence that television, movies, pornographic literature, and other forms of mass media, are significantly related to delinquency.'[12] A diametrically opposed view to this assessment is voiced by the American authority on child behaviour, Arnold Arnold, who, having examined the available literature up to 1969 says: 'The majority of independent research indicates that television, comic books, movie and war-toys inspired violence seriously and adversely affect children.'[13]

In my opinion not only is television different from other media such as books, papers, cinema, radio, but it is so different as to make any comparisons with other modes of communication both misleading and irrelevant. Its uniqueness consists in its possession of three elements which *in combination* affect the individual, and particularly the very young, in a completely fresh and unprecedented way. The first element is the sheer volume of the television intake, the insatiable appetite in countries like Britain and America for the electronic fodder of the box. The second element is its moving visual content. The third is the conditions in which it is normally experienced — the *familiar environment* of the home.

First let us consider volume. In Britain the average home has its set switched on between four to five hours a day. Since maximum programme hours were until 1972 legally limited to 50 a week, with additional time in the mornings and afternoons for educational, children's and outside broadcasts, there were approximately 65–70 hours of television available on each of the major channels per week. Since all channels transmit at roughly the same time, it seems that the average British home is tuned in to receive about half of the transmitting time. It is clear, too, that since four to five hours a day is an *average* figure a great many homes have their sets on for an even longer period. Out of this total of hours beamed into the home, it is calculated that the average individual actually watches about two hours per day. Children between five and fifteen look at television for about three hours per day.[14]

In America where there is almost round-the-clock television, viewing figures are higher. Sets in homes are switched on for about six hours a day. The average American child starts watching television at the age of two and by nine years old he is watching it three to four hours a day. In homes of the poor and ill-educated, children spend five to six hours a day, on an average, in front of the box.[15] These again are average figures. Some children clearly watch much more.

If you extrapolate these daily figures, you get some awesome statistics about how much of an American's life is spent doing nothing but watching the set. In his statement to the Commission on Violence, Federal Communications Commissioner Johnson estimated that the average male viewer, between his second and sixty-fifth year, would be watching television for over 3000 entire days — roughly nine years of his life. He said that by the time an average child enters kindergarten — before he has had any formal education at all — he has already spent more hours learning about the world from television than the hours he would eventually spend in a college classroom earning a B.A. degree. And when one balances the hours of television involvement against formal learning involvement, it appears that by the time the average American child graduates from high school, he will have spent about 10,800 hours in school and more than 20,000 hours with television. In other words, the television set has occupied his time almost twice as much as his school during his most intensive educational phase.[16] The same can be said of children in Britain.

It is apparent, then, that in terms of sheer volume alone there is no medium in man's history that has taken up so much of his time. Although there is no mathematical formula that equates the importance of an environmental factor with the number of hours spent in it, it is obvious that time is a significant aspect of the influence of environment. It is probable that home, neighbourhood, school and church are generally accepted as the most powerful environmental factors in a child's life simply because, between the four of them, they occupy practically all his time.

If that is so, then television in time terms has ample justification to be listed as the fifth factor. Do any of the other influences in a child's life command full attention for three to four hours a day? Does he listen to his parents four hours a day, pay attention to his teachers, focus on his neighbourhood for that many hours with the same intensity as he devotes to watching television?

Nor can it be convincingly argued that what comes out of the box is merely an echo, a reflection, a synthesis of the four other factors; that television is at most a part of a child's home and neighbourhood, reiterating and reinforcing the messages and pressures he is already receiving from those factors; that television is not something different but more of the same thing. The statement, the vision, the message of television in Britain and America is radically different from anything he experiences in home, neighbourhood, school or church. No one's neighbourhood is anything like the active, anarchic, compelling mosaic of the small screen. No one's school gives anything like the telly curriculum with its emphasis on entertainment, relaxation, its selling pressures, its excitement. And as far as the home is concerned, it is for nearly all children the television set that takes over the living room rather than the living room counteracting the impact of the television picture.

In addition to the unprecedented volume of television that is consumed by the individual, the second distinctive feature of television is its visual element with its compulsive attention-commanding quality which print certainly does not have. It has been generally accepted that sight is the most compelling of all the senses. Our own personal experiences tell us that when we are confronted by an event that could simultaneously stimulate a number of our senses, it is usually the visual impression that takes precedence and dominates our recollection of it.

At a spectacle such as a football game or a bullfight or a carnival, it is what we have seen that remains more vividly with most of us than what we have smelt, heard or touched. If we are present at a bank robbery or involved in an automobile accident, the law places more credence on our testimony as an eye-witness than it would if we were merely a smell-witness or a hear-witness. True, there are some people whose olfactory senses are more acute and dominating than their visual senses. Marcel Proust's memory of things past was unlocked by the taste of a cup of tea and a piece of cake, and Norman Mailer's fiction is obsessed by the smell of bodies, food and streets. But for most of us, seeing is the predominant sense amongst theoretical physiological equals.

Of course, just before the arrival of television it was the cinema, with its arrangement and juxtaposition of moving images, that was the most popular medium or art form. But isn't television merely a smaller, less competent cinema? That is the question most often asked by those who refuse to believe that television can be anything more than a minimal influence for changes in society. If the social consequences of the cinema have been neither deep nor important, they ask, why will television be any different?

The difference, in my view, is that compared to television the amount of moving pictures seen was tiny (three hours per week; probably six or seven hours per week for addicts) and the cinema was never part of the natural continuum of one's home environment. If children lived in a cinema, had their meals in a cinema, went to bed in a cinema, and all during their waking

34

hours their attention was focused on a succession of visual images purporting to portray a comprehensive picture of life, no doubt the impact of such conditions would have been as important on such a generation of children as the impact of television upon our own telly babes.

The third element — in addition to volume and its visual quality — that makes television different from other media is its pervasiveness in the home. Because it appeals directly to the gullible sensory apparatus of the eye — seeing is believing — and because it is experienced in the familiar, reassuring atmosphere of the home, television is the least alien of all mass media. Its very existence in the most trustworthy, comforting milieu for the individual — the home — makes television an integral part of the nest, the family, the retreat where familiarity has provided the individual with reasonably reliable guides for filtering out, by his own standards, the true from the false. Every survey comparing the reliability of media shows that the greater percentage of viewers believe that television is more impartial and trustworthy than the radio or newspapers. Blumler and McQuail in their study of the 1964 British General Election campaign found that twice as many people thought television more reliable than the press and radio (45 per cent to about 18 per cent each for the other two) and surveys in America have found the same disposition to trust the small screen.[17]

Because of its visual element, its familiarity and its being there, being on, almost all the time that the child is actually in the house, television is more than merely moving wallpaper. It is part of the room, an extension of the home, a private neighbourhood in itself. In other media there is a distinct consciousness of a separation between the individual and his involvement with that particular medium. Because most media demand a deliberate act of choice about where, when and for how long he is going to be involved, the individual has more control, more critical detachment from them. You *pick up* a book or newspaper or a comic strip. You narrow your range of choice to *that* book and *that* paper and you can cut them off when they cease to be interesting. You *go* to the cinema or theatre. You leave the home to experience something foreign and different. But you *step into* television. You immerse

35

yourself in it and it surrounds you, takes you over, like the all-pervasive atmosphere of your home.

Theoretically, there is a freedom to switch on and to switch off. To choose one programme over another. But few people, and very few children, exercise it. The statistics show conclusively how unselective television addiction is. There may be variations in choice of programmes — although even these are rarely very great — but the total number of viewing hours remains constant. The sets flicker away the same number of hours per day, per month, per annum — with occasional dips and rises because of the weather — in the same number of homes no matter what is on or what is being said. Just as you do not lock up your living room from time to time so you do not expel television from your home. In its persistent, continuous activity only radio, amongst all the media, compares with television. But the way in which radio has been overtaken in popularity by the small screen — radio-listening figures have fallen drastically since competing directly with television for attention — is another piece of indirect evidence of the compulsive power of the visual medium over an aural one.

One can cite numerous illustrations to prove that people react to television in a markedly different way than they do to other media. I remember a man complaining in a television discussion about the rough treatment Harold Wilson, then Prime Minister, had received in an interview on the Panorama programme. 'I did not pay my licence fee,' he said, 'so that the Prime Minister could be insulted in my living room.' Had he read the same interview in the *Daily Express* — in his living room — he would never have felt that sense of being personally related or involved with the incident. The newspaper report cut him off from that interview. The television made him part of it.

If then a case has been made out for establishing the credentials of television as an important environmental factor in our society — for children important enough to be ranked, *pari passu*, as a fifth factor — then one must ask what specifically is the environmental message of the box. Not what each individual programme is saying, what each splinter of the whole is transmitting, but what the entire mosaic of television looks like, what the totality of the small screen's vision is all about. The mosaic is the message, not the medium.

I do not believe that single programmes like *Panorama* or *Civilisation* or *The Selling of the Pentagon* make serious contributions to the total cultural, social or political awareness of the viewers that watch them. Nor do I believe that single programmes like *The Untouchables* or *Peyton Place* or *The Avengers* or *Hawaii Five-O* significantly reduce cultural standards, stimulate violence or dull sensitivity amongst audiences that watch them. There are few, if any, individual programmes — no matter how boring, incompetent, vulgar, shocking, perverse, radical, trivial, silly or salacious — that can by themselves make any lasting imprint on the resistant hide of society. They can annoy, irritate, soothe, even hurt for a moment but in the long run they are little more than fading tattoo marks or momentary pin pricks on the body politic.

What counts is the manner in which the components are presented and arranged in the total television mosaic. If all television, for example, were devoted to informing viewers about current affairs and nothing else, the impact of the box would be far different from that of a system of television devoted entirely to the transmission of programmes about art, music, poetry, drama and other cultural matters. If all television were monopolised to propagate Communism, its effects would be quite different to a television system designed exclusively to promote Fascism. I am not concerned here with whether such a concentrated diet of anything would in the long run drive people away to alternative forms of media stimulation or information gathering, but merely with the proposition that (to contradict Marshall McLuhan) such divergences in the content of television would inevitably lead to divergent effects.

Television in Russia — state-controlled, conformist, part of the total apparatus of Communist indoctrination — clearly produces different results from television in America where the over-all purpose of the box is directed towards selling goods through the entertainment of viewers. The philosopher, Herbert Marcuse, far from deprecating the effect of the contents of television, considers it to be one of the powerful media factors forming 'the material base of domination' in advanced industrial societies. According to Marcuse, television is part of the apparatus used, probably unconsciously by the ruling class to stifle dissent and protest by proclaiming the virtues of affluence. A society conditioned to the satisfaction of its material needs becomes a passive tool of the dominating system. 'Can one really distinguish between the mass media as instruments of information and entertainment,' he asks in *One Dimensional Man*, 'and as agents of manipulation and indoctrination?'[18]

While it is true that Marcuse lumps all mass media together in his indictment of their role in repressing and limiting individual freedom in the interests of American capitalism, it is television that he always lists in the forefront of these media influences. Suppose all advertising and all media of information and entertainment were suddenly to disappear from the American scene, he asks towards the end of *One Dimensional Man*. This would plunge the individual into a traumatic void where he would have the chance to wonder and think about the nature of himself and his society. 'Deprived of his false fathers, leaders, friends and representatives he would have to learn his ABC's again. But the words and sentences which he would form might come out very differently, and so might his aspirations and fears.

'To be sure, such a situation would be an unbearable nightmare. While the people can support the continuous creation of nuclear weapons, radioactive fallout, and questionable foodstuffs, they cannot (for this very reason!) tolerate being deprived of the entertainment and education which make them capable of reproducing the arrangements for their defence and/or destruction. The non-functioning of television and the allied media might thus begin to achieve what the inherent contradictions of capitalism did not achieve — the disintegration of the system.'[19]

Thus we see how two such formidable leaders of contemporary thought, Marcuse and McLuhan, can argue themselves into diametrically opposed positions about the social consequences of television. To Marcuse, it is used by American capitalism as the hidden persuader and electronic comforter of the system; to McLuhan, anyone like Marcuse who thinks that it is the 'use' of television that counts, takes up the 'numb stance of the technological idiot'.

Fundamentally Marcuse is saying that television can be used

by society to help its course and nature. Without agreeing with his conclusions that the mass media play a determinant role in holding American capitalism together, the logic and the facts tell us that his view of the function of television makes more sense than McLuhan's. In Russia, the effects of television are deliberately calculated; in America and Britain, they are accidentally spawned. In Russia, television is an integral part of an ideological Communist culture; in America, television is an integral part of the profit-making system; in Britain, television is neither one nor the other, but tends to look more and more like the benign rump of the status quo. In Russia, the state knows exactly where television is going; in America and Britain, the state has no idea where television is going.

The only incontrovertible fact about television in America and Britain — judged from its over-all output — is that its primary purpose is to entertain. In America it is quite clear why entertainment has become the main function of the box. American broadcasters are in the business chiefly for profits through the selling of advertising space. The most efficient way to deliver audiences for that advertising is through programmes that entertain the public.

In Britain the reason why television is entertainment-dominated is not so clear cut. The commercial channel, of course, has much the same philosophy as the American networks. Except for a perfunctory genuflection towards some public service responsibility, it endeavours to sell advertising by guaranteeing that the viewers will be 'entertained' most of the time. The reason for the BBC's adoption of exactly the same philosophy is a little more complex. In order to justify its monopoly of the licence fee that finances it, it must also deliver a substantial part of the total audience to its programmes. How substantial a part that has to be has never been laid down. But through some magic rule-of-thumb the statistical quota which the BBC feels it must enjoy to vindicate its licence fee is about 40 per cent of the viewing audience. To acquire such a figure, it must produce almost as many entertainment programmes as its rival.

Naturally the competitive spirit — the quest for ratings — begins to dominate the thinking of those in charge of BBC programmes. Everyone is pleased when figures go up — for

39

no other reason than that the other channel has been beaten. The 40 per cent norm becomes a minimum. Why not push for 50 per cent or even 55 per cent? Ego inflation insidiously takes over from objective consideration of the broadcasting purpose of the Corporation. And since the politicians, too, prefer a non-involved, non-controversial BBC, the entertainment ethos is encouraged. In this way the two major channels — BBC-1 and ITV — vie with each other in giving the public what it wants, and what the public wants is to be entertained.

Most of the entertainment and sports programmes are jammed into the peak-time viewing hours — between 7 and 10 p.m. — because the potential audience is about four or five times larger in those hours than at any other time of the day. The commercial channel concentrates about 90 per cent non-serious programmes in this segment of the day. BBC-1's ration of light entertainment and sport in prime time is 78 per cent; in America, if one eliminates the news bulletins, the peak-time formula is about 97 per cent entertainment. The one channel that does reverse this balance is BBC-2 where the most popular hours are filled with only 40 per cent of light entertainment with serious programmes taking up no less than 60 per cent of its schedule. But so conditioned are British viewers to expecting entertainment on the box that BBC-2, which can now be seen by over half the houses in the country, still only attracts little more than 5 to 7 per cent of the potential national audience. In America the entertainment element of programming so swamps all scheduled hours that there can be no possible argument about what it is actually doing.

However, there is a considerable attempt in Britain, particularly by the BBC, to deprecate the significance of the entertainment ration at peak-time. They point out that programmes like *Panorama* and weekly documentaries exist in peak-time and that the children's hours between 4 and 6 p.m. as well as early and late current affairs programmes like *Nationwide* and *Midweek* could be totalled up to show an over-all statistical prevalence of serious over non-serious programming on BBC-1 during the day. But what is relevant is not how many hours of serious programming there are but how many people see them. The average audience for peak-time programmes on BBC-1 is roughly about 10,000,000 people over the 3½ hour segment. On ITV it is about 13,000,000 people watching between 7 and 10.30 p.m. Outside those hours, the audience average drops drastically. There is, perhaps, an average total of 4,000,000 for non-peak viewing for *both* major channels together. And just as there are some serious programmes in peak hours, so there are non-serious programmes in off-peak hours. Taking a statistical high-dive it is possible to guess that the average Briton takes in six to seven times more light entertainment and sport from television than the combined total of everything else transmitted by the box.

For children under twelve (many of whom watch well past the so-called nine o'clock watershed which is supposed to separate adult from children's viewing) this statistical proportion might be slightly less because the BBC's children's slot between 4.30 and 6 p.m. is probably the most intelligently organised and serious sector of all British television. When someone asks how can one assess the effect of a stimulating programme like the BBC's *Blue Peter* or the American *Sesame Street* on a child's mind, the answer is that the *Blue Peters* of the box are swamped by at least five or six times as many hours of programming, seen by the child, with an impact far different from that conveyed and intended by the intelligent educational children's shows.

Thus even though British television is not as saturated with entertainment as American, amusement is still predominantly its chief purpose. What, then, are the likely social consequences of this powerful environmental influence — nothing less than a fifth factor — dedicated towards the projection of life as primarily amusing, trivial, uninvolved, escapist, bland and only marginally concerned with reality?

CHAPTER THREE

The Television Factor: Positive, Probable and Peripheral

I believe TV is going to be the test of the modern world, and that in this new opportunity to see beyond the range of our vision we shall discover either a new and unbearable disturbance of the general peace or a saving radiance in the sky. We shall stand or fall by TV — of that I am quite sure.

E. B. White, July 1938

Television has no monopoly over the mind. Even over the youngest mind. It jostles with other environmental conditions for influence over some of an individual's thoughts and actions. Its importance is obviously less where neighbourhood and parents and education provide counteracting, selective, concerned pressures. In tightly-knit, isolated towns or villages where the mores of the community cast a restraining influence on change, the impact of television is likely to be less than where population mobility has produced large conurbations without a clearly recognised community ethos commanding as much fear or respect.

What, then, is the television factor? If one cannot isolate it — and social scientists are not having much luck in that field — can one at least grade it? Are there certain effects more likely to be caused by the television factor than others? Can one produce a scale not only of the likelihood of these influences being felt but of their significance? For example, television has certainly changed people's eating habits. But does that matter very much? It has stopped people going to the cinema as often as they used to. Does that matter very much to anyone but the cinema industry? Are there more profound changes that it has brought about — changes that go to the very heart and nature of a society?

Where it seems to me that definite and profound changes have taken place in Britain and America and that such changes would clearly not have taken place to the same degree or intensity had not television been operating, then I contend that a *positive* television factor is at work. Where definite but less profound changes have taken place and it is plain that television has played some significant part in those changes although it is too difficult to sort out from other influences the magnitude of its contribution, then I believe that a *probable* television factor is at work. Where television is operating not as a direct influence on changing attitudes and values but indirectly through the fact that its existence has brought about changes in other media, art forms and cultural institutions, then I claim that a *peripheral* television factor is at work. Before I attempt to show in more detail how such changes might be related to television, let me summarise a few of the areas in which I believe a positive, probable or peripheral television factor could operate.

The image most people have of their leaders — particularly politicians — comes from their appearances on television. In making those appearances they are seen as part of a mosaic of life which is essentially trivial and facetious. In the early days of American vaudeville it was a hook wielded from back stage that yanked unpopular performers out of the sight of hooting audiences. Now it is the switch-off button that rudely dismisses the most powerful figures in the land from the living room. We have cultivated a society that nightly obliterates with casual contempt the faces, the voices and arguments of its leaders. We have produced a population that prefers the company of variety artists, comics, actors, sportsmen and commercial hucksters to that of the men who shape its destiny and that of its children. Even worse, we have encouraged our leaders to become television performers in order to gain our attention, our vote or our sympathy. Can all this happen without authority belittling itself in the process? Is there not a prima facie case for assuming that a positive television factor is operating in the current disillusionment and scepticism about the ability of our leaders and the workings of our institutions?

A positive television factor can also be detected in the area of violence. There can be no doubt that Britain and America have become in the past decade more violent societies than at any time in this century, always excepting, of course, the organised and approved violence of the two World Wars. Statistics show that the rate of violence amongst the under 21s — the telly generation — has risen at a much faster rate than amongst those who were not conditioned in their early years by the box. Nor do we need statistics to establish that all round us violent behaviour that has not been classified as criminal — student demonstrations, hooliganism, crowds at sporting events, children's play at school — is more prevalent and more vicious than anything experienced in recent times.

When one moves from the areas in which a positive television factor can be said to operate to those where a *probable* television factor can be detected, the variety of contending explanations for any social phenomenon becomes greater and the influence of television more difficult to isolate and establish. Does television share any responsibility for the increase in drug-taking, particularly amongst the young? Does television help create a narrow, xenophobic society, through its fostering, particularly in Britain, such a passion for sport that it encourages lop-sided values about a nation's aims and achievements? Does television have anything to do with the increase in gambling in Britain? Does it help widen the generation gap?

Another criterion by which the impact of television must be judged — as well as its positive and probable effects — is its indirect influence on other media and art forms. The very existence of television and its unprecedented ability to command the time and attention of most people has forced significant changes upon media that have to compete with it. These changes I have tried to lump together as being due to the *peripheral* television factor. In this context 'peripheral' means external rather than superficial. These are spin-off effects from the circumference of television rather than anything emanating directly from its centre.

The disappearance of the picture magazines, the shrinkage in national newspapers, the alterations in the contents and make-up of newspapers and magazines, the plight of the novel, the revolution in the subject matter of the cinema, are some of the changes that, as I shall try to show, can be traced to the peripheral television factor. The changes that have been wrought in these cultural fields have in turn had considerable consequences on the social pattern of life in Britain and America.

No doubt it will be said that in listing this catalogue of positive, probable and peripheral effects, I am a Cassandra prophesying chiefly anguish and confusion as television's major contribution to society. Only in the sense that rapid change produces confusion, and anguish is often caused by an inability to cope with change, would this charge be remotely true. There is nothing inherently evil or demoniac about television as a medium.

Most people would contend that their personal experience with television has been benign and harmless. It provides relaxation for the tired working man and housewife. It is a constant joy and companion to the sick, the lonely and the elderly. It broadens the horizons of the young, brings them into contact with lands and sights they could never possibly have seen before, encourages them to take up interests, hobbies, adventures that might never have inspired them had it not been for something seen on the box. It brings to millions the cultural heritage of the past — plays, concerts, opera, ballet — that were denied their forefathers.

All this is true. But whether, either in the long or short run, these 'good' effects will add much more to the sum total of human happiness than did the 'good' effects of the printing press, the radio or the moving picture, would be impossible either to prove or to establish.

I would like to stress that when considering the social consequences of the small screen, I am not concerned with attributing value judgments to whatever it is doing. It is not logically and indisputably 'bad' to have a society in which we have a greater degree of violence than has been the norm up to now; in which authority and institutions are treated with more scepticism and disrespect than hitherto; in which the majority adopts values and attitudes radically different from those held by the élitist or informed minority; in which a drug culture has some place in the social pattern; in which the media encourage and stimulate a more permissive and libertarian attitude towards sexual mores and behaviour.

Learned and concerned people could be found to argue the merits of any one, and even all of these changes. Society will not undergo some convulsive cataclysm should they all take place. But what is intolerable and painful and costly is that these changes should occur without those in charge of our institutions knowing why they are happening or the speed at which they are happening. It is my argument that the pace of these changes is in itself significant. Man can adjust to almost anything given enough time. He is still — after 500 years — in the process of coming to terms with the consequences of the printing press.

It would be difficult to show that television's existence in America or Britain has made our societies more humanitarian, less cruel, more tolerant, significantly wiser, more than marginally better informed, more accomplished or more understanding than they would have been had television never been invented. Whatever it has done in these fields must be balanced against the frightening contribution it has made to increasing the pace of change and escalating its consequences.

One last word before I go on to examine in more detail the manner in which the television factor works. Too often the consequences of television are dismissed because people within their own experience cannot see it affecting either themselves or their children. 'I never watch it myself . . . my teenage children never look at it . . . my children watched it as kids but they are perfectly normal adolescents today — no hang-ups, no dope, no alienation . . . my daughter's love of animals comes directly from seeing *Blue Peter* . . . have you ever found anyone who would admit that they personally have ever been changed by television?' These are some typical reactions of the pooh-pooh brigade to suggestions that the small screen might be having some impact on society.

Few social scientists would care to be so dogmatic about the nullatory influence of television. The most complacent of them would admit that some individuals — the mentally unstable, the ultra-sensitive, the profoundly ignorant — react to the small screen in a different way from the norm. Even this minimal acceptance of the impact of television could mean that very

46

large numbers of people are involved. With mental ill-health becoming one of the growing anxieties of Western societies and with statistics revealing its terrifying extent, it is clear that in Britain if television's effects were confined solely to the mentally ill it would still be affecting millions of people. In 1970 47 per cent of Britain's hospital beds were occupied by the mentally ill. It is calculated that every fifth family in the land will be directly affected by some immediate member of that family (i.e. grandparents to grand-children) becoming a patient suffering from some form of mental illness. It is estimated that in Britain one in nine women and one in fourteen men during their lifetime will enter a mental hospital.* American statistics reveal a similar situation. In view of such facts, can one dismiss the impact of television by saying that it merely concerns the unbalanced and unstable?

But, of course, television's effects are not confined merely to the mentally ill. It would be a very wise man to detect even in himself how television may have affected him, let alone confidently assert that he has sorted out its influence on the development of his family or his neighbours. The stability, the style, the values, the quality of life of any society do not necessarily depend upon the views of the majorities or even of substantial sections of the population. Minorities, too, can shape the direction and tempo of change in a society. If 10 per cent of the people decide they can only accept the ethos of violence as a basis for change or decision-making, then you have an almost ungovernable society. If 10 per cent of the young become heroin addicts, or opt out of the main stream of social activity, or violently reject the ethics and values of their elders, then there will be costly, painful and convulsive repercussions in the land. If 10 per cent of the electorate grow so disillusioned with their leaders and their institutions that they set out to subvert it, the democratic process becomes difficult, if not unworkable.

It is essential, therefore, to understand that even if a statistical majority of the population has been unchanged or unaffected by the box, it provides little reassuring evidence that significant changes in that society are not taking place because of it. Anyone who doubts the importance of minorities need

* Statistics supplied by British Mental Research Fund.

only look at how an aberrant doctrine like Nazism under Hitler, with its patently psychotic appeal, eventually took over the mind and conscience of a nation.

The social scientists are slowly coming round to the view that their previous methodology for studying the social impact of television has led them up many blind alleys. 'There has been a tendency to confuse effects with effectiveness,' write the authors of *Television and Delinquency*, analysing this type of research. 'An absence of change in the expected or intended direction has been interpreted as an absence of influence. There is much more to the influence of television that can possibly be assessed through direct changes in attitude and opinion, as these have normally been measured ... Influence must not be equated with attitude change and, in general, the tendency to do this in the past has probably led to both *an underestimation of the extent and a misunderstanding about the nature and direction of the influence of television* [my italics].'[1]

One can detect then a shift by social scientists from the view that television has only minimal consequences on society to a position in which it is conceded that television's consequences may be more than marginal or minimal. Would it be possible to look at the matter from another viewpoint? Instead of examining individuals for effects and deducing from such samples what television is doing to a society, might it not be productive to examine a society as a viable organism where social changes have taken place coincidental with the arrival of television. One day there was a minor drug problem and then there was a major one. One day there was a general acceptance of authority amongst the young and then there was a general rejection of it. One day violence had escalated to proportions that defied normal explanations. Suppose that such changes took place in relatively the same degree in all countries that had the same system of television — countries that used it primarily for entertainment purposes and to sell goods as do America, Canada and Britain. Suppose that countries like Russia, Holland, Czechoslovakia, Sweden, with a more integrated system of media control designed less for entertainment and more for propaganda or value indoctrination, had other social problems but not more violence, more drug-taking, more scepticism of authority. Would such a divergence of effects be some evidence of the consequences of television or would it be merely the result of the different cultural and political bases on which television was superimposed?

Finally, like any other environmental factor, television's social effects are neither rigid nor consistent. Indeed, just as the influence of parents, schools and neighbourhood can produce both good and bad social behaviour, so can television produce contradictory effects. A church can turn out saints and sinners; a university can spawn sages and fools. The depiction of violence on the box may convert some of the young into flower people revolted by such violence while others are encouraged to become vandals, hooligans and criminals. But it is the latter group — even if they are only a minority — that gives society most serious concern. Similarly television can stimulate reading while discouraging many more from ever opening a book. It can enhance authority as well as demean it. It can reinforce attitudes, weaken them and form them. These pages attempt to set out only what television does to some people — not all people. Our civilisation will stand or fall — as E. B. White predicts at the beginning of this chapter — by the values promulgated and disseminated by television. Society, in the last resort, will have to decide whether the beams of the ravenous eye, directed as they now are, produce beneficial or malignant effects. And what to do about it.

CHAPTER FOUR

The Day President Kennedy was Shot

It was TV more than anything else that turned the tide.
John Kennedy on how he defeated Richard Nixon in
the 1960 Presidential Election

*Never in recent times have the politicians of every
party commanded so little credence from the public.
Never has the status of Parliament sunk so low.*
Rt. Hon. Reginald Maudling, Conservative Chan-
cellor of the Exchequer and Home Secretary, *The
Times,* October 1967

In English-speaking Western countries like America, Britain,
Australia and Canada, performers, entertainers and sportsmen
dominate, practically monopolise, television. Although theoretically, and by statutory injunction, in Britain the medium is
supposed to cater for a troika of social interests — to inform, to
educate and to entertain — it is generally accepted that its
primary purpose is to fill, in a relaxed and undemanding
manner, the increasing number of leisure hours available in
highly industrialised Western societies.

The group that is given the next largest volume of time on
the box and most ready access to the medium is politicians. It is
not merely that their activities and pronouncements are reported in great detail in the news bulletins, but all current
affairs programmes like *Panorama, Midweek* and *This Week* in
Britain or *Meet The Press* and *CBS Reports* in America devote
most of their attention to questions that involve topical political
decisions and therefore require the comments and appearance
of politicians. Politicians are also given access to the small
screen for party political and ministerial broadcasts — the
latter reserved for matters of grave national interest. In

America the President can get television time almost on demand and whenever he has an important speech or statement to make. What is considered 'important' is sometimes a matter of bargaining and discussion between the White House and the broadcasting authorities.

Yet in spite of this seeming plethora of programmes about politics, it adds up to very little, particularly at peak-time. I would guess that politicians get less than two or three per cent of the total television time and in America their share is even smaller. Richard Crossman, ex-Labour Minister of Social Services, reflected the dissatisfaction of the politicians with their treatment on the box when he said in his Granada Lecture on October 21, 1968: 'I do sometimes wonder whether the people interested in politics and current affairs cannot establish a right to be given equal treatment with all-in wrestling — sixty minutes a week of straight outside broadcasting would seem a lot to us!'

Between them the entertainers, the sportsmen and the politicians occupy something like 95 per cent of the most important hours of television. The rest of society has to squabble for the remaining electronic crumbs. The Church is probably third in the hand-out queue in Britain with its hour-and-a-half preserved area on early Sunday evenings and its midnight epilogues for insomniacs. Industry, farming, trade unions, students, housewives, science, medicine, engineering, finance, teachers (as distinct from education), the academic world, are denied any serious allotment of television time. Facilities, of course, are given during the day for schools broadcasting and the Open University but these are adjuncts of Britain's educational system — usually watched in a classroom — and do not provide opportunities for segments of society to participate in the totality of the medium.

Politicians have reluctantly crept into the television age. Their first reactions to the small box were a mixture of contempt and indifference. Churchill thought of television as 'a penny Punch and Judy Show'. Harry Truman refused to allow television cameras into his press conferences. The Nixon–Kennedy television debates of 1960 changed all that. Although social scientists might find it difficult to come up with any concrete proof that television had any serious influence on

51

voting patterns, politicians in their bones felt that it did. While they might discount television's impact upon every other aspect of society, politicians have taken no chances with their own personal relationships with the medium. They have since 1960 assumed that in the political field television is a potent opinion-former, image-maker and, above all, vote-getter.

Not only have such institutions and procedures as political conventions and congresses, Presidential press conferences, Senatorial committee hearings, techniques of Governmental announcements, been radically changed in tone and method because of the presence of television cameras, but electoral campaigns themselves have undergone transformations so startling and fundamental as to call into question in America the impartiality and justice of the democratic system.

An even more drastic consequence of television is the changes it has wrought in the kind of men who will henceforth be expected to govern the country. The qualities demanded of leaders by a telly electorate have been imperative enough to disqualify from high office men whose natural abilities have not been conveyed through their performances on the box. Similarly the telegenic personality, or the candidate with financial resources large enough to provide him through the use of commercials with a popular image, has in America advantages never contemplated by those who framed the Constitution and the electoral process.

Confronted by a medium dedicated to entertainment and frivolity which by some intangible process had become essential to their survival, politicians decided not to fight it but to join it. The methods, the values, the attitudes, the techniques, the philosophy of the box have been adopted by politicians and parties to win support and popularity.

Party political broadcasts are produced so that they look like commercials or television quiz games. Leaders with urgent statements to give the public edit them into the required ten or fifteen minutes' precise segment needed to fit exactly into the schedule. Politicians are ready to debate and discuss the most complex and controversial issues in six- or seven-minute garbled sessions because producers are terrified their viewers will become bored with anything more. Politicians have become increasingly eager to ingratiate themselves with the viewer through appearances on light entertainment talk shows where they can be identified as equals with pop singers, actors, comics and other folk heroes of the telly public. Individuals who cannot perform on the box, cannot meet the necessary telegenic qualifications, cannot act the required role demanded not only by the public but by the selection process, have little chance of attaining real success in politics. The commandments of show business, the catechism of the talk shows, the litany of the television producer have become the articles of faith on which the career of a politician depends.

'It can be argued that for the whole American nation, television has made the actor-politician inevitable,' writes Robert MacNeil. 'Television is indispensable to politicians, and the television audience is conditioned to like glamour and style. Therefore, politicians become glamorous and stylish.'[1]

Since the glamour of the television idol is almost always associated with an image of energy and youth, viewers now look to politicians for the same television qualities. Harold Wilson and Edward Heath fought out the 1970 British General Election when they were both aged 54 — probably the youngest pair of political leaders to contest an election in modern British history. In the 1968 Presidential election Hubert Humphrey was 57 and Richard Nixon 55. Even Lyndon Johnson, when he contested the 1964 Presidential election, was only 56. Men like the late John Kennedy, Pierre Trudeau of Canada and Harold Wilson, when he first became Prime Minister in 1964, are even more striking examples of the attractions that youth has for electorates in those telly democracies. It can be predicted with reasonable certainty that elder statesmen like Gladstone, Churchill, Mackenzie King, who were elected to the highest office when over 70, would not accomplish the same electoral feat in the television age.

Lord Butler, who had been both Foreign Secretary and Chancellor of the Exchequer in post-war Conservative administrations, reflected in a television interview that, if the heavily-bearded Moses had had to announce personally the message of the Tablets on the small screen, the sight of his venerable figure would have certainly diminished the significance and impact of the Ten Commandments. It was his opinion that the electorate had now been conditioned, because of television, to the view that 'youth is vital to the transaction of public business'. A decided contrast to the words of that other elder statesman, Cicero, who claimed that reason and judgment were found in old men and 'had it not been for old men no state would have existed at all.'

Anyone who believes that television will not make any serious difference to the type and calibre of men who will be voted to leadership in Western democracies should cast his mind back over the last 50 years and ask himself which of the former Presidents or Prime Ministers in America and Britain would have been selected for the highest office if the television screen had been available in their time. Can anyone convincingly contend that in the ruthless stare and glare of television cameras, fixed on them from the battle of the primaries to the party conventions themselves, that the taciturn Coolidge or the pompous-looking Hoover would have made it to the White House? Would Roosevelt, a cripple in a wheelchair who had to be supported physically whenever he walked, have been chosen by a Democratic Convention in 1932 if they had realised that the visible handicaps of their Presidential candidate could be seen by the entire electorate?

I suspect, too, that in Britain the careers of Bonar Law, Neville Chamberlain and Clement Attlee might not have led them to Downing Street had they pursued their ambitions in a television era. The florid rhetoric of Ramsay MacDonald might have diminished his chances if persistently subjected to the attentions of the small screen. And the fate of Sir Alec Douglas-Home, whose features and manner were so mercilessly ridiculed in the BBC's satire programme, *That Was The Week That Was*, makes it doubtful if ever again the Tories would choose as their leader someone whose looks and style so clearly identified him as an aristocrat and who represented to a majority of the electorate a member of a class they considered inimical to the task of leading a modern-orientated, technological democracy. In the quick cutting down of Douglas-Home as Prime Minister, television was probably the major assassin.

Whether any society is best served by excluding the elderly from the pinnacles of political leadership is a moot point. Would the British have been wise in 1940 to reject Winston

Churchill as Prime Minister because he was then aged 66? It is patently obvious that no nation can afford to dispense with the wisdom and experience of great men merely because they do not happen to fit into some arbitrary age bracket.

This trend towards electing the telegenic candidate reached its apotheosis in California where it was not men who merely looked like actors but the actual actors themselves who were elected to responsible political office. The Western star, Ronald Reagan, was made Governor of California in 1966 and the song-and-dance trouper, George Murphy, was elected Senator. Commenting on this phenomenon, the American magazine *Newsweek* said that behind Reagan's television manner was 'his unmatched ability to convince people that the honest face they see on the TV screens is an accurate reflection of the inner man ... His rise sometimes seems an eerie fulfilment of those prophecies of the early 1950's that TV would revolutionise American politics, producing comfortably charismatic candidates cast very much in their Reagan mould.'[2]

Although politicians have become more wary of television than they used to be, most of them are egotistical enough to believe that they can manipulate it to their personal advantage. They can rarely resist an invitation to appear on it. Many of them, particularly heads of governments, fall into the trap of over-exposure; many of them take on appearances in conditions that are unsuitable and demeaning. Like their fellow performers, the actors, they are tempted to believe that the show must go on with themselves prominently in the cast. They rationalise their eagerness to be seen on the box by insisting that it is their duty to be available in a crisis to explain and reassure. Sometimes, as in the case of George Brown on the day President Kennedy was shot, an appearance by a politician can lead to embarrassing and unforeseen consequences.

This incident, which received considerable publicity at the time but which has never been related in detail, is almost a perfect morality tale about the pitfalls that await politicians who assume they are always capable of coping with the demands of the box. George Brown, now Lord George-Brown, was easily the most volatile, unpredictable and controversial member of Harold Wilson's Labour Government. His activities at the Foreign Office and his rows within the Labour Cabinet, which eventually led to his resignation, have been well documented in press headlines and in the memoirs of his colleagues.

'His strengths far exceeded his weaknesses,' wrote Harold Wilson in his record of the Labour Government, 'but it was his weaknesses which ended his Ministerial career.'

Nine months before Kennedy was shot, George Brown had contested the Labour Party leadership against Wilson and was defeated by 144 votes to 103. After so much support from his colleagues, it was natural that George Brown should be made Deputy Leader of the Party and the likely heir-apparent should there be any serious revolt against Wilson's leadership. But I believe that Brown's performance on television on the day of President Kennedy's assassination effectively put paid to any chances he might have had to succeed to Labour Party Leadership.

On November 22nd, 1963, I was having an early evening drink in the dining-room for senior programme executives at Rediffusion Television's offices in Kingsway, London. With me was Mr. Geoffrey Whitaker who, like me, was one of five Assistant Controllers of Programmes in the company. Usually seven or eight executives could be expected to forgather for gossip and a drink before slipping off home, but that evening most of them were attending the annual dinner of the Guild of Television Producers and Directors where awards for the best performances of the year were to be announced and handed out. The news that President Kennedy had been shot in Dallas, Texas, was given to us by a rather diffident waitress who had heard it over the radio and wasn't sure that she had got it right. It was several minutes before we could get confirmation that a shooting had taken place and not long afterwards we heard that the President was dead.

Switching on the television set in the dining-room to pick up further details of this numbing news, we saw to our horror that while the BBC had discontinued their regular programmes and were transmitting solemn music out of respect for Kennedy's death, Rediffusion was still merrily churning out the bi-weekly medical soap opera, *Emergency Ward 10*.

Racing round to the office of Cyril Francis, the executive at that time responsible for co-ordinating the programmes of the

14 companies on the commercial network, we protested that Rediffusion could not go on pumping out *Emergency Ward 10* and that something more appropriate to such a serious occasion should be substituted. If the BBC's screen had gone dead, we said, we would have to follow suit or be subjected to severe criticism in the morning. Francis pointed out, however, that his hands were tied by the formal Obituary Procedure that had been laid down to apply whenever the death of a prominent figure occurred.

According to these rules, different transmission arrangements were to apply depending upon the importance of the deceased. In category A, covering the immediate members of the Royal Family from the Queen to the Prince of Wales, all normal programming would cease immediately after the formal 'Announcement To The Nation' was made and all commercials would be cancelled for the remainder of the day. The death of lesser categories of individuals would not have such drastic repercussions on the scheduled programmes or the commercials. For instance, the death of the Duke of Gloucester, who was in Category C, would mean only the cancellation of commercials in the programme break in which the formal announcement took place.

President Kennedy was in Category D along with the Pope, the Archbishop of Canterbury, Harold Wilson, the Duke of Kent, Khruschev, Nehru, and a few others. For their deaths no commercials were to be cancelled and no programmes would be altered or amended unless it was felt that their theme was unsuitable in some specific way related to the death of that particular individual. It was this procedure that was being conscientiously carried out by the entire ITV network immediately after the announcement of Kennedy's assassination.

Whitaker and I insisted that if we persisted in carrying out this obituary procedure, we would be affronting the mood of the nation which we felt would be extremely disturbed and shocked by the tragic circumstances surrounding the death of this much-admired and much-loved youthful President of the United States. Francis agreed.

Emergency Ward 10 was taken off, the commercials cancelled and a stand-by programme of Sir John Barbirolli conducting the Hallé Orchestra substituted. The rest of the companies on the commercial network followed suit. It was a decision that meant the loss of something like £60,000 in advertising revenue. Oddly enough, the BBC who had in the first instance made the right decision by taking off their regular programmes, saw that Rediffusion was still transmitting *Emergency Ward 10* and decided to return to their ordinary schedule. This meant that while the ITV was displaying an appropriate sense of tragic decorum, the BBC was insensitively showing a Harry Worth comedy at a time when the nation was not very disposed to laughter. The next day the Press gave the Corporation a bad time over its display of bad taste. ITV was praised. Nor did the companies lose any revenue because they were given permission to recoup the lost advertising minutes on subsequent days.

In the meantime it had been decided to mount a special programme in which some attempt would be made to assess the implications of Kennedy's murder. Who had done it and why? Was it the signal for a right-wing take-over of the American government? Was it a left-wing plot? What sort of a man was Lyndon Baines Johnson? How would America react? What did it mean to Britain and Europe?

Under Jeremy Isaacs, an experienced current affairs producer, every secretary and programme executive available was rushed to the telephones to contact as many appropriate Americans and authoritative figures as could be assembled in Rediffusion's studios as quickly as possible. The programme was scheduled for 10.30 p.m. which gave us just three hours to put together the necessary film about Kennedy, bring in the commentators, invite participants and write the script. In normal circumstances such a programme would have required at least a week's preparation.

Since it was a Friday night, London was denuded of both politicians and experts. Every former ambassador to Russia or Washington was called without success. Politicians like R. A. Butler, Selwyn Lloyd, Peter Thorneycroft, Edward Heath, Jo Grimond and Patrick Gordon Walker were 'phoned and were unavailable. In the course of these frantic proceedings, we were told that both the Prime Minister, Sir Alec Douglas-Home and the Opposition leader, Harold Wilson, would be making national TV statements. Neither was in London.

Through sheer persistence, however, some appropriate figures were finally located and tracked down. Professor Sir Denis Brogan, an expert on American history, was available. Mr. John Crosby of the *New York Herald Tribune* was approached during the interval of the ballet at Covent Garden and persuaded to come to the studios. Two other Americans, the film producer, Carl Foreman, and the actor, Eli Wallach, also agreed to appear. George Brown, the Deputy Leader of the Labour Party, was traced to a Mayor's dinner at Shoreditch which he agreed to leave in order to make his contribution to the programme. To all of us, Brown's availability was most gratifying, not only because of the weight his presence would bring to our hurriedly-assembled programme, but because he had only recently returned from a trip to America where he had met both President Kennedy and Vice-President Johnson.

Jeremy Isaacs had planned the shape of the programme. It would include a short account, illustrated by as much film as was available, of the controversial issues facing Kennedy at the time — right-wing bitterness in the South, race riots — then the three Americans —Wallach, Crosby and Foreman — would be asked to give their reactions to the event, followed by interviews with Professor Brogan and George Brown.

The participants assembled in the company's hospitality room and I briefed them about what was wanted while Isaacs sorted out the technical problems of production. Although there tends to be a great deal of easy chit-chat and cynical banter during the behind-the-scenes preparation of a current affairs programme, on this occasion the mood was intense and sombre. Kennedy's death had seemed to touch something deep and personal in those involved in the programme and few were inclined to talk very much.

George Brown, however, was as talkative and communicative as ever. Having first expressed his views that the assassination was a great tragedy for both Britain and America, he then went on to assure everyone within earshot that Lyndon Johnson would be a great successor and that, having just met him in America, the presidency would be in safe and good hands. To this optimistic assessment, Professor Brogan slightly demurred. Brown brushed aside the Professor's misgivings.

During the pre-programme briefing I gave to Professor

Brogan and Brown, I said that we would like the Professor to confine his remarks to an assessment of the constitutional and political implication of the new regime while we hoped that Brown's contribution would be in the nature of a tribute to Kennedy. Something I said suddenly raised Brown's suspicions.

'Is this going to be one of those 15 second statements on the air?' he asked me. 'If so I'm leaving the building now.' I assured him he would have a reasonable time to make a statement and, mollified, he went off to discuss with Kenneth Harris, who was going to conduct the interview, the general drift it was to take.

At about this time, Eli Wallach, the American actor, arrived. He was clearly upset about the news and was in no mood for small talk. He was introduced to George Brown who immediately told Wallach how much he admired the actor's work. Wallach accepted Brown's compliments with good grace but was not anxious to chat about himself. Brown, however, persisted in trying to steer the conversation in that direction and when Wallach did not respond, Brown asked why actors were so conceited. Someone like Wallach, said Brown, always carried a newspaper in his pocket with his name in prominent headlines. On the contrary, Wallach was finally stung to reply, he was always meeting people who said they recognised his face but could not place his name. It was all meant to be light-hearted banter but Wallach, emotionally upset by the President's death, clearly wanted none of it.

'Have you ever been in a play by Ted Willis?' asked Brown.

'No,' said Wallach. 'Who's Ted Willis?'

'You've never heard of Ted Willis?' said Brown.

Ted Willis, now Lord Willis, was created a Life Peer in 1963 not long after this incident. An ardent Labour supporter, he has written such plays as *Woman in a Dressing Gown* and is probably best known for his popular police television series, *Dixon of Dock Green*.

Wallach's curt denial of any knowledge of Ted Willis evidently annoyed Brown. Wallach, in an effort to break off this pointless conversation, walked over to the drink cupboard and poured himself a whisky. This did not stop George Brown. The

American actor returned to his seat and said nothing while Brown continued to mutter about American actors, Ted Willis and Eli Wallach. Suddenly Wallach lost his temper. He rose from the sofa, pointed at the Labour Deputy Leader and shouted, 'I didn't come here to be insulted. Is this bastard interviewing me on the programme? If so, I'm leaving now.'

Brown said something deprecating which infuriated Wallach even more. Wallach began to strip off his jacket. 'Come outside!' he said to Brown, who was sitting on a low chair looking up at him. 'Come outside and I'll knock you off your can!'

Undeterred, Brown shrugged the threat away and told Wallach to shut up and sit down. The American actor rushed forward as if to hit him when I leapt between them and pushed Wallach back on to the sofa. At that moment, the American film producer, Carl Foreman, arrived to see me wrestling with Wallach. Foreman told me afterwards that his first reaction on seeing us locked together in this way was to assume that Wallach was trying to hit me because of something I may have said about him in some film or theatre review.

Although he had no idea what it was all about, Foreman joined me in restraining Wallach and trying to pacify him.

'He's not going to interview you on the programme,' I hissed at Wallach. 'He's one of the guests.'

'Well, who is he? Who is he?' Wallach kept asking. Although there had been formal introductions when he arrived, Wallach had obviously not worked out who everyone was.

'He's George Brown! Deputy Leader of the Labour Party!' I whispered, trying to prevent my voice from carrying across the room where Brown was imperturbably watching the tussle.

'That's right,' confirmed Carl Foreman, becoming aware of what was going on. 'Don't be a fool. Sit down. He's an important man in the Labour Party.'

'I don't care who he is,' said Wallach, still trying to break loose from our restraining efforts. 'I'll still knock the shit out of him.'

By now George Brown was reduced to silence. Wallach, realising that his anger had been directed at an important politician and not some aggressive interviewer, allowed himself to be pacified. It was quickly decided that the best course was to cool the temperature by getting Wallach and Brown as far apart as possible. The three Americans — Wallach, Foreman and Crosby — were asked to go downstairs to the studio where the programme would be on the air in about fifteen minutes time. As they rose to leave, Brown got up from his chair and extended his hand to Eli Wallach. 'Brother, brother,' he said, 'I don't think we should go into the same studio feeling this way. Let's shake hands.'

In subsequent comments on the incident some publications implied that Rediffusion was at fault for allowing Brown to appear in that sort of mood. But Brown's ebullience and aggressiveness are part of his character. Kenneth Harris and myself — both with some previous experience of Labour's Deputy Leader on other programmes — did not think that his behaviour, until the Wallach affair, was so unusual as to assume he would not be able to acquit himself reasonably well on the box. He had displayed the goodwill and good grace to ask Wallach to patch up their misunderstanding. Wallach shook Brown's hand, they exchanged a few terse words, and I thought that was the end of the matter. I was wrong. Just as Wallach was leaving the room, in the wake of Foreman and Crosby who had preceded him, Brown could not resist one final word.

'And now you'll know who Ted Willis is!' he shouted, after the retreating figure of the American actor.

I spent the next fifteen minutes trying to make light of the whole incident by explaining to George Brown that Wallach had obviously not known who he was and had not realised that the banter was not unkindly meant. By the time he turned up in front of the cameras the intensity of the occasion, the wait under the hot lights and the quarrel with Wallach, inevitably had their combined effect. His talk with Kenneth Harris was a disaster. His enthusiasm for Johnson, based upon a short meeting between them which he described in some detail, struck a jarring note of complacency and optimism. His rambling, inconclusive remarks indicated a remarkable insensitivity to the mood of the moment.

It was not until over a week later that the storm over Brown's appearance blew up into a first-class political row. According to Walter Terry of the *Daily Mail*, it was members of the Labour Party, rather than the general public, who reacted 'with horror at the effect it might have on party prestige'.[3] It was their concern that caused Harold Wilson to ask George Brown for an explanation of what had happened that evening and the Deputy Leader, on the Thursday following the broadcast, made a brief personal statement about it to the Parliamentary Labour Party.

But things really began to simmer when the *New York Herald Tribune*, on their front page on November 30th, 1963, reported that 'there was trouble at the studio even before the programme began. Mr. Brown got into a verbal row with Mr. Wallach and friends had to intervene to stop it from coming to blows. Neither of the men had met previously.'

Wrote Derek Marks in the *Evening Standard* of December 2nd, 1963: 'Now it should be said at once that Mr. Brown made an ass of himself in his television appearance on the night of President Kennedy's death — at least, to be more accurate, he did in the view of every single person I have met who saw the programme. But he is not the first, and will certainly not be the last, politician to make an ass of himself on television.'

George Brown's value as propagandist, energiser and catalyst was too great for an incident like this to exclude him from the high councils of the Labour Party. Under Harold Wilson he was given the formidable posts of Secretary of State for Economic Affairs and Foreign Secretary. But this television performance most certainly cast a shadow over his political future, if not amongst the general public, undoubtedly amongst his Parliamentary colleagues.

Of course, the ability of television to mar as well as enhance a politician's image was made evident as far back as 1954 when Senator Joseph McCarthy revealed the ugly, bullying side of his character during his investigation of security charges against the American Army. Not only did the cameras show McCarthy being bested in an exchange with an image of elderly respectable integrity in the person of the eloquent lawyer, Joseph Welch, but by some clever cutting of the cameras to McCarthy's hands as they nervously clenched and unclenched, the pictures insidiously suggested an uncertain, unstable, devious character.

Whether this revelation of McCarthy as a demagogue rather than a true-blue patriot was the beginning of the end of his political career is doubtful. After all, in 1954 only 60 per cent of American homes possessed television sets and probably only a fraction of these actually witnessed these hearings. But if the public did not turn against the Senator immediately, as the polls indicated, these television programmes became part of the accepted indictment of the Senator, evidence used in the press and by commentators to damn him, and when the Senate eventually turned against him, the reports of what he had looked like on television were amongst the important shovels used to dig his political grave.

Politicians have learnt a great deal about television since the McCarthy hearings in 1954 and even since George Brown's unhappy experience in 1963. In America an important television appearance is planned with as much caution as a walk through a minefield. In Britain the political parties employ experts to deal exclusively with the problems posed by television and to advise politicians on the pitfalls that may await them. There are even courses to teach M.P.s the ingredients of relaxation, familiarity, cosiness which are considered so essential for a successful television image. The chances of a politician ruining his career by some unwitting revelation of a weakness or by some unprepared outburst are becoming smaller as the techniques of image-making take over. Yet the sight of Senator Muskie, bursting into tears because of a newspaper attack on his wife, was probably the beginning of the decline of his chances of getting the 1972 Democratic Presidential Nomination. Before television such a demonstration could have been decently buried in the press. But in the telly age it was enough to sow suspicion in millions about Muskie's stability in a crisis. It did not mean that the people had discovered the truth about Muskie's ability. In spite of these tears Muskie might yet have made a firm and resolute President. But the image — true or false — sealed his political fate in 1972. It is an even greater indictment of the power of the box that this affair was cooked up by the 'dirty tricks' department of the Republican Campaign Committee. Watergate showed how easily television could be used as an unwitting pawn of sinister political forces.

Although the perils of immediate availability have been considerably reduced by an increased awareness of the dangers of the box, politicians are still prone to treat the small screen as a sort of public Wailing Wall whenever they are in trouble. In the past a politician with something significant or embarrassing to reveal would make a personal statement to his colleagues either in Congress or Parliament. Alternatively, he might have called a press conference or issued a statement to the press. Today his first instinct is to turn to the television cameras. What is more, the electorate now expects such an immediate direct explanation from their representatives. Anyone who is not prepared instantly to explain himself on television is automatically assumed to have something to hide.

This practice of instant accountability results not only in hurried, ill thought-out statements but tends to encourage explanations that are couched in the emotional, over-simplified and dramatic language of the television medium.

The best known illustration of television to muster sympathy for a politician's plight was Richard Nixon's 'Checkers' speech in 1952. The 39-year-old Senator, who had made a reputation for himself as a member of the Un-American Activities Committee, had been chosen to run as the Republican Vice-President alongside their esteemed Presidential candidate, General Eisenhower. During the course of the election, it was discovered that Nixon had accepted the sum of 18,235 dollars from 76 wealthy Californian Republicans. Since Eisenhower's image was that of sea-green incorruptibility, the suspicion that his young running-mate had been using this money improperly led to a vociferous campaign to get him dropped from the Republican ticket. In order to explain himself, Nixon went on a television network of 256 stations and told his story. As a tear-jerker, his broadcast rivalled anything ever achieved by *Peyton Place* or *Coronation Street*.

The half-hour talk, which was produced by an advertising agency, contained just those folksy ingredients which Americans, conditioned by the mass media, have identified with sincerity, honesty and integrity. Something like 25 million viewers heard him first of all dispose of the 'slush fund' charge and then reveal the details of his home life. Not a cent of the money he had received had been used by him personally. Indeed, the Nixon family was in debt, their house was heavily mortgaged and Pat, his wife, didn't even have a mink coat. 'But she does have a respectable Republican cloth coat,' said

65

Nixon defiantly, and one could almost hear the throb of violins, 'and I always tell her that she'd look good in anything.'

But the moment that won the hearts of America, the master touch of the consummate public relations man, came when Nixon admitted that he had received a gift of a political nature.

'A man down in Texas heard Pat on the radio mention the fact that our two youngsters would like to have a dog,' he said. 'And, believe it or not, the day before we left on this campaign trip, we got a message from Union Station in Baltimore saying that they had a package for us. We went down to get it. You know what it was? It was a little cocker spaniel dog in the crate that he sent all the way from Texas. Black and white spotted. And our little girl — Tricia, the six-year-old — named it Checkers. And, you know, the kids love the dog and I just want to say this right now, that regardless of what they say about it, we're gonna keep it.'

Although Nixon then went on to promise to drive 'the crooks and Communists out of Washington' and said a few admiring words of Eisenhower, it was this tale of a dog that his viewers could not resist. How could such a homespun character, who talked the same simple language as the people, who had a pretty wife and two young children, who had a mortgage on his house and who loved dogs — in short Mr. Average Family Man — be anything but decent, God-fearing and honest? Wasn't he doing just what James Stewart or Spencer Tracy or Mickey Rooney — cinema symbols of folksy integrity — would have done in similar circumstances in dozens of MGM and Paramount domestic sagas?

As if this display of mawkish self-justification were not humiliating enough, the viewers were then asked to write to the Republican National Committee and say whether or not Nixon should be dropped from the Republican ticket. It was, in its way, the electronic equivalent of the mobs in the Roman Colosseum being asked to give a thumbs up or a thumbs down sign about the fate of an intended victim. The Republicans gleefully announced that there was a 350 to 1 vote for keeping Nixon as their Vice-Presidential candidate. 'You're my boy,' said General Eisenhower, embracing Nixon a few days after the broadcast.

'While there was much criticism of Nixon's unscrupulous use of theatrics, his "soap-opera" appeal, the low level of intelligence at which he had pitched his defence, and the use of show business methods in politics, no one could deny that his political technique had been effective,' wrote sociologists Kurt and Gladys Engel Lang.[4]

Since Nixon's Checkers speech, it has become almost accepted practice that politicians will speak to the people through television whenever they are in a jam. If they do not get a half-hour to themselves as Nixon did, they will be interviewed by reporters or appear on current affairs programmes such as *Meet The Press* or *Panorama* to account for their actions. These appearances are more likely to determine the resolution of their problems than speeches made to their political peers in Congress or Parliament. It might even be said that as Nixon lived by television so did he die by it. It was the direct lies he told to the American people through TV — their effrontery and their brazenness — that ultimately discredited him in the eyes of the nation.

Another example of instant accountability through the box — and almost as dramatic — was Senator Edward Kennedy's nationwide broadcast in July 1969, in which he attempted to explain his involvement with the death of Mary Jo Kopechne at Chappaquidick and his failure to report the accident for nine hours. Before television it would have been appropriate and seemly for such a personal statement by an important politician to be made either in the form of a statement to the press, a press conference or a speech in the American Senate. But in 1969 none of these methods would have been considered as effective, as satisfactory or even as honorable as a direct confrontation with the people through the small screen. It was the people themselves who had to decide whether he was speaking the truth and after watching him on television make up their minds whether he deserved forgiveness or ostracism. Thus television had taken the place of the medieval trial by hazard. A man's destiny would hang on a performance. And woe to the man who performed badly!

'By God, he told the truth!' was the immediate reaction of Senator George Aitken of Vermont to Edward Kennedy's television confessional. It was typical of the response of millions who saw Kennedy's appearance. Like Nixon, he had, it seemed, triumphed in this ordeal by television.

Unlike Nixon, Senator Kennedy had not resorted to sentimental gimmickry but plumped for an image of staid, sombre forthrightness. Eyes fixed firmly in front of him, hands indulging in a minimum of movement, face a mask of suppressed anguish, he offered his explanation of those dreadful events in a voice that never faltered into pathos nor cracked under the burden of his humiliation. If the penalty for high office was the need to pass through such a shattering test in moments of personal crisis then Kennedy came through his ordeal splendidly. There was an overwhelming flood of support in his favour from viewers, particularly from Massachusetts, the Senator's electoral state.

But was the electorate in a better position to decide on the fitness of Edward Kennedy as a potential Presidential candidate? Had the small screen illuminated or obscured the truth? The blunt fact was that what millions of Americans saw on that Friday night was not a man revealing himself in a moment of crisis but a man who was *acting* the part of a man revealing himself in a moment of crisis. Even the words he spoke were not his own. The speech had been written by expert phrasemakers and which of the phrases and sentiments came out of his own heart and mind, the public had no way of knowing.

Would the viewers have reacted as sympathetically as they had if they had known in detail the advance preparations that had gone into the making of this programme? How many times did the Senator rehearse his speech? What instructions was he given as to how he should look, how to sit, what to do with his hands? Was he reading his speech through an Autocue or Tele-Prompter device which flashed before him line by line? Or were the words all written on huge placards — known as idiot boards — held beside the cameras by studio hands? What could such an appearance, sifted as it probably was through so many technical aids and second-hand devices, have to do with the reality of a man baring his soul spontaneously and honestly to the nation? Wasn't the public being treated, instead, to a *performance*, an enactment, a skilled professional version of what a politician *ought* to look like when revealing his soul to the nation?

Whether Kennedy was or was not telling the truth is less important than the fact that people should so readily accept such a patently contrived and theatrical means of determining the fate of public men. Suppose Senator Kennedy had been a bad performer instead of an able one. Suppose he had stumbled over his lines, looked shifty and uneasy, made a thoroughly unpleasant impression. Would this have been a fair basis for condemning him and sending him into political limbo? Some day an honest man, unable to cope with the demands of the box or the questions of a ruthless interviewer, will be publicly crucified by such an ordeal. As will be discussed later on, some men have already suffered the unhappy fate of trial by television. Is it not both unfair and dangerous that a politician should be judged a villain because he is a bad actor or that he should be acclaimed a saint because he happens to be a good one?

Relying as it does on an emotional, one-sided presentation of the facts, this sort of electronic circus is a crude and primitive way of determining a man's honesty. By preferring the test of instant accountability on television to the slower rules of judicial or legislative process, politicians are encouraging what Walter Lippmann called 'Mob law by modern electronics'. The end product must be a diminution of respect for politicians and the authority they represent.

The men, however, who are likely to be most diminished and quickest tarnished by television in Britain and America are those who reach the very pinnacles of leadership. They face the most intractable of all communications problems. How can a President or a Prime Minister steer an intelligent course between the Scylla of instant accountability and the Charybdis of immediate availability and still retain his authority and credibility with the electorate? How can they avoid the temptations of over-exposure? How can they report mostly bad news to the nation without at the same time acquiring the image of a man beset by problems too big for him to solve? How can they prevent themselves being identified, because of their constant immersion in it, with the triviality and frivolity of this primarily entertainment medium?

Undoubtedly, it was radio that gave political leaders the illusion that through broadcasting they would be able to manipulate public opinion more effectively than through any other medium. The ranting harangues of Hitler whipped up the German nation to frenzied support of Nazi ideals. The firm stirring voice of Roosevelt in his fireside chats reassured the Americans during the Depression years. The magnificent rhetoric of Churchill sustained the British in their most perilous and finest hours. Even the thin, reedy voice of Chamberlain, the blunt tones of Baldwin, the earthy views of Harry Truman acquired, when transmitted on radio, a mysterious and impressive authority. A politician could hardly fail on the wireless.

Mistakenly believing that television was merely radio with pictures, politicians after the war assumed that the small screen would similarly provide them with a convenient device for enhancing their prestige. But the mystical properties of the face and voice are quite different — as the Jews discovered long ago. For over 5000 years the Jews have been in awe of a God they have never pictured or envisaged. Instinctively they realised that the voice of Jehovah thundering down on them from above — even if it was only His words rather than His voice they heard — was a more impressive symbol of Almighty Authority than any graven image of their God.

Political leaders have still to learn how much the voice is belittled by the body. The corporeal appendages to a voice make us realise only too plainly how vulnerable is the creature who is claiming to lead us. The face reminds us of our doctor, our grocer, our uncle. If we see it too often, we grow accustomed to its mannerisms, its expressions, its sameness. The immediate result of identification with the personality and problems of a politician — as we have seen in Nixon's Checkers speech and in Kennedy's Chappaquidick television appearance — may be favourable. But in the longer run there is the danger of diminishing returns. Awe, wonder and respect diminish with familiarity. We identify more readily and more closely with a face than with an invisible voice. And with identification comes a recognition of the limitations and weaknesses we see in ourselves. If a leader is just like me, why should he be leading me? People want someone wiser, stronger, more courageous, less fallible than themselves to guide their destinies. The radio voice — remote, aloof, unidentifiable — provided such an illusion; the television face does not.

Political leaders still cling fondly to the assumption that television, like radio, is the best medium available to them for communicating with the people, for explaining away a crisis, for seeking the co-operation and understanding of the electorate. In America successive Presidents in the telly age have escalated their use of the small screen and increased their reliance upon it not only to gain support from the public but to enable the Executive to put pressure upon Congress for some course of action.

Harry Truman hardly used television at all. He would not allow television cameras into his press conference. This disdain of the medium is hardly surprising since for most of Truman's Presidency from 1945 to 1953 less than 10 per cent of American homes possessed sets. It was only in the last two years of his incumbency that something like one-third of Americans could have heard him on the box.

Eisenhower in 1955 held the first televised press conference and then only under strict rules that the final edited version of the Conference be approved by his Press Secretary, James Hagerty. Even these supervised editions of the press conference caused dismay amongst some viewers as they heard for the first time Eisenhower's long-winded, rambling, confusing, grammatically erratic answers to questions put to him by journalists. Inevitably, to ensure that the President be seen to best advan-in these confrontations with the press, entertainment experts were brought in to stage-manage the occasion. 'By this time, the President had employed Robert Montgomery as a television consultant,' writes Robert MacNeil, 'and the actor had become the first show business personality with an office in the White House. Under his influence Ike's television performances were noticeably more relaxed and natural. Montgomery also introduced some lighting changes which gave the President a warmer appearance.'[5]

It was President Kennedy in January 1961, who brought the live television conference to the White House. Risky because of the consequences of an inadvertent, off-the-cuff answer to an important question, these conferences, too, had to be manipulated so that the viewers could get an impression of being informed without actually realising that little of significance was really being revealed.

71

President Johnson was never very keen on having his press conferences televised. In the first place, they were too identified with the Kennedy image and Johnson was eager to make his own mark on the nation. Secondly, he preferred a more private method of briefing the press in which his intimate, robust, racy style of speaking would not be inhibited by the presence of cameras. The President seen in these bull sessions, replete with anecdotes and expletives of a Texas cowhand, was a far different figure from the earnest, drawling, schoolmasterly figure the public had become accustomed to seeing on the box.

But if he was shy of the televised press conference, it by no means indicated that Johnson was against the medium as a device for communicating with the electorate. On the contrary. Johnson was more telly conscious than any other American President before him. His own family fortune, through his wife's ownership of television station KTBC in Austin, Texas, was largely based upon profits made in television. He had a naïve faith in the persuasive power of the small screen and insisted on his right to appear on it whenever he felt he had something important to tell the nation.

'Under President Johnson, a fully equipped television studio was installed in the White House for the first time, located in the old movie theatre,' wrote Robert MacNeil. 'The networks actually agreed to keep a camera "warm" there at all times at a joint cost estimated at one million dollars a year. The studio, which had a director and camera crew constantly on duty, was on a five-minute alert.'[6]

There are, of course, a number of constitutional issues which are raised in America by this ability of the President to have such immediate and constant access to the television screen. Since the Executive and Congress are part of a power balancing act — often in conflict about legislative actions and decisions — the President, through his use of the box, is seen as having an unfair advantage in being able to present his point of view to the people while opposing Senators and Congressmen have no like opportunity for putting their arguments to the electorate under similarly favourable conditions. It also unbalances the party system in that an incumbent President, being the head of his party, can be seen to be having millions of dollars worth of free television time justifying his actions which in turn is theoretically helping the party he leads. In Britain it is only on matters of national significance — 'appeals to the nation to co-operate on national policy' — that the Government can have access to television without the Opposition having a right to reply. Such occasions might number two or three a year.

President Nixon was even more television conscious and convinced of its effectiveness as an instrument of Executive persuasion than President Johnson. His fear and respect for the television cameras was no doubt engendered by his political history. In each major crisis of his political career television played a major role. The Checkers broadcast saved him from being dropped as Republican Vice-Presidential candidate; the Nixon–Kennedy debates probably lost him the marginal votes he needed to defeat John Kennedy; the shrewd packaging of his image on television during the 1968 Presidential campaign was a significant factor in getting him to the White House. Watergate wrote the electronic finish to his political career.

Like Johnson, President Nixon was not very keen on the televised press conference. He preferred the direct confrontation with the viewers provided by either a speech straight to camera or a question-and-answer session with journalists. He made such frequent use of the box for policy statements about Vietnam, the economy and civil unrest that complaints about 'government by television' became more loud and persistent.

Eric Sevareid, a respected CBS-TV commentator, firmly declared that it was wrong for three television networks to grant a President a free platform whenever the White House wanted one. He thought the networks were much too 'amenable' to frequent Presidential demands and 'the White House acts as though it has a proprietary right to it — and it doesn't'.[7]

Coupled with the excessive use of television by Nixon was a campaign, provocatively led by Vice-President Agnew, to deter the networks from subjecting a President's television address to any objective or outside criticism immediately after it was made. In a speech in November 1969, in Des Moines, which has since been interpreted as a veiled declaration of war by the

Nixon administration against its critics in the press and broadcasting, Agnew accused news broadcasts of persistent bias and hostility to the President. He was particularly incensed about the reception on television to Nixon's speech on Vietnam made on November 3rd, 1969.

'When the President completed his address — an address incidentally that he spent weeks preparing — his words and policies were subjected to instant analysis and querulous criticism,' said Agnew. 'The audience of 70 million Americans gathered to hear the President of the United States, was inherited by a small band of network commentators and self-appointed analysts, the majority of whom expressed in one way or another their hostility to what he had to say.

'One commentator twice contradicted the President's statement about the exchange of correspondence with Ho Chi Minh. Another challenged the President's ability as a politician. A third asserted that the President was following a Pentagon line. Others, by the expressions on their faces, the tone of their questions, and the sarcasm of their responses, made clear their sharp disapproval.'

The speech went on to attack the unrepresentative nature of the men who were selected to analyse and dissect political news. Appealing to the anti-intellectual, anti-Eastern-seaboard prejudices of the American masses, he sneered at the parochial, incestuous environment of Washington and New York inhabited by men like Walter Cronkite, Chet Huntley, and David Brinkley. 'It's time we questioned such power in the hands of a small and unelected élite,' said the Vice-President. 'The great networks have dominated America's air waves for decades. The people are entitled to a full accounting of their stewardship.'

Such an unprecedented and ferocious assault on the medium could not be brushed off as an aberration by an exhibitionist Vice-President seeking some attention. 'By the time the Vice-President was finished,' commented the American news magazine *Newsweek*, 'There seemed little doubt that the onslaught had been long in planning, carefully orchestrated, and patently designed to force US television news programmes into a mold more clearly to the liking of the Administration of President Richard M. Nixon.'[8]

The networks indignantly denied Agnew's charges and made

bold statements about not yielding to intimidation. 'Whatever their deficiencies,' said Dr. Stanton, president of CBS, 'they are minor compared to those of a press which would be subservient to the executive power of the government.' Nevertheless, in the short run, Agnew's attack succeeded in restraining still further the already strictly limited area of political discussion exercised by American television.

Six months after Agnew's Des Moines speech, Henry Brandon in the *Sunday Times*, commented on the subtle way in which the medium had retreated in the face of the Vice-President's onslaught.

'The leading professional television critics are convinced that, even though it may be difficult actually to document it, the networks are looking with agonising uneasiness over their shoulders,' wrote Mr. Brandon. 'And some commentators — not those with an established national reputation — admit they have become more careful ... The Agnew salvoes have had an effect not so much because of his accusations but because of the public support they engendered ... Even if the national television networks have not been strikingly influenced by the Agnew broadsides, it seems certain that the local stations, whose licences are up for renewal every three years, have reacted. WTOP., one of Washington's four television stations, is now giving 50 per cent more time to its conservative commentator, James Kilpatrick, than it did before the Vice-President began to throw his rocks ... Whether by coincidence or not, after President Nixon's two last Press conferences, the instant commentaries were virtually uncritical.'[9]

It should be noted that television played little part in the investigating journalism that helped to end Nixon's presidency. Cowed by fear of White House wrath, the American networks did little but report the findings courageously dug out by publications like the *Washington Post*, the *New York Times* and *Time* and *Newsweek* magazines.

The obsession of the Nixon administration with the power of television and its determination to deter it from any unwelcome criticism of the Government was bluntly outlined by the Federal Communications Commissioner, Nicholas Johnson, in a speech he gave in London to the International Association of Political Consultants on December 14th, 1970.

75

'What emerges is the overwhelming impression of an administration whose fixed focus is on the little glass screen, beginning with the media campaign of 1968,' said Mr. Johnson, 'President Nixon surrounds himself with advisors whose principle experience is in advertising, public relations and broadcasting; his appointments to the federal communications commission and related agencies are designed to foster administration control and industry orientation. The full panoply of governmental power is available to use on the broadcasting medium. An office of "Director of Interior Communications" is established in the White House to survey the media and co-ordinate the attack. Broadcasters are kept off-balance by the one-two punch of barely camouflaged intimidation and acts of censorship, together with the promise of an economic pay-off for those who co-operate.'

From Truman to Nixon there has been an increasing involvement and concern with the medium by every President in the White House in the television age. Truman was indifferent to it. Eisenhower was wary of it. Kennedy was sceptical and extremely sensitive about it. Johnson was almost hysterical about it. Nixon at times verged on paranoia over it. Ford quickly became a victim of TV exposure. But none discovered a sure formula for handling it or a guaranteed technique for taming it. The fact is that in spite of all the show biz methods adapted to give them amenable and attractive images, each President has found it more and more difficult to retain his popularity and lovability in the glare of the television cameras.

The same process of diminishing popularity for political leaders is evident in Britain. Although illustrations are yet few in number — Johnson, Alec Douglas-Home, Edward Heath — it seems certain that television has drastically curtailed the longevity of power. Contrary to the view that frequent direct contact with the people through the small screen raises the credibility and acceptability of Prime Ministers and Presidents, a formidable statistical case could be made for showing that exactly the reverse process takes place. Up until now no such leader has been able to survive six consecutive years of television coverage. Over-exposure had become one of the most deadly killers of political ambitions. Why is this so?

The rules of the political game in Western democracies do not encourage leaders to come to the television screen when they have something to boast about or something that will enhance their prestige in the eyes of the electorate. The Opposition strongly resists the use of the broadcasting media as a public relations device to be available to the Government at all times. In Britain 'Ministerial broadcasts' can only be used, without giving the Opposition a right to reply, when they can be interpreted as 'appeals to the nation to co-operate on national policy'. In other words, the Government has only a right to the box on its own when it has something of national — as distinct from Party — significance to broadcast to the people. Thus when Edward Heath appeared in a Ministerial broadcast to urge support for the Government's White Paper on the Common Market in July 1971, it was still considered a partisan enough issue to entitle Harold Wilson to a reply on television the following night. The use of the word 'appeals' in the *aide-mémoire* setting out the rules for Ministerial broadcasts indicates the general nature of the issue that would justify such a one-sided privilege. It is usually bad news that vindicates such a need for an 'appeal' to the nation rather than good news.

Even in America, where no such explicit ground rules restrict the President's access to the small screen, it has been matters of an urgent, critical or depressing nature that have usually provoked a television address. They have been designed to reassure, mollify or explain some Governmental action when the nation was troubled and uneasy about some course of events.

President Eisenhower's major television appearances dealt with the state of his health when seeking re-election in 1956; a school integration clash between Federal and State authorities at Little Rock, Arkansas; a warning to Communist China that America was ready to intervene if it persisted in trying to conquer the Nationalist off-shore island of Quemoy.

President Kennedy, who was undoubtedly the most telegenic President of the television age, treated the medium as if it were a ticking bomb. Except for his press conferences, he tried to avoid using it as a means of informing or arousing or warning the nation. He was actually conscious of the dangers of overexposure.

But even he was forced to use the electronic box as an ally in taking arms against 'the sea of troubles' that constantly threatens to overwhelm an American President. There was the continuing crisis of school integration, the Cuban missile threat to world peace, the Bay of Pigs débâcle, rows with Congress and the steel industry — all matters of gloom and anxiety that brought the Kennedy television image to the electorate.

The harassed, over-earnest, hang-dog face of President Johnson reporting on difficulty after difficulty over the television screen was a decided feature of his administration. Johnson resorted to television so often and so indiscriminately that on occasions some of the networks refused to broadcast a so-called 'Major Speech' live and had it taped for transmission in the late, non-prime-time hours. Thus an important address about Vietnam on September 29th, 1967, was only carried live by NBC and it had to face the competition of a Hitchcock film and a Western from the other major networks.[10] The intractable Vietnam war, violence in the cities, student riots, racial conflict, a difficult Congress occupied most of the appearances Johnson made on television. Sometimes he used the box to herald a heartening or optimistic event such as his happy meeting with Kosygin at Glassboro, New Jersey in 1967, but for the most part the American public could expect that the presence of President Johnson in their living-rooms was evidence that things were going wrong rather than right.

President Nixon, too, was faced with this Cassandra role of a bearer of bad tidings on the box. The American invasion of Cambodia, the depressed state of the economy, civil strife, the menacing drug problem have been the subjects of most of Nixon's major addresses on television. Like all his predecessors in the telly era, he felt obliged to explain himself on the small screen when national events were going through an ugly, depressing or difficult phase. Not least, he used television time and time again to try and ward off the enveloping tide of Watergate.

What is the cumulative impact of these persistent appeals by leaders asking for support, understanding, sympathy, tolerance, patience for the actions they are taking over a seemingly unending parade of national crises? I believe that each time they appear they leave behind a psychological negative residual.

Most viewers, of course, are not drastically affected by such appearances. Their loyalties and antipathies are not likely to be changed by a single television speech. Another justification of the bombing of North Vietnam will not seriously shift most people's views about a leader like President Johnson or President Nixon. But amongst the uncommitted voters, voters with no hard political loyalties, the young who have voted for the first time or are about to become eligible for voting, the sight of a democratic leader explaining himself, justifying his policies, displaying his fallibility, must be evidence to some people that the man in charge is more pathetic and less omniscient than they assumed. Each explanation he gives must displease someone as being either inadequate or unconvincing. Trust in the ability of the leader to control events begins to ebb; suspicions about his competence and even honesty begin to harden. A nugget of doubt is lodged in the viewer's mind and consciousness. This negative residual, left behind by a television appearance, is extremely difficult to eradicate. Since the next time the leader appears on the small screen, once more asking for sympathy or support over some depressing issue, the earlier scepticism about the President's ability to handle affairs is confirmed. The negative residuals accumulate with time until a positive hostility or dangerous cynicism develops not only towards the leader but the Party and views he represents.

In their book *Politics and Television*, the sociologists Kurt and Gladys Lang found in their case studies that television, not only in the way it treats politicians but in the way it disseminates news, can contribute to a disillusionment with the political process.

'The way television handles the day-to-day flow of news by presenting a series of headline stories tends to highlight the unusual and extraordinary,' they wrote. 'Conflicts and crises predominate. Balanced presentation, that hallmark of good television reporting which gives equal time to charges and counter-charges, can, where contextual interpretation is inadequate, create a feeling that political events are beyond the scope of ordinary comprehension. Nor is the full coverage of an event enough to neutralise the inclinations of the chronically distrustful. It may only abet the tendency of viewers low in political competence to see in what they cannot understand

79

proof that they are being manipulated . . . The media, we contend, can stir up in individuals defensive reactions by their emphasis on crisis and conflict in lieu of clarifying normal decision-making processes. Thus, the individual's resistance to appeals for political support is often rationalised by disgust about the low state of political ethics.'[11]

It is not only the content of his speeches that build up negative residuals for a leader in a telly democracy but familiarity with his mannerisms, his voice, his gestures, his style. What may begin as an attractive, reassuring, even endearing characteristic — Johnson's evangelical earnestness, Wilson's pipe and chatty phrases, Nixon's flashing smile — becomes with repetition and constant association with news of crises and concern, evidence of smugness, complacency, insensitivity and insincerity. Just as a husband who has become disenchanted with his wife can build up the sound of the way she crunches Corn Flakes at breakfast into a justifiable cause for homicide, so do the repetitive mannerisms of politicians build up irritation, suspicion and even loathing amongst viewers who have become disenchanted with their leaders.

Thus the 'performance' becomes an essential ingredient of a politician's worth. In an attempt to put across the so-called 'real person' — which is merely a euphemism for 'likeable' person — every kind of artificial, show-biz device is recruited. Thus President Johnson was equipped with contact lenses to give him a less austere image. He was advised to speak faster to offset the drawling, languid effects of his Southern accent. He was widely praised for a press conference, not because of anything he said, but because he was equipped with a microphone device which enabled him to escape the confines of the lectern and walk about freely as he answered questions. This made him look 'more natural'.

But just as make-up men, speech therapists, lighting experts are now the essential backroom boys of a leader's retinue, so does the 'performance' become judged and assessed not on its political content but on the success or failure of the performance. The more sophisticated viewer, the more aware voter, becomes an amateur television critic searching for telltale signs of fallibility behind the mask, confirmation of suspicions, evidence of the visual tricks being used to influence him. The politician as actor becomes as vulnerable as any other actor to this cynical scrutiny. The sense of being manipulated grows the more often the leader is seen with his techniques showing. The suspension of disbelief which is essential for successful theatre becomes in the case of politicians who have been seen too often a heightening of disbelief. Over-exposure in the actor role snowballs with alarming velocity the growth of negative residuals. An example of just such a reaction to a politician's performance can be seen in the report by William Millinship, the *Observer*'s chief correspondent in the United States, to a live television interview given by President Nixon in July 1970.

'President Nixon's eyes twice flicked away from his questioners, as if to check which camera was on him,' wrote Mr. Millinship. 'These were the only technical flaws in an otherwise supremely professional performance in Wednesday night's live television interview on American policy. Mr. Nixon was fluent, firmly relaxed and courteous ... But the involuntary sliding away of the eyes sharpened the feeling that the appearance was a performance, calculated and self-monitored, carefully designed to create a certain impression. The famous Nixon smile was allowed to appear only occasionally and then as if on a prearranged cue.'[12]

In Britain no politician has suffered the consequences of television's negative residuals more severely than Harold Wilson. Praised as the man more adroit and professional at manipulating the mass media than any previous Prime Minister, Wilson could not resist the temptation of exercising his skills on the box. A compulsive self-justifier and acutely suspicious of the press, he saw in television a device to suit both his needs and his temperament. As part of the technological revolution that was to be introduced with the Labour Government in 1964, broadcasting was to be recruited as a more modern method of communicating with the people. There were to be the equivalent of intimate fireside chats on television and radio. 'We shall speak freely to you and tell you what needs to be done,' said Mr. Wilson in his first television broadcast as Prime Minister in October 1964.

For the first two years of office, he more than kept his word. In 1965 on the BBC alone he made seven major television appearances discussing such a variety of subjects as Vietnam, the economic situation, Rhodesia and the United Nations. Since he was also seen on the commercial channel, the Wilson image turned up in Britain's living-rooms almost once a month. Even the most popular actor thinks he is tempting fate if he appears in a series of 13 programmes a year. This rate of appearances is bordering on saturation. Particularly when they are added to the usual news coverage that a Prime Minister gets as normal routine.

It is clear that the fresh image that Wilson offered viewers in his first year of power did him a lot of good. Although he had a good deal of dispiriting news to broadcast about Rhodesia, the economy and Vietnam, there was no way of testing in the short run whether his solutions were logical or effective. Most of the nation's problems could be attributed to '13 years of Tory misrule' and the British electorate thought it only fair the Labour Government be given a reasonable time to get things right. When in April 1966, after just over a year in office, they asked for another mandate, it was generously accorded them. The negative residuals had not yet begun to take hold.

In 1966 Wilson made six major appearances on the BBC — i.e. Ministerial broadcasts and appearances on *Panorama* — with a somewhat similar number on commercial television. In 1967 his television appearances had shrunk to four on the BBC. And in 1968, except for a personal tribute to the late Robert Kennedy, he did not make a *single* major broadcast on either channel.

Now it was not as if 1968 was a year devoid of political events justifying a British Prime Minister's use of television to communicate with the nation. On the contrary. It was a year of almost traumatic uncertainty, violence and disruption not only in Britain but in the world at large. There was a railway go-slow; Enoch Powell's controversial speech on race relations with its visions of rivers of blood; riots in France bordering on a state of revolution; and the Russian invasion of Czechoslovakia. Each of these events gave rise to enough anxiety, concern, uneasiness to warrant a statement from the Prime Minister about what the Government was going to do about them. Yet the man who had been hailed as the wizard of the media, the politician who believed the public should always be kept in intimate touch with his closest thoughts, did not resort to television once in that worried year. What had happened to the exhibitionist Mr. Wilson?

Clearly the negative residuals had begun to take their toll. The years 1966–7 were bad for Labour with deteriorating economic conditions which culminated in the devaluation of the pound. Wilson's appearances on the small screen merely compounded his own and his Party's unpopularity. His buoyant optimism became irritating in the face of rising unemployment and the worsening balance of payments situation. His vistas of a technological millennium began to sound like so much pie in the sky. His appeals to the nation's Dunkirk spirit raised only yawns instead of enthusiasm.

There was a sameness about his voice, his mannerisms, his phrases that made him irresistible material for satirists and impersonators. There was a psychological backlash, too, over the image that Wilson had been at such pains to cultivate in his early years as Prime Minister. Although his opponents tried to portray him as a slippery, devious confidence man manipulating propaganda gimmicks for a short-term political advantage, he consistently concentrated on emphasising the humble ordinariness of his tastes and style. The Gannex mackintosh; the pipe; the holidays in the Scilly Isles; the taste for the North Country television serial *Coronation Street* and his admiration for the Beatles who were given an MBE for services to the arts; the homely speeches devoid of heightened language or inspirational phrases; the talking down on television; the picture of a hard-working clerk with his finger on every statistic. These were the ingredients of the electronic jig-saw that made up Harold Wilson's image on television.

But this identification with the average man began to pay diminishing dividends as the practical problems of government became more intractable and more insoluble. Wilson's emphasis on the simplicity of his life resulted in his being lampooned on television — not nearly as severely as he would have been had the BBC satire shows in 1967 possessed the bite of their predecessors — and in magazines like *Private Eye* which were widely read by the young, as a tasteless philistine with a passion for HP sauce and whose reading outside of official papers was confined to a biography of Lincoln, *The Making of the President* and Kipling's *If*. At the London Palladium, where one might have expected to find Labour supporters, the laughter at Wilson jokes was no longer good-natured. The reception to his television speech in November 1967, in which he tried to reassure viewers that devaluation did not mean that 'the pound in your pocket or purse or in your bank' had been devalued, was so damaging that it was clear that Mr. Wilson's image was reaching a nadir of unpopularity.

It was now self evident that the Wilsonian media magic had evaporated. A holiday from the box was essential. In an attempt to make people forget the personality associated with such unpopularity, Wilson spent 1968 in the shadows. The disappearance of the Prime Minister from the television screen took on the aspect of a national joke. Cartoonists were beginning to draw faceless pipes and mackintoshes to symbolise him. In the satirical play, *Mrs. Wilson's Diary,* which had a short run in London's West End, he was depicted hiding away in an attic in 10 Downing Street with his only outside means of communication a large basket which he lowered from time to time to receive his newspapers and groceries.

With an improving economic situation and the opinion polls indicating more support for Labour, Wilson began to venture back to the box in 1969. Conscious of a coming election, Wilson's performance during that year concentrated less on the harsh realities of politics and more on the friendly, likeable personality of the Prime Minister and his home life.

This build-up of Wilson on television as the sincere man to be trusted, the avuncular figure just like everybody else, the good-natured wit with a riposte for every heckler, continued right into the 1970 election campaign. The walk-about policy adopted by Labour's strategists was deliberately designed with an eye on the box. Catering to the demands of the small screen, the strategy was to damp down concern over issues and concentrate on the personality of the leader. As we shall see, it was a British version of Nixon's television campaign in the 1968 election.

Peter Jenkins in the *Guardian* on June 3rd, 1970, described the technique: 'In a few more days, if not already, the mass of viewer-voters will have had it impressed on their minds' eyes that the Prime Minister's election campaign consists chiefly in "meeting the people". By contrast, Mr. Wilson cunningly hopes, their image of Mr. Edward Heath may be of a man making the tediously repetitive speeches which voters have come to expect from politicians. . . .

'Do not be misled by Mr. Wilson's innocent folksy account of what he is up to. He is not "meeting the people" at all, either in large numbers or in any representative capacity. He is showing himself to small crowds in the streets and meeting small gatherings of the party faithful in tiny committee rooms . . .

'The concept is a simple one: moving pictures make better television than talking heads. That's how most news and current affairs producers see it. Mr. Wilson is the first politician to grasp the full potential of the hand-held camera . . .

'While Mr. Wilson was in motion in North London I asked him if he wasn't risking losing the impact on television of the big speech made to the packed hall. "No," he said. "This makes much better pictures. People are sick of politicians on the box making speeches. If I want to make a statement I can put out a 700-word handout at any time with just as much effect."

' "Meet the people" is the message and the message is the medium. It would be better described as a meet the camera campaign.'

Unfortunately for Labour, this campaign misfired. The defeat of the Labour Party in 1970, against all the evidence of the opinion polls and all the predictions of the pundits, has still not been convincingly explained. In their detailed analysis of that campaign, *The British Election of 1970*, the psephologists David Butler and Michael Pinto-Duschinsky confess their inability to find a satisfactory explanation as to why and when the electorate turned against Harold Wilson. The most that they can claim for their investigations is that they offer 'evidence which proponents of any point of view can cite.'[13]

Since any theory on this issue is as plausible as any others that have been advanced, let me offer one which has not yet been seriously considered. It is generally accepted that it is the uncommitted, floating or new voter who determines election results in Western democracies.

The die-hard party supporter in Britain will vote for his side whether it is led by a belted earl or a chimpanzee. It can

85

generally be assumed that about 35 per cent of the electorate will vote Labour and 35 per cent Tory no matter what issues are at stake or who is leading the party. It is the uncommitted middle — somewhere about 30 per cent or less of the total vote — by their abstentions or shifting preferences that decides on the day who is to govern the country.

It is amongst this group of floating voters that the impact of television's negative residual is at its most potent. A proportion of them had decided long before the election that they would not vote Wilson come what may. And that decision was largely taken because of Wilson's image on the small screen. They had become disenchanted with his mannerisms, disillusioned with his methods and explanations, antipathetic to his phrases, his style, his looks, his voice. How large this group was, it is impossible to estimate. But anything from 3 per cent to 5 per cent of the electors would have been enough to swing the election in the direction it took. Traditional Labour voters abstained because they could not take Wilson any more; undecided voters chose Heath because they disliked him less than Wilson.

There is little doubt that the unpopularity factor is becoming increasingly relevant in democratic elections. The electorate now tends to vote to keep somebody out rather than to put somebody in. Their vote is a symbol of rejection rather than approval. To a certain extent this has always been true, but in the telly age this rejection process is more significant than ever. In a survey carried out by the sociological magazine, *New Society*, R. L. Leonard found that on recent evidence the longer a leader remained on the scene the less popular he became. Conversely, Mr. Leonard noted that political parties usually improved their standing when there was a change of leader and that a substantial fund of goodwill was allotted to a new leader no matter what people had thought of him before he was chosen. In Britain, for example, Home, Macmillan and Wilson were all beneficiaries of this flood of approval on taking over as heads of their parties.[14]

In a letter to *The Times* on June 25th, 1971, the late Lord Salisbury indirectly gave his aristocratic imprimatur to this view when he quoted with approval a speech given by Professor Geoffrey Dobbs in which Dobbs said, 'Very few people actually believe in or approve of the party for which they vote.

Their vote, in fact, is normally a negative vote, a vote to exclude from power whichever party is deemed more disastrous.'

Lord Salisbury then went on to comment: 'These words, I believe, enshrine a great truth and one very applicable to our own General Election last June. The real reason why the British people put in the Conservative Party in that election was surely not because they thought that the Conservative manifesto would provide a cure for all their ills. It was because they could not endure the Labour Government any longer.'

Since it is conceded that the 1970 election was fought not on any burning issue but largely on the personality of Mr. Wilson — whose face, voice and activities during the campaign overwhelmingly eclipsed any other personality in the Labour Party — Salisbury's comment might logically read 'because they could not endure Harold Wilson any longer'.

The public opinion polls during the campaign consistently showed Heath lagging far behind Wilson as a figure who was satisfyingly leading his party. The gap was so wide as to convince the experts that only a miracle would defeat Labour. The miracle duly arrived. What the experts failed to realise was that if 65 per cent of people were satisfied with Wilson as leader of his party and only 35 per cent were satisfied with Heath as leader of the Tories, this did not mean that they wanted Wilson to head another Government. Many voters did not choose Heath in preference to Wilson. They voted against Wilson. That was their only positive act. The Conservatives merely happened to be the beneficiaries of that choice of lesser evils. So evident was this mood of disillusionment with both parties, and presumably both their leaders, that Butler and Pinto-Duschinsky thought that their book on the British General Election of 1970 might logically have been subtitled 'The unpopularity contest'.[15]

Although Harold Wilson, again in a surprise result, regained power in the 1974 February General Election and consolidated his position in another General Election in October of the same year, this was no evidence that the TV electorate had taken him back again into their hearts. The Labour victory, very slim in both cases, was largely due to the effects of the Tory Government's confrontation with the trade unions which resulted in the miner's industrial action in the winter of 1973–74 and the attendant miseries of a three-day working week. Again it was less due to faith in Wilson's ability to deal with the unions and loss of faith in Heath's ability to deal with the unions and inflation. And, as far as the leaders of both major parties were concerned, the 1974 elections were both 'unpopularity contests'.

Just how far both Wilson and Heath had fallen in the esteem of the British people was illustrated by a Confidence Index, based upon the monthly findings of the Gallup Poll stretching back over the ten years when both men were chosen to lead their respective parties in 1965.

Richard Rose in the *Sunday Times* of February 16th, 1975, analysed this 'long legacy of mistrust of party leaders in which both Edward Heath and Harold Wilson have shared'.

'Under a two-party system, the electorate's confidence in the Leader of the Opposition ought to rise as the standing of the Prime Minister declines,' wrote Mr. Rose. 'But while Heath and Wilson were slogging it out, both of them slumped in public favour. By 1968, two voters out of five actively disapproved of the leaders of both parties . . . For the rest of the time, one or the other — both in 1968 — has slumped so low in public trust that more voters have sometimes disapproved of both of them than would offer either one support.'

Again, as in the case of Alec Douglas-Home, the inability of a Tory leader to cope with his TV image led to his downfall. No matter what was done to mellow and humanise Heath's stiff and plummy TV personality — walk-abouts, chummy chat-ins, casual clothes — his advisers were unable to remove that aura of aloofness and remoteness which is unacceptable to a TV electorate that cherishes loveability above all. In every analysis of the cause of Heath's two electoral defeats in 1974, his inability to communicate on the small screen was included as one of the major factors responsible for the Conservative collapse.

The *Observer*'s comment on 20th October 1974, reflected a consensus of editorial opinion about the causes for the Tory party's second electoral defeat in a single year. 'Mr. Heath's public personality lacks some kind of empathy or capacity for easy communication,' it wrote, 'and that puts him at a disadvantage, particularly on television. This is an important, even if imponderable, factor.'

Trying to combat the view that Heath should be discarded because of his TV image, Lord Hailsham, one of the elder statesmen of the Conservative Party, vigorously attacked the idea of a democracy that selects its leaders on the basis of their electronic appeal. In a speech on 9th November 1974 to key party organisers he said that a leader should not be a sort of disc-jockey, chosen for his patter or his sex appeal.

'It is no good aspiring to be a political leader unless you have a first-class brain, bags of courage and endurance, absolute integrity and total commitment. To worship the television potential of one possible leader, to concern oneself unduly with the relatively unfavourable image of another is the classical error of the immature and the superficial.'

Nevertheless, in spite of Lord Hailsham's admonitions, when the Tory party had to face the question of whether Heath should stay or go, it was his TV personality that probably influenced the result as much as any other factor. Perhaps typical of the way many of the Conservative MP's were thinking was this letter in *The Times* on October 19th, 1974, by Mrs. Elizabeth Holt, a defeated Conservative candidate. 'It is a sad thing when the choice of a party leader depends on how well he/she can communicate to the electorate by way of TV but this now is a fact of life.' And in a leader in *The Times* on December 31st, 1974, it was ruefully conceded that while Mr. Heath was a man who possessed great force of will and executive ability, 'it is now widely supposed, he is a doorstep loser at election time.' And since political parties are in business to win elections, Mr. Heath on February, 1975, was duly ditched to be replaced by Mrs. Margaret Thatcher, the first woman to lead a major political party in Europe. Her chances of ever becoming the first woman Prime Minister would obviously depend to a major extent on how she manipulated TV and how the box handled her.

What part television plays in this growth of suspicion and cynicism about party leaders cannot, of course, be statistically assessed. But it is clearly an important catalyst in the cauldron of unpopularity in which democratic politicians now stew. The chances of political leaders surviving in such an atmosphere for

a long time are very remote. The prospects of political longevity enjoyed by men such as Gladstone, Walpole or Mackenzie King — 14 to 25 years as heads of government — are
almost unthinkable in the television era.

The national elections in America and Canada in 1972 contributed some further evidence to the relatively meagre store of
information we have about the mysterious and contradictory
impact television has on the electoral fortunes of politicians in
telly democracies. On the face of it, the narrow victory of
Pierre Trudeau's Liberal Party in Canada — a 109 to 107 lead
over the Conservatives but no overall majority against all opposition parties — would seem to confirm the view that TV char-
isma is a short-lived asset. Trudeau's leadership was no match
for such big issues as high unemployment and inflation which
were probably the main causes of his party's loss of votes. But,
one might ask, what negative residuals accumulated around
Trudeau's personality during four years of office? The swing-
ing Trudeau image which television brought to the electorate in
1968 could not be sustained in power. The handsome, party-
going bachelor annoyed those who expected an aura of responsibility from a Prime Minister; when he married and
spoke to the people in the sombre, respectable tones of a head of
state, he annoyed those who had turned to him because he was
something fresh, different and youthful on the Canadian political scene. Trudeau was trapped by his image and negative residuals accumulated whenever he tried on the box to sustain that
image or discard it.

Richard Nixon's overwhelming presidential victory in
1972 — an almost unprecedented 61 per cent of the popular
vote against Senator McGovern's 38 per cent — would seem to
indicate that in spite of his constant use of television no serious
negative residuals accumulated around his image. At least, not
enough in any way to diminish his electoral chances. But even if
Nixon was re-elected in this decisive manner, can it be truly
said that this vote was a testimony to Nixon's popularity? Did
all those television appearances increase the public's faith and
trust in him? Or was his election simply an unhesitating choice
of a lesser evil, a fear of the change and uncertainty that McGovern seemed to stand for?

The commentators and the pollsters agreed that Nixon was

re-elected in spite of a great deal of distrust and suspicion about him. James Reston, the political journalist, described the election as an 'unpopularity landslide'. A Louis Harris poll, scientifically measuring public preferences early in the campaign, had this to say: 'It would appear from President Nixon's early lead that the negatives about him at this stage of the campaign do not cut as deeply as those against Senator McGovern. More significant, however, may be the fact that in 1972 voters are in a highly critical mood about both men running for the White House, as indeed they are about leadership of the country in nearly every major private and public area.'

Analysing the results *Newsweek*, on November 20th, 1972, said, 'Casting a shadow over Mr. Nixon's lien on power was the suspicion that his victory was a shallow one, built less on affection for him than on antipathy toward McGovern and his New Democrats ... Mr. Nixon had only to stand on his substantial record and stay out of sight, with just eleven days of campaigning and thirteen radio talks (to two on TV). The choice between his disembodied non-campaign and McGovern's apocalyptic rhetoric brought out fewer than 54 per cent of the voters, the lowest turn out in 24 years.'

The ultimate rejection of Nixon because of the Watergate affair was probably made more likely because the American people — even though they preferred Nixon to McGovern — already had a built-in and hard suspicion and distrust of the man himself.

Professor Sir Denis Brogan, the distinguished British writer on America, confirmed the anti-Nixon element in the result. 'The completeness of President Nixon's triumph in 1972 cannot conceal the fact that he is not a popular *triumphator*,' wrote Brogan in *The Spectator* of November 18th, 1972. 'People trusted his sense, including his sense of his own interests, more than they did George McGovern's sense of American or his own interests, but it was a very tepid support and would not stand much wear and tear if things went wrong.'

Significantly, then, the special circumstances of Nixon's triumph do not invalidate the theory that the way television is used in countries like Britain, America and Canada contributes to the hardening of suspicion against leaders. It should also be noted that in the 1972 campaign Nixon, the most TV conscious

President America has ever had, decided, probably on shrewd advice, that appearances on the box could only do him electoral harm. The power of television to tarnish a political reputation, already recognised in Britain by Prime Minister Heath in his sparse use of the medium, was given further recognition by Nixon's electronic abstinence in the '72 elections.

The limited evidence we have would seem to point to the view that democratic leaders risk losing much more than they are likely to gain by frequent appearances on the box. The negative residuals left behind by a political performance can be decisive in closely-fought elections where the public is evenly divided about the issues.

What still remains disturbing is that in countries where politicians are reflected in an escapist TV environment, all leaders — Trudeau, Wilson, Johnson, Nixon, whether they are returned to power or not — become unusually disliked and suspect after only a few years in office. Such antipathy acquired so quickly was not the lot of politicians like Eisenhower, Truman, Baldwin, Mackenzie King or Attlee whose personalities and images were conveyed to the people chiefly through radio and press rather than television. Parenthetically, it should be noted that in West Germany, where television is more intelligently balanced between information and entertainment, the negative impact of the box did not appear to affect Chancellor Willy Brandt, who was returned to power in 1972 with both an increased majority and enhanced popularity.

The hypothesis, then, that certain systems of television by their very nature persistently belittle and denigrate heads of state would seem to be supported by most recent evidence. Does it not follow that such swift disillusion with political leaders resulting in elections which are little more than unpopularity contests will eventually erode faith in the democratic process? Even the victors of such elections cannot view their future prospects with equanimity.

But if television in Britain and America has so great a potential to cheapen and demean Prime Ministers and Presidents, it is capable of providing the same dubious service for lesser politicians and the political process in general. We have already seen how a miscalculated television appearance can have unforeseen consequences in sudden crises such as those faced by

George Brown and Edward Kennedy. It is in their desire to mould their thoughts and words and actions to fit the demands of a medium that aims primarily to entertain that politicians constantly trivialise themselves and their profession.

The commandment that dominates the thinking of most current affairs producers is 'Thou shalt not bore.' Instinctively aware that political programmes run counter to the entertainment ethos of the medium, producers are always terrified that they are making too many intellectual demands on audiences impatiently waiting to watch a Western or threatening to switch over to an old film. Their success, just as that of the most lowly and vulgar comedy series, ultimately depends on the ratings. If ratings sink below a certain tolerable point — even the most unpopular current affairs programmes are expected to attract audiences three times the size of the combined circulations of the *Guardian* and *The Times* — it will be yanked off because it affronts the economic criteria of cost effectiveness.

Since they are visually oriented, producers assume that pictures are less boring than words. They therefore insist that words be kept to a minimum. Also that the words spoken should be distributed amongst as large a number of talking heads as possible. If the discussion is between two politicians and a chairman then every effort will be made by the director in the control room to switch from face to face as often as possible to provide facial and pictorial diversity. The fact that such juggling with images inevitably distracts the viewer from concentrating on what is being said does not bother most television producers.

When I produced current affairs programmes in the middle 1960s it was generally accepted that a six-minute discussion between two politicians was long enough to cover the most intricate and involved political topic. This gave them each 350 words of argument — hardly enough to provide a leader in a popular newspaper like the *Daily Mirror*. Programmes like *Panorama* will often provide double this time — 12 minutes for an item involving politicians — but usually this will entail three or four participants in the discussion leaving them each with a pathetic fragment of time to justify their case.

Mr. Richard Crossman, Minister for Social Services in the

1970 Labour Government and a frequent contributor to broadcasting, forcefully criticised the 'trivialisation effect' of television in his Granada Guildhall Lecture on October 21st, 1968.

'The coverage of politics, outside the news bulletins,' said Mr. Crossman, 'consists chiefly of interview, arguments and confrontations between the spokesmen of the two parties which play up the gladiatorial aspects of politics and give the impression that it consists of a mere conflict of personalities rather than a conflict of ideas carried by personalities . . .

'A television interview under normal conditions merely leaves the viewer with a vague impression of the speaker. "Saw you on telly last night", your friends will say. "Jolly good." I always leave it at that, because if I ask them what I was talking about, few of them have more than the vaguest idea.

'The fault, I suspect, lies in the first place with the producer, who feels he must popularise what he regards as a dull, musty subject. The Housing White Paper can be made more palatable by staging a shouting match between the Minister and some studio hecklers . . .

'Of course, on all channels we can from time to time see a politician seriously interviewed, or a political subject treated in depth. But I do contend that recently there has been a steady decline in the seriousness and depth of the treatment given to current affairs . . .'

Most politicians are well aware of the hopeless and humiliating task that confronts them when they are asked to justify their position on some intricate and controversial issue in three or four minutes of television time. The baffled, frustrated look of a politician being cut off in mid-sentence and mid-thought by the words, 'I'm afraid, Mr. So-and-So, that is all we have time for' is one of the commonest features of current affairs programmes. Aside from occasional carping about it in speeches like Mr. Crossman's, politicians have co-operated only too readily with the broadcasting authorities in accepting these show-biz limitations on their appearances. They rarely insist on a reasonable time to present their arguments. They frame their contributions in stark, bald terms recognising there is no time for qualifications. They do not protest when they are frequently made fools of by the cursory and abrupt fashion in which they are dismissed from the screen and the viewer's attention. They ruefully pocket their fees and console themselves with the thought that no one has in any case remembered what they said.

Just how eager politicians are to tailor their language and their ideas so that they will accommodate the receptivity potential of the mass telly audience was demonstrated in Mr. Harold Wilson's famous Ministerial broadcast about devaluation on November 19th, 1967. In his memoirs, Mr. Wilson explains the genesis of that phrase 'the pound in your pocket will not be devalued' which his political opponents have used as a typical example of the Labour Prime Minister's deviousness. This, claims Mr. Wilson, is a distortion of the actual words he did use.

But why was such a phrase thought necessary at all? According to Mr. Wilson: 'I was aware that there would be timid and frightened people thronging the post office and bank counters, pathetically believing that for every pound of their savings they had invested there, they could now draw only seventeen shillings. I was anxious to allay these fears.'

Treasury officials who drafted the first speech were also obviously aware of frightening people about the real value of the pound. 'Devaluation does not mean that the value of the pound in the hands of the British consumer, the British housewife at her shopping, is correspondingly cut,' read the Treasury draft. 'It does not mean that the money in our pockets is worth 14 per cent less to us now than it was this morning.'

This reassuring statement was, says Mr. Wilson, the only sentence of the Treasury's version that he incorporated in his final speech. He rewrote 'money in our pocket' with the more alliterative 'pound in your pocket'. Although cautioned by a civil service adviser against using it, Mr. Wilson decided to include it when he heard that the maiden aunt of one of his staff 'had telephoned to express concern that her Post Office Savings Bank holdings had been slashed by three shillings in the pound'.

Another decision Mr. Wilson took, because he was talking to the people on television about the consequences of devaluation, was to adopt a chirpier and more optimistic tone than the occasion warranted or that the public thought appropriate. His original idea was to adopt a sombre tone and frankly admit that devaluation was a set-back. But at a meeting of ministers he claims he was pressed 'above all by Dick Crossman, to alter the tone of the broadcast, and to drop the references to set-back and defeat, and almost exult in our decision. I believe I was wrong to accept this advice ... I believe I made an error, in that desperately unreal weekend, in toning down, as compared with my original draft, the extent of the defeat we had suffered, whatever the cause.'[16]

It cannot be said that Mr. Wilson has an enviable record for graciously and generously admitting error on his part. The fact that he did so in these memoirs indicates the telling blow that this unfortunate television speech, its phrasing, its tone, its manner of delivery, made on Wilson's reputation. In other days — when television did not exist — so complex and con- troversial a matter would have been first explained by a speech in the Commons where there would have been no need to adopt a phoney tone of optimism or to shape sentences, designed to be understood by simple maiden aunts, that would eventually have been open to misconstruction and abuse. As an illustration of the way in which politicians can demean themselves by framing their ideas to suit the lowly, over-simplified quality of political expression demanded by the small screen, Mr. Wilson's devalu- ation speech is a vivid object lesson.

Although politician's speeches on the hustings have rarely been noted for their intellectual or logical content, television has lowered still further the quality of the dialogue that takes place between politicians and the electorate. David Wood, the Political Editor of *The Times*, pointed out how during the General Election of 1970 the speech styles of Mr. Wilson and Mr. Heath differed from 'the controlled periods of Gladstone, the verbal power and pomp of Churchill, the weight of manner that Eden could bring to a Foreign Office feather of fact, or the elegance that turned a Macmillan statement into something close to wit'. According to David Wood, the British leaders had both adopted 'anti-stylist' speech mannerisms because that was the style thought to be obligatory for television.

'Mr. Wilson speaks in Cardiff and Mr. Heath in Bexley,' wrote Mr. Wood, 'but the audiences they play for are the millions of television viewers and the skimmers of streamer headlines in tomorrow's newspapers ... The contemporary party leader's speech is made up of verbless slogans, and the adjectives, if any, are all sound and fury, like "massive", signifying nothing in particular. The slogans are machine-turned to be fired off staccato into a microphone, after the manner of those amiably mild, self-doubting television reporters who go into a studio to be transformed into aggressive dogmatists ("Do not qualify," an adviser once told me in a studio. "You are here to speak captions to pictures".) Nothing succeeds like excess.

'So far as this may be reckoned a style of political speech at all, I suspect it to be a style that is unfriendly to truth and alien to anything that deserves to be called reason ... Having first studied with distaste the Cardiff and Bexley texts, I watched their delivery in the television news. They were so false to Mr. Wilson and Mr. Heath that they both looked like amateur actors reading a play script on sight for the first time.'[17]

The other electronic arena in which politicians disport themselves is the talk show. This phenomenon, which keeps millions of Americans glued to the tube in the late evenings and which is most often seen in Britain at late hours during the weekends, is designed primarily to amuse. Its most ardent supporters would claim that the talk show is an effort to revive the lost art of conversation and to reveal in a spontaneous and intimate manner the real personalities of those taking part. The viewer is presumed to have a keyhole view of a choice dinner party loaded with brilliant and articulate guests. His eavesdropping should reward him with delicious bits of gossip, witty repartee, indiscreet disclosures.

The reality, alas, is far different. The guests are recruited predominantly from the world of entertainment with a sprinkling of popular sportsmen, authors wanting to plug their books, visiting celebrities and occasional locals who have happened to be the centre of a newspaper item. The talk usually consists of an exchange of gags or anecdotes conducted in an atmosphere of good-natured bonhomie and mutual backslapping. Although the conversation looks spontaneous, it is carefully planned in advance with the host having ready-to-hand a list of questions and a supply of jokes to make sure the event doesn't sag too disastrously.

It is into this potpourri of amiable small talk that the politician is often immersed to give the show a semblance of meaningfulness and responsibility. The politician agrees to take part, not only because there is usually a small fee involved, but because he wants to demonstrate his friendly, human and jovial qualities.

In a perceptive analysis of the American talk show in the American magazine *Esquire*, Chris Welles provided a number of illustrations of the erratic and unpredictable fate that can await politicians who wade in these shallow conversational waters. Mr. Welles is quoting Jonathan Reynolds, a man who worked on the Dick Cavett and David Frost shows, about a chat panel that consisted of Ramsey Clark, the former US Attorney General, a recently resigned chief of police, and a lawyer who had been robbed a number of times. Said Reynolds: 'If you read the transcript, you'd have thought that Clark came off best because he had a high verbal content. But if you watched the show, the guy who'd been robbed came off best because of his personality. He was enthusiastic and upset and he seemed to have all sorts of specific plans and remedies and ideas. But Clark (the Attorney General) seemed kind of cerebral and uninvolved and kind of fuzzy thinking, and the police chief, well, he just seemed to wash out altogether.'[18]

Sometimes politicians come off remarkably well on these shows. But not because of what they say but because of how they look on that particular night and how they conform to the audience's image of a successful performer. Thus Mr. Welles quotes the views of Marshall Brickmann, the producer of the *Dick Cavett Show*. Said Brickmann: 'We had a show with Herb Klein, Bob Finch and John Mitchell, the Attorney General. Now Mitchell came on and, like, his delivery was good. He got a couple of laughs. He looked right. He smoked a pipe. There was a little bit of fire between him and Cavett, but it was all good-natured, you know, the loyal opposition, and all that crap. So the show came off, and everybody on the staff said, Gee, that was a good show. These were the same people who were saying before the show, Let's *get* Mitchell, he's a bastard. They wanted to get him and show he was wrong and his policies were crazy. But he was on the show and he sort of *did well*. He gave a good performance. He came off good. And the show was good because there was a nice feeling about it, but it had

nothing to do with information or politics or anything like that
... The kind of information we're disseminating is not so much
words and ideas as how people look, how they act, what their
face is like, their delivery, their sense of humour, all that kind of
murky stuff. It all adds up to what works on a show like this
and what doesn't work. Somebody can come on with the most
brilliant ideas in the world, with the most challenging, perceptive, provocative thoughts, and be just a boring guy. You'd
tune him out like bad narration. It's too bad.'

Considering what has since happened to Mitchell through his
involvement in Watergate, this turns out to be a particularly apt
illustration of how the talk show can prettify even the most
dubious and unattractive politicians.

As a means of putting their personalities and views across to
the British public, politicians were undoubtedly attracted to the
usually bland, informal environment of the talk show. Whenever their images were in need of refurbishing, it was assumed
that a cosy chat with David Frost would do wonders. Thus
George Brown, Edward Heath, Ray Gunter, the late Iain
Macleod, were all given the Frost humanisation treatment. On
the *Eamonn Andrews Show*, which was even more flippant and
show-biz concentrated than the Frost programmes, politicians
could often be found engaged in the most humiliating confrontations with the most unlikely adversaries.

The effect of such appearances on some members of the
public can be judged by a letter sent to the *Evening Standard*
by the author, Giles Playfair: 'The transmogrification of
statesmen into entertainers on the Frost Programme only contributes to the country's reputation for giggling frivolity, which
partly accounts for its economic ills,' wrote Mr. Playfair. 'But
the Frost Programme is not quite the worst of it. The other
night, Mr. Duncan Sandys [former Tory Cabinet Minister] on
the Eamonn Andrews show discussed the death penalty with
Miss Dora Bryan, Mr. Peter Cook and Mr. Dudley Moore [all
comedians]. I personally happened to consider Mr. Sandys's
views on this somewhat serious and difficult topic only minimally better informed than Miss Bryan's. But that is, perhaps,
the point. Isn't it time statesmen were prohibited from appearing in such programmes, whatever the attraction for them
in publicity (or money)?'[19]

On the particular programme that distressed Mr. Playfair so much, the former Minister for Defence had been jeered at by some of his fellow guests and had many of his remarks hooted at with derisive laughter by a studio audience. Politicians on the Frost programmes have suffered similar demeaning experiences.

Thus the medium, geared to making performers of all who appear on it, distorts and perverts not only the nature of the political debate but the contributions of those who are seriously involved in the political process. But isn't it healthy that we should see politicians as they really are? Doesn't telly do democracy a service by showing up the stupidity, egotism and pettiness of men in power? That is the argument advanced by those who believe that all rulers should be subjected to the full glare of publicity at all times and that they should be accountable day by day for their weaknesses, their foibles, their errors and their mistakes. It is a very dubious thesis.

In the first place, no advanced society has ever functioned on the basis of such detailed supervision of the leader by the led. The contract between the electorate and their rulers in Western democratic societies is a relatively long-term one — four years for an American President, up to five years for a British Prime Minister — and Government policies are the subject of scrutiny and harassment by the elected opposition. It is largely an act of faith and trust that politicians on all sides will carry out their responsibilities in what they see as the best interest of the public. If it is assumed by the electorate that all politicians cannot be trusted to perform these duties reasonably and honestly and that they are to be persistently subjected to an assessment of their stewardship and activities by appearances on television then the entire framework of the democratic process is seriously undermined.

In the second place, if politicians under this sceptical glare are inevitably found disappointing and wanting — their mere presence in the entertainment environment of the box demeans them — what politicians waiting in the wings are likely to do any better? If television seriously helps to destroy trust in *all* politicians who resort to it, won't it provide the same corroding service for the politicians who replace them? And those who replace them? If no politician over a reasonably long run can hope to retain the affection and respect and trust of his countrymen, where does democracy go from there?

And in the third place, what the viewer sees of politicians on television is not the truth but a distortion of the truth. Because the entertainment ethos of the small screen forces him to adopt the unnatural mannerisms and standards of those who run it, it does not necessarily mean that if he fails in such tests he is of no value to the electorate. If Lord Hailsham behaves boorishly on the box, it does not mean that he will not function as a wise and tolerant Lord Chancellor. If the American Attorney General, John Mitchell, is good at exchanging quips and banter on the *Dick Cavett Show* and comes across as an exceedingly pleasing fellow, it does not mean that he will not function as a repressive and unsatisfactory statesman in office.

The view that television provides the truth about those who appear in front of it is as valid as saying that an audience can detect the true character of an actor in spite of his make-up, the lighting, the part he is playing. Television, as it now operates in Britain and America, has produced criteria for judging the intelligence and sincerity of politicians which are less reliable and more inefficient than the electorate had at its dispoal when only press reports of their activities and an occasional glimpse of them in a town hall determined their judgment. That such a basically dishonest device as the television screen should help discredit and undermine the democratic system is a sad reflection on the consequences of the technological age.

That politicians are uneasily aware of this insidious dry-rot in the system — although they are at a loss to know what to do about it — was reflected in the words of Richard Crossman, speaking in a BBC television programme on October 24th, 1968, which discussed the views he had expressed in his Granada Guildhall lecture. This quotation pieces together a number of statements he made in his opening remarks.

'We are faced now with a period, and we cannot deny it, when a large number of people feel that democracy is in decline,' said Mr. Crossman. 'Every politician knows very well that a large number of the public think they are liars; they think that we break promises; they have a very low opinion of us and we can see it in the Gallup polls.

'I think the causes of this are very profound and they are

much deeper, of course, than anything to do with the media of mass communications. But I do think that though there are deeper causes, television and the way television treats politics and the image that television creates in the public mind of the politician and how he behaves, is a factor.'

There is, finally, another way in which politicians are cheapened by television as it is used at present in Western democracies. This is the reliance upon television as a direct vote-getting device. Although politicians in current affairs programmes and in talk shows are largely at the mercy of the system, during an election campaign they organise the presentation of themselves fairly much as they would like. In Britain tight rules about exactly the kind of programmes that will be transmitted and who should appear on them during a campaign are agreed between the parties and scrupulously adhered to by the broadcasting authorities.

In America the equitable distribution of television time to all candidates in a campaign is virtually impossible. Oddly enough, it is Section 315 of the Federal Communications Act, which insists that equal free broadcasting time be given to every candidate seeking office, that makes it impossible. Although it would be reasonable to give the official Republican and Democratic candidates a half hour in which to explain their policies, under the Act this would entail giving a half hour each to every other candidate representing anything from the Socialist Party of America to the Vegetarian Party or the American Beat Party. Broadcasters are naturally loathe to give up valuable commercial time to such a proliferation of candidates and the result is that, in the name of equality, none of them gets free time.

Since the Equal Time law does not apply to time bought by candidates or political parties — the broadcasting companies must be ready to sell time to any candidate — this has become the accustomed method by which political campaigns are fought on television. Inevitably this means that the party personality with the deepest purse will get most exposure on the box. There will, of course, be some free time available in the regular news and current affairs broadcasts — and considerable ingenuity is used by candidates and their advisers to get themselves reported on these programmes — but by the year of the 1968 Presidential Election, it was generally accepted that the way to appeal to the electorate for votes was by purchasing minutes on the box. And the manner of that appeal, its style, its intellectual level, its method, its philosophy, was shaped to suit the tastes of a society conditioned to identify reality and truth as they saw it on commercially-sponsored, entertainment-dominated television.

Electioneering has never been one of the more edifying aspects of democracy. Grubbing for votes by using lies, impossible promises, intimidation and even bribery is something we have had to live with in order to permit each man his free say about his rulers. The corruption described by Charles Dickens at Eatanswill has had its counterpart in boss rule in Illinois and Louisiana. The bombast, the half-truths, the accusations, the baby-kissing antics, hand-shaking bonhomie, the whole vulgar spectacle of vote-getting did not seriously undermine the democratic process because it was expected that the average man would discount the clowning and the bluster, recognise his own self-interest, and vote accordingly. In pre-television days, however, only a small fraction of the electorate ever caught a glimpse of their candidates during a campaign and what impression they received of the man asking for their support was largely dictated by the candidate's own views and own personality. Television has blurred even more that limited ability of the voter to make an intelligent choice about what to do with his vote. In America the candidate has become a product of market research, a puppet of public-relations thinking, an end result of advertising techniques. The voter in many cases no longer chooses between personalities and policies; he chooses between a number of professionally created electronic images.

The trend towards marketing politicians like consumer products was already evident in the 1956 Presidential contest between General Eisenhower and Adlai Stevenson. The kind of political information upon which presumably the electorate would be expected to make a rational decision had to be reduced on television to thirty-second or one-minute spots. Typical was the following Republican spot television commercial:

Voice: Mr. Eisenhower, what about the high cost of living?

Eisenhower: My wife, Mamie, worries about the same thing. I tell her it's our job to change that on November 4th.

In the closing stages of that campaign, the sensitive, intellectual Adlai Stevenson, whose image was never quite right for a television-controlled electorate, was heard to complain that he felt he had been competing in a beauty contest rather than a solemn debate. 'The idea that you can merchandise candidates for high office like breakfast cereal . . . is the ultimate indignity to the democratic process,' said Stevenson.[20]

By the 1970s the reliance upon paid television commercials to project the merits of political candidates in America had accelerated to such a degree that it had become the normal mode of electioneering. The cost of such campaigning had mounted to such proportions that only rich men or men with rich backers could contemplate entering politics. The narrowing of political recruitment to the wealthy could in time convert America's broad-based, egalitarian democracy into a thinly-disguised plutocracy. Congress became concerned enough about the problem to pass a bill restricting within certain limits the amount of money that could be spent during political campaigns. It was vetoed in December 1970 by President Nixon who, at the same time, promised he would cooperate on a different bill that was not so narrowly centred on the question of restricting spending only on radio and television. He thought that other media should also be included in any decision to limit campaign expenditure. In August 1971 the Senate passed another bill to keep campaign costs within reasonable limits. This, too, has not yet, at the time of writing, been approved by the President or Congress.

Nixon, of course, was the politician who, more than any other, relied upon the selling power of television to get him into the White House. The way in which it was done was described in detail by Joe McGinniss in his book, *The Selling of the President*.[21] It is a disturbing story for anyone who believes that democracy can only operate as a viable political system if most men exercise their franchise according to some rational, independent exercise of free will. If the manipulative and persuasive power of television is so great as to deceive people into voting irrationally or against their own interests then disenchantment and resentment against the system and its leaders will be a likely consequence. Nixon might have beaten Hubert Humphrey without the aid of such a television campaign. The fact that it was thought necessary is the truly frightening aspect of this electioneering development.

McGinniss shows how with ruthless efficiency and cynicism a group of advertising and television men, with a budget of £4 million, set out to sell Nixon to the American public as if he were a can of beer, a deodorant, or a Ford car. The methods they used were the time-honoured ones of the Madison Avenue advertising agency — market research, psychological analysis, consumer demand, professional projection.

They did not ask themselves what were Nixon's qualifications to be President. They asked what did the American public want in a President and set out to sell their man as a cast-iron, genuine, beautifully wrapped, money-back-guaranteed replica of every American's vision of the perfect Presidential article. They based their electronic tactics on the McLuhan thesis that television is the triumph of the blurred outline, the low definition, the muffled truth, the persuasive omission, the convincing blank. 'What you leave unsaid becomes what the audience brings to it,' wrote William Gavin, one of Nixon's staff. 'Lead 'em to the brink of the idea, but don't push across the brink. It's not the words, but the silences where the votes lie.'[22]

Thus it was essential that Nixon's campaign should not be cluttered up with such inessential matters as issues. Issues were complicated, difficult, intimidating and boring for the average voter. They should be replaced by an aura, an essence, a sympathy for the likeable guy who could do the job. That's all.

They were, unfortunately, confronted with a flesh-and-bones candidate called Richard Nixon with certain obvious attributes that did not conform to the theoretically ideal President as 'a combination of leading man, God, father, hero, Pope, King, with maybe just a touch of the avenging furies thrown in.'

One of the television producers, Roger Ailes, faced with this task of image-transformation was depressingly pessimistic about his prospects. 'Let's face it, a lot of people think Nixon is dull,' he said. 'Think he's a bore, a pain in the ass. They look at him as the kind of kid who always carried a bookbag. Who was 42 years old the day he was born ... Now you put him on television, you've got a problem right away. He's a funny-looking guy. He looks like somebody hung him in a closet overnight and he jumps out in the morning with his suit all bunched up saying: "I want to be President." I mean this is how it strikes some people. That's why these shows are important. To make them forget all that.'[23]

There were other problems, too. He was known as Tricky Dicky, the man with a devious facility for getting out of jams. He had no sense of humour. He lacked warmth. Above all, he was a born loser having lost two vital elections already — one for President and one for Governor of California. The voters had to be persuaded to forget all that. Nixon was to be projected as a man of vigour, toughness, experience, integrity, understanding. The man to provide the lost leadership for which America was crying. The man for law and order, the return to true American values, the unifier of the nation, the figure respected and feared abroad.

How was that to be done? By exposing an image of a President rather than a guy called Nixon. The image would get the vote; the man was incidental. A variety of technical methods were used to achieve these effects. Their common denominator was to deny to the electorate any glimpse of the true Nixon that might distort or contradict the picture of an ideal President for whom the viewer was expected to cast his vote. The Nixon public-relations staff produced a series of minute-long commercials composed entirely of fast-moving, brilliantly juxtaposed stills about violence, welfare, poverty, race. Over these kinetic, mind-blurring images was the voice of Nixon uttering massive clichés. He wasn't seen but people felt he was there. The illusion was the presence.

In conformity with the view that issues on television were best handled as obliquely, as non-committally as possible, Nixon generally spoke on television panel shows for about two minutes about such subjects as agriculture, education, foreign aid, income tax, law and order. 'Some answers are still too long,' complained the producer.

Fundamental to the policy of the campaign was keeping the

prying eyes of the press as far away as possible. Nixon and his aides distrusted newspapers and they felt that their interests could best be served by relying upon the manipulable facilities of television rather than the less pliable, less buyable, more suspicious and more recalcitrant ranks of the press.

Nixon, himself, distrusted what his television boys were up to but played along with the concept because it was obviously successful. One of his most endearing assertions was his insistence that he was not, like other politicians, a showman or a television personality.

On the Democratic side, of course, the same image-selling campaign was being pursued on behalf of Hubert Humphrey. It started later, had less financial resources and was less efficient. Recognising that the Republicans were trying to hide the real Nixon, the Democratic forces made a half-hour film in which they claimed to be revealing the true Humphrey. Who do you want for President, it asked. A man with heart or an impersonal political machine? The film was called *The Mind Changer* and Joe McGinniss describes it in these words: 'It was awful in many ways. It showed Hubert Humphrey and Edmund Muskie crawling down a bowling alley in their shirt sleeves. It showed Humphrey wearing a stupid fisherman's hat and getting his lines snarled on a lake near his home and it took shameless advantage of the fact that he had a mentally retarded granddaughter. It was contrived and tasteless. But it was the most effective single piece of advertising of the campaign.'[24]

The successful selling of Nixon to the American public accelerated an irreversible trend. American elections in the 1970s were bound to be turned into electronic bazaars in which media hucksters peddled their products to the electorate. Aside from the ethical problems that this sort of campaigning raised, the costs were escalating to stratospheric proportions. The audited figures for the 1970 mid-term election for Congress and State Governors — in which a Presidential contest did not take place — showed that 42,386,035 dollars had been spent by the various candidates. Since these audited figures have always been recognised as a gross underestimate of the actual money disbursed, it is estimated that no less than 100 million dollars was spent on this election. Most of it was due to the cost of television time and television commercials. This sum was more than five times the money spent on the 1960 Presidential election between Nixon and Kennedy.

No wonder American politicians have become frightened of this economic monster that television has mothered. Yet even the bill passed by the Senate in 1971 to curtail these vast expenditures was resigned to the fact that electioneering by television was in America to stay and that it was bound to be an expensive business. The Senate bill, said Henry Fairlie, 'to put it crudely, will stop multi-millionaires having much advantage over mere millionaires'.[25]

What the American people were getting for their money was what a new breed of publicists and television technologists was whipping up for them. Professional, cynical, articulate operators, they brought to the democratic process all the morality of slick salesmanship and the ethics of mass persuasion. Politicians put themselves in their hands and kept their fingers crossed. If a miscalculation was made by the experts, if a television commercial struck a wrong note, a man could watch his money and his election hopes go down the drain. Thus in Utah, the Republican Senatorial candidate, Laurence Burton, was posed sitting on a horse, his shirt open. 'The candidate looked so uncomfortable that Utah's cowboys and city folk laughed him off the screen and out of the race,' reported *Time* magazine on November 16th, 1970.

The advertising men are completely cynical about how they wrap up their particular political package. If a candidate is handsome, they will try to convince the public that handsome men are more honest and straightforward. If he is an ugly man, they will do their best to cast suspicion upon handsome men as reliable politicians. Thus Robert Goodman, one of the more successful practitioners in this new form of wizardry, when faced with putting over square-jawed, regular-featured Spiro Agnew in the 1966 election for Governor of Maryland, concentrated on projecting Agnew's good looks. 'He was a beautiful, beautiful body, and we were selling sex,' said Goodman. When in 1970, he had as his client the less exciting, 64-year-old Senator William Prouty, who was trying to hold his seat in Vermont, the Goodman campaign went about 'making a virtue out of non-charisma. In image terms,' said Goodman, 'we're saying "Do you want a pretty boy or solid honesty?" ' According to *Newsweek* magazine, the music on Prouty's commercials was harpsichord and string quartets.[26]

In the event, did the results of the 1970 mid-term elections confirm the view that media experts were now the real king-makers, that they possessed the secret of eternal success at the polls, that America would henceforth be governed by men with enough money to buy the most television time and the best image-makers? Not according to *Newsweek* magazine, November 16th, 1970: 'In the months immediately preceding last week's elections, the nation's politicians and pundits almost uniformly accepted the proposition that television merchandising was the high road to the voters' affections ... Thus of all the surprises that occurred on November 3rd, none was so unexpected as the deflation of television's political image-makers — the highly paid television consultants who make a speciality of 'handling' candidates. In race after race, the candidate with a carefully planned and lavishly financed television campaign saw the office he coveted snatched away by a far less sexily merchandised adversary.'

Satisfaction, then, with the fact that richly-backed television campaigns could not automatically win elections is misplaced and very premature. The worry is not that they don't always work but that they exist in their present shape at all. The failures of media experts in 1970 did not discourage more money being spent on this form of campaigning in 1972 and 1974. Again some campaigns will succeed with little television promotion; others will flop with lots of it. But what will such a display of electronic dog-fights — reducing debate to huckster slogans, refusing enlightenment about issues as a matter of policy, exaggerating or distorting a candidate's personality as cynically as if it were bubble-gum — do to our faith in democracy as a political system that, with all its shortcomings, is still fondly believed to be the most equitable, most humane, most responsible, most logical way of choosing governments yet devised by man?

Anxiety about what television, exploited in this manner, is doing to the American state is not new. Said historian Arthur Schlesinger Jr. in 1966: 'This development can only have the worst possible effect in degrading the level and character of our political discourse. If it continues, the result will be the vulgarisation of issues, the exaltation of the immediately ingratiating personality and, in general, an orgy of electronic demagoguery. You cannot merchandise candidates like soap and hope to preserve a rational democracy.'[27]

Other voices — academics, journalists, broadcasters, even advertising men — have echoed this concern.[28] Only the politicians seem powerless, or unwilling, to do anything about it. Blindly, almost mesmerically, they have adapted their outlook and their style to suit the demands of the show-biz Frankenstein monster they have themselves created. It is a spawning they are already living to regret.

In Britain it is impossible for political parties to buy air time. Thus British elections have not been dominated by the ad man's values as they have been in America. Nevertheless, there was disquieting evidence in the 1970 General Election that the existence of television was a dominating influence on the shape of the campaign and that influence was generally directed towards trivialising or vulgarising the arguments and the debate.

Even before the election, the Labour Party was indicating through its Party Political Broadcasts that it *wanted* to be assessed as an adjunct of the entertainment business, *wanted* to have its policies interpreted in fun-and-games terms, *wanted* to have its achievements condensed into easy-to-take capsules like chocolate-coated laxatives. It had produced two of these broadcasts — over which it had complete control — which resembled in tone and format the lowest common denominator of television programming.

In one of these broadcasts no less than seven Cabinet Ministers, sternly facing the camera, were allowed about one and a half minutes each to describe what their Departments had achieved in four years. In a way, it was almost a parody of the most irresponsible current affairs programmes. Everything that Labour politicians like Richard Crossman and Anthony Wedgwood Benn had been attacking as representative of the harm television was doing to democracy was being produced by the Labour Party itself. In another of these party political broadcasts, the Government touted its record in the form of a quiz game not much different in format from *Top of the Form* or *A Question of Sport*, except that the questions were simpler.

Had any of the broadcasting organisations treated politics in this patronising denigrating fashion, the moans and groans of politicians would have been long and loud. Its intellectual level set the tone of Labour's campaign on television which was to follow a few months later. 'The television coverage of the election has concentrated on the two leaders and had trivialised the election process to a remarkable degree. In place of argument we get physical snippets,' said a *Times* leader.

The impression that the General Election was an unnecessary intrusion on the social scene was enhanced by the fact that most of the campaign took place in direct competition with television's coverage of the World Cup. The nation, fanned to a point of mass hysteria by the BBC's obsession with sport and its determination to devote hours and hours daily to these football games in Mexico, could hardly be expected to take a General Election seriously under such circumstances. After all, England was the World Cup holder. What else could be more important than her ability to win it again? Thus in the decisive week before polling day — a crucial moment in the life of any democracy — BBC-1's sense of priorities dictated that it should devote almost four times as many hours to the World Cup as to the General Election — $26\frac{1}{2}$ hours of football to 7 hours of politics inclusive of party political broadcasts.

When it is contended that in its sense of news values television was not much different from the press, it might be pointed out that even on the vital day when England lost to West Germany, the most popular and frivolous newspapers devoted three to four times as much space to the election as to the World Cup. Television merely reversed these proportions.

Indeed, it has been seriously contended that so mesmerised was the country with football, and so euphoric about the team's victories, that the nation's success or failure was identified in many people's minds with how England did in Mexico. Not only did this preoccupation with sport suit Wilson's plan of obscuring and nullifying the issues — pub talk was about Bobby Charlton and not Eddie Heath — but a World Cup victory would convince many voters that any Government that could produce it was worth supporting. The country couldn't be so bad after all. Alas, for Wilson, England was eliminated four days before polling day.*

* For a fuller account of the impact of too much sport on television see M. Shulman, *The Least Worst Television in the World* (London 1973), pp. 108ff.

'During and after the campaign the parties were charged with avoiding the real issues,' wrote Martin Harrison. 'But Mr. Hogg and Mr. Healey (among others) vigorously objected that they frequently talked on Vietnam, EEC, pollution and education, but the media showed little attention. Though it was hard to see where justice lay, it was clear enough that television's election was increasingly taken for "the" election, at least in the sense of being a faithful microcosm. Yet the drastic selectivity time imposes on newsmen, enhanced by technical financial and political restraints, means that television is always liable to be holding a distorting mirror to reality.'[29]

The British General Elections of February and October, 1974, took another giant step towards the domination of the electoral process by the small screen. And it also demonstrated how the major parties were concerned, above all, with manipulating their appeal in terms of electronic images. Because the February, 1974, election was taken in the midst of the three-day week and a miner's go-slow when restrictions on the use of power — limited lighting, travel and television — had made social life very uncomfortable, the aim of all parties was to show that their chief desire was to get the country back to normality, unity and industrial peace. This resulted in a surprisingly pacific campaign with a minimum of thumped tables, political accusations and scaremongering as Tories, Labourites and Liberals alike exuded sweet reasonableness in an effort to establish themselves as the most moderate, the fairest and the most unifying party in the land.

Again it was television, and the values of television, that dictated what issues were discussed and how they were treated. If Mr. Wilson, at his morning conference, faced the cameras to announce that North Sea oil was the question of the day, then all through that day North Sea oil dominated the news scene in all media. If Mr. Heath decided trade union militancy needed airing, the TV reporters and commentators made that the dominating topic of the Tory campaign.

In other words, the big parties circumscribed the debate by swamping television with the problems they wished to highlight. As a result a vast range of vital matters were hardly discussed and, as far as the electorate was concerned, they did not exist. The only reference to foreign affairs was made by Sir

Alec Douglas-Home 15 days after the election campaign had begun. There was barely a word said about Britain's Middle East policy, the Atlantic Alliance or the relationship with Russia or America. Such controversial measures as defence cuts, immigration, the increasing crime rate, hanging and the drug problem received hardly a whisper of attention.

And because of the domination of television as an electoral forum — even though it was constantly restricting and trivialising the issues because of lack of time and the need to be instantly popular — the political meetings throughout the land were sparsely attended or supported. Only the major political luminaries attracted reasonable audiences — and often because they had become a telly star. The average candidate, unhallowed by the favours of the box, found himself addressing in village halls more empty chairs than potential voters. The contact with the local candidate, the opportunity to question him intimately about his policies, was replaced by the remote apparatus of the telly show as the main lever in the democratic process.

But the telly show itself had begun to bore so acutely by the time of the second General Election in October, 1974, that even the fragmented and superficial dose of six months before was drastically curtailed by the broadcasting authorities.

'How to cover the second General Election of 1974 adequately and responsibly without boring the pants off the electorate was the peculiar problem facing television,' wrote Richard Last in the *Daily Telegraph* on October 14th, 1974. 'In the event ITV, whose audience is usually considered to be more sensitive to boredom, backed away so far that on some nights (except for individual regional contribution) the Election hardly featured at all, even when ITN was not on strike.

'The BBC, mindful of its responsibilities as a "public service", reached what I thought was a nice compromise. You could watch the Election if you stayed up late enough: before 10.25 p.m. or thereabouts, normal service was maintained as far as possible.'

Thus, except for the dedicated or the concerned, the television service was becoming of less and less help in fostering or educating an informed public about the nature of the democratic choices available to them. Indeed, by actively discouraging them from attending local meetings and listening to their local candidates because of the counter-attractions of TV entertainment and without providing a responsible quota of political programmes at peak times, they were creating an electorate inadequately equipped to select what was best for themselves and society.

There is formidable evidence to suggest that the manner in which television uses politicians and the manner in which politicians use television is a two-way denigrating process bound ultimately to bring disrespect and distrust to the democratic concept both in Britain and America. Whether they take part in current affairs programmes or talk shows or election campaigns on television, politicians are bound to be demeaned by the conditions under which they are required to appear. A positive television factor undermining authority is relentlessly at work.

Reflecting on the fact that the public now demands too much of its politicians, Thomas Griffith in *Time Magazine* of January 27th, 1975, considered the part television plays in the inability of American Presidents to live up to the hopes reposed in them by the electorate.

'The gap between the public's expectation of Presidents and the reality has grown so great that it can only be bridged, if at all, by a public relations campaign of pretense and concealment,' wrote Mr. Griffith. 'Television has given an unsettling emphasis to a certain kind of publicity skill. George Washington would have made a dull TV performer. As the first effective television President, Kennedy proved how important it was to be fast on his feet. This helped to set a demanding new standard that elevates flash over substance. The effect of television — which in one year can make an unknown face tiresomely overfamiliar — has been to disqualify able but uncharismatic men, and to make others (Humphrey and Muskie come to mind) glib parodies of their once impressive selves. In the present atmosphere, no one seems good enough to be President.'

Of course, suspicion of rulers goes back a long way and is universal. An ancient Burmese saying has it that fire, water, storms, robbers and rulers are the five great evils. And that was said a long time before democracy. A healthy democracy encourages the questioning and suspicion of those in power. It assumes that the system will produce men and women capable of ruling competently, humanely and reasonably honestly. If one set of politicians fails in this task, there is always an alternative set to take its place. It is when contempt and disgust is felt by a large section of the electorate for *all* politicians, for the motives and manners of all those seeking popular support, that democracy is threatened.

But in neither America nor Britain is there any sign that any significant changes in the way in which television is run are being remotely contemplated by politicians. Instead there is increasing pressure upon broadcasters to refrain from independent comment, to keep out of controversial affairs, to act merely as a neutral channel for the transmission of the voices and deeds of the political Establishment.

In America it was Vice-President Agnew who tried to shift the blame for the nation's ills from politicians on to television by accusing the major networks of biased, sensationalist reporting. Although it is true that the presentation of news and the comments upon it have the heightened, intensified, shallow values of a show-business medium, these are the inherent qualities of a system relying for its financial existence upon the need to sell goods in a private enterprise economy. It has nothing to do with a conspiracy to discredit the Administration or a sophisticated cabal amusing itself by mocking authority. If Vice-President Agnew had his way and criticism of politicians was more muted, if the news was presented without scrutiny or analysis of any kind, if the small screen became merely a conduit pipe for official comment and opinions, then television would do much more damage to politicians than it already does. For then the medium would be making life even more frivolous and unreal, would be patently lying to the people, would be building up resentment against any leaders reflected in it.

Another attempt to browbeat American broadcasting into responding to the dictates and pressures of politicians was over Columbia Broadcasting System's documentary, *The Selling of the Pentagon*. This was a hard-hitting tendentious account of how the American War Department publicised its activities and justified its role as guardian of the state. Its purpose was to decry the fact that the Pentagon was spending 190 million dollars a year trying to influence the public about the merits of the Vietnam war when its duty was restricted to merely informing them about its functions.

Instead of being indifferent to this statement of the obvious, some American politicians were affronted by it. This documentary was blown up into a full-fledged confrontation between Congress and broadcasters over the right of television to broadcast such a programme. The fact that such concern should be aroused amongst politicians over such a minor expression of dissent reveals how limited are the areas in which American television can truly examine and criticise the activities of the Administration.

A Congressional Committee chaired by Mr. Harley Staggers of West Virginia, was so incensed by what it deemed the unfairness of the programme that it demanded from CBS all its background material, its unused film footage, its scripts and research so that it could examine the detail upon which the programme was based. CBS consistently denied that these technical changes had in any way seriously distorted the facts. Standing on its right to freedom of speech under the First Amendment to the Constitution, CBS refused to comply with the subpoena of the Congressional Committee and turn over its unused film material. In a historic reversal of the recommendation of one of its own Committees, the House of Representatives by a vote of 226 to 181 supported the view that a broadcasting organisation did not have to reveal the sources upon which it based one of its programmes.

CBS may have won this victory, but who has won the war remains a more dubious proposition. It is likely, as happened after Agnew's Des Moines onslaught, that the networks would become even more cautious and timid over controversial issues than they were before. The politicians will have once more pushed television that much closer to becoming the media eunuch they mistakenly assume they can live with.

A similar campaign to deter television from becoming a serious investigative and questioning medium of the activities of politicians has been waged in Britain. During Mr. Wilson's regime there have been numerous rows and allegations of bias about the people chosen to appear on current affairs programmes and the subjects they should discuss.*

* I have discussed Mr. Wilson's relations with television in more detail in *The Least Worst Television in the World*, op. cit.

In 1966, fury with the BBC's reporting of that election resulted in Wilson refusing to talk to a BBC reporter on the day of his victory. Following the 1970 election there were more complaints from Labour politicians about the unfair way in which the BBC had treated them. 'Labour anger about "BBC bias" flared afresh, even though Mr. Wilson had said just before polling day that he had no complaints,' said Martin Harrison. 'However, as in 1966, the party offered no detailed substantiation of its charges of deliberate unfairness ... After watching or hearing well over a hundred election bulletins as well as every major current affairs programme during the campaign, I found a number of errors of judgment on all channels but nothing which could reasonably be categorised as bias for or against any of the major parties ... The greatest immediate danger was probably the threat to the broadcaster's independence.'[30]

The persistent harassment of the BBC by the Left — the commercial channel rarely fought over-enthusiastically on such matters of principle — triggered off a similar reaction from the Right. It was probably done to remind the BBC that if they bent too readily to Labour's pressures, similar pressure could be exerted by the Conservatives.

Thus during the 1970 General Election the late Iain Macleod, a senior Conservative politician, said he would not appear on radio's *World At One* or television's *24 Hours* 'because of their Left bias'. Quintin Hogg, who became Tory Lord Chancellor, said *24 Hours* was coloured by its recruitment of extremely Left producers. Mr. Eldon Griffiths M.P. accused the BBC of engaging in a subtle attempt to undermine the capitalist system.

After the Conservative victory, the Right-wing pressure on the BBC did not stop. There was a pamphlet written by Mr. Julian Critchley M.P. outlining the Left tendencies of BBC programmes. Mr. Harold Soref M.P. and Mr. Evelyn King M.P. bombarded the press with complaints about the BBC's Left-wing bias.

Mr. G. K. Young, a former Under-Secretary at the Ministry of Defence, speaking to a conference of the Right-wing Conservative Monday Club, made no bones about the ultimate object of this campaign of intimidation by Tory politicians. 'We must begin to scare the pants off those pansies at Broadcasting House,' said Mr. Young. 'We have got the BBC on the run. They are getting scared.'[31]

A programme called *Yesterday's Men*, transmitted by the BBC's *24 Hours* stimulated as much chest-beating and hair-tearing amongst Labour politicians as *The Selling of the Pentagon* had amongst American Congressmen. The first the public was aware of this programme was a story that made the front page of most papers on June 11th, 1971. Mr. Wilson had become incensed about a question put to him by David Dimbleby, one of the regular front men of *24 Hours*, about how much money he had made out of his memoirs. (It was reputed that with serialisation rights he was getting something in the region of £170,000.) When Dimbleby pressed the question, Mr. Wilson not only refused to answer but insisted that everything already filmed about this section of the programme should be eliminated from its final version. He made his views known forcefully not only to those in the studio but those in higher echelons in the BBC.

What is surprising about this part of the controversy is Wilson's assumption, and that of his colleagues, that he had every right to insist on the destruction of a filmed section of the programme merely because it displeased him. Thus explaining Labour's side of the story, Mr. Joe Haines, Wilson's Press Secretary, wrote in the *Guardian*: 'On 12th May, Mr. John Crawley, special assistant to Mr. Charles Curran, the Director-General, telephoned me to say that he had "no hesitation in saying that the whole of that section will be destroyed formally, lost sight of and forgotten . . ." I still possess my original short-hand note of that conversation.'[32]

In the row that followed after the programme was transmitted on June 17th, 1971 the principle that leading politicians could by right demand the destruction of filmed matter that concerned them — where presumably nothing libellous or improper had been said — was glossed over and side-tracked.

The programme itself was a mild, sardonic look at what happens to politicians when they are forced by the electorate to relinquish power. Its title, *Yesterday's Men*, was a rather crude jibe based upon the phrase used by Labour's advertising men to discredit Conservative leaders during the 1970 General Election campaign.

There were snippety interviews with a number of ex-Cabinet ministers — Mr. Jenkins, Mr. Healey, Mr. Crosland, Mrs. Castle and Mr. Callaghan, as well as Mr. Wilson — in which the chief impression was that financially things were much rougher for most of them now than in the good old days of Ministerial salaries, chauffeur-driven cars and Government financed residences. No serious issues were tackled. There was a pop tune accompanying the entire 50-minute programme with sly digs at politicians in general.

Waving threats of legal action and behaving as if a major constitutional crisis were at stake, the leaders of the Labour Party insisted that something should be done. What was wanted was not explicitly stated. An abject apology? Somebody's head on somebody's platter? Of course, nothing of this had anything to do with the BBC's freedom, as the Labour Party's memorandum to the BBC pointed out. 'It ought to be unnecessary to say — but nevertheless should be said — that nothing in this controversy is concerned with freedom of speech,' read the memorandum, 'and the right of disclosure to the public of knowledge *to which they are entitled* [my italics].' But who is to decide to what knowledge the public is entitled? Only politicians? Or governments? Are they the ones to regulate what the public are *not* entitled to hear? Isn't the essence of free speech that anyone, even the BBC, is allowed to decide what the public may hear so long as it does not transgress the laws of privilege, libel, obscenity, and other boundaries to free comment?

Was the Labour Party right in taking the affair so seriously? Said the *Guardian*: 'It ill behoves those who live by the sword to bleat when they cut themselves shaving. So few will feel for Mr. Harold Wilson in the latest of his interminable haggles with the BBC. If a Leader of the Opposition does not wish to appear on television he need merely say no.'[33]

The Times took a sterner view. In a leader headed 'The Voice of the Trivial', it said: 'The BBC's coverage of political affairs has been lacking in depth in recent years but this programme was too shallow to be tolerated. It is much more dangerous to trivialise than it ever is to criticise politicians.'[34]

The consequence of all this vociferous displeasure was that the BBC was forced to conduct an enquiry into the affair. Issued by the BBC Governors on July 8th, 1971, the report insisted on the right of the BBC to exercise its own independent editorial judgment and contained no apology to Mr. Wilson or anyone else. It found that it was 'permissible and proper' for David Dimbleby to have asked Mr. Wilson how much he received for his memoirs, which was 'a matter of public interest'. It did not feel that the Labour politicians were seriously misled about the nature of the programme they were invited to take part in or about where the emphasis would lie.

It did, however, think some major mistakes of judgment had been made on the part of the producers. There were also some pious hopes that the damage done by the incident to relationships between the BBC and politicians would soon be rectified and that understanding would be restored.

The suspicion of Labour politicians once more manifested itself following the October, 1974, General Election. To the surprise of almost all objective observers the BBC was once more accused of bias and a special enquiry was set up to examine the evidence. Months after the election not a word had been heard of either the enquiry or the evidence.

Was the trivialisation in *Yesterday's Men* much worse than the trivialisation that politicians themselves indulge in when they resort to the box? The trivialisation of avoiding issues at election time, talking down to the public on the box, giggling away with comics and starlets on chat shows?

Nothing less than a rigid, State-controlled censorship could guarantee that something of a similar nature, displeasing to politicians, would not occur again. The instinctive reaction of all politicians — both here and in America — when faced with some affront to their dignity is to look for more methods of controlling the medium, restricting its independence, narrowing its area of comment. They will not see that so long as television functions as it does in English-speaking Western democracies, disrespect for and distrust of authority in general and politicians in particular will continue to grow and flourish. This scepticism will become as integral a part of the telly generation as the acceptance and awe of authority was part of the consciousness of their parents and grandparents. In the demeaning of politicians in our time there is at work a powerful and positive television factor.

CHAPTER FIVE

Television's Bit Part Players: God, the Queen, Trade Unions, the Law and Others

> *The power which rests on the love of the people is un-*
> *doubtedly the greatest, but is precarious and*
> *contingent; and princes will never be satisfied with*
> *it.*
> Jean-Jacques Rousseau, *The Social Contract*, 1762

Authority, of course, in any society is not the exclusive prerogative of politicians. It stems from a number of sources beginning with the family and is exercised by institutions and
groups such as the Monarchy (where one still survives), the
Law, the Church, the universities, the armed forces, the police,
the trade unions, the employers, and others. Parliament or Congress in a democracy may have the last authoritative word.
This is because theoretically it represents the will of the people.
But its power to enforce its laws and regulations depends in the
final analysis upon the co-operation and consent of all the other
voices and arms of authority. Authority is not a single thread,
but a thick rope holding society together. If it binds too tightly,
society will strive to burst out of its repressive grip. If too many
of its strands unravel at the same time, the state will become
weak, tenuous and indecisive. Authority has to be flexible
enough to accommodate change and firm enough to prevent the
entire social structure from coming apart.

Plato in the *Laws* thought there were certain titles to authority. He took it as axiomatic, for example, that parents would
exercise control over their children, high birth govern low birth,
the elderly lead the young, the ignorant obey the orders of the
wise, the stronger control the weak. It was not until the eighteenth century that these basic concepts were seriously challenged. Today in Western democracies hardly one of

them — perhaps parents are still assumed to have some control over very young children — would be accepted as an unquestionable qualification for the exercise of authority.

No one is naïve enough to assume that wielders of authority are always wise, just and humane in the exercise of their prerogative. Inevitably many are stupid, ignorant, unjust and cruel. But government depends upon a degree of assent and tolerance amongst the led about the follies, mistakes and even wickedness of those in authority.

'Where is the man that has uncontestable evidence of the truth of all that he holds, or the falsehood of all that he condemns; or can say that he has examined to the bottom of his own or other men's opinions?' asks John Locke in his *Essay Concerning Human Understanding* written in 1687. 'The necessity of believing without knowledge, nay often upon very slight grounds, in this fleeting state of action and blindness we are in, should make us more busy and careful to inform ourselves than to restrain others.'

But if leaders are fallible, often less informed than those from whom they demand trust and obedience, how have they managed to impose their will and decisions upon those they lead? That shrewd Italian thinker, Machiavelli, had the answer. By deception and disguise. 'But it is necessary to disguise this character well, and to be a great feigner and dissembler; and men are so simple and so ready to obey present necessities, that one who deceives will always find those who allow themselves to be deceived,' wrote Machiavelli in *The Prince* in 1513. Thus he concluded it was not necessary for a prince to have all the conventional virtues, 'but it is very necessary to seem to have them'.

Although one would like to believe that in an open democracy of the latter part of the twentieth century Machiavelli's cynical precepts have little relevance, one needs only to be reminded of the recent revelations in the Pentagon papers about how Presidents Kennedy and Johnson secretly expanded the Vietnam war, to realise how little the people really know about what their politicians are doing. The Watergate affair and the final undoing of President Nixon is further evidence of the ability of democratic leaders to hide their machinations from the people. It is true, however, that democratic leaders have to be accountable for their actions in a manner never dreamed of by Machiavelli and his medieval princes. We have seen in the last chapter how politicians use television to give an illusion of accountability and forthrightness. We have also seen how television adds its own patina of deception to the normal layers of guile that a politician must use to remain in office.

What, then, is television doing to the other forces and institutions of authority in English-speaking Western democracies? It is corroding their stature and credibility just as relentlessly as it corrodes the authority of politicians. Much more slowly, of course, because such institutions have so much less access to the small screen.

Just as disguise and dissembling are essential attributes of politicians so are they imperative aspects of authoritative institutions. The reason is quite simple. All authority is wielded by fallible men. They could not function if those who were led realised how many stupid, ignorant, ill-informed, incapable men gave them orders and instructions. We assume judges are wise even if many of them are stupid. We believe generals know how to conduct battles even if many of them are incompetent strategists. We have faith in the understanding of priests even if many of them are bewildered or insensitive.

Institutions like the Law, the Army and the Church command authority in spite of the incompetence and ineffectiveness of many of their officials, servants and practitioners. Their power is based on the assumption that the whole is greater than any of its parts. It has therefore been necessary throughout the ages to provide such institutions with an image that is superior to and independent of the transient nature of the individual agents who organise and administer such authoritative bodies. Such images have usually been shaped by ritual and a deliberate aloofness from close scrutiny by those over whom they exert authority. Remoteness and ritual generate awe and respect and discourage investigation and scepticism.

Thus the Law is wielded in hushed courtrooms by lawyers and judges garbed in gowns and wigs using a code of formal conduct that cows the average citizen into respectful submission. The armed forces have uniforms, bands, flags and ceremonials that imbue the people with confidence that the nation's security is in the right hands. The Church communicates with its adherents in a reverential, sacred place with the priest emphasizing his authority by his vestments, his lofty pulpit, his distance.

Now what effect have the electronic media had upon these formidable and commanding images? Radio probably enhanced and strengthened them. The disembodied voice, as I suggested earlier in this book, brought its own mystique and wonder to those using the microphone alone. By nature a distancing medium, radio added another dimension of remoteness to the institutional image. Just as Jews have never asked what Jehovah looked like — assuming that the echo of His voice through His words was enough — so did politicians like Hitler, Roosevelt, Churchill gain in stature and authority through the awe generated by their faceless voices. Similarly priests and professors and trade-union leaders and other figures of authority found that radio, in the days before television, generally advanced their reputations and prestige.

Television, on the other hand, does not work like radio. It tends to shrink the distance between the performer and his audience, between the watcher and the watched. According to McLuhan, it is a participant medium. It engages you. It invites participation; unlike radio which serves as background sound. Just as politicians are eager to have themselves identified as representative average men, so do other representatives of authority, when they appear on television, want to portray themselves in a manner sympathetic to the tastes of the ordinary viewer. To be liked — the creed of the performer — is the aim of all who cavort on the small screen. And this means stripping themselves of the robes and paraphernalia of authority — which are the symbols of separation rather than sameness — whenever figures of authority set out to use television.

Thus the field-marshal, deprived of his epaulettes and medals and imposing hat, turns out to be a thin-faced, rodent-like man with a piping voice who might easily be a bank clerk. The archbishop, chatting to a television reporter away from the grandeur of his cathedral, reveals himself as a chuckling, avuncular, tolerant figure so different from the firm servant of God demanding adherence to His principles and His commandments. Similarly the judge, the senior civil servant, the ambassador, the university head, away from the imposing atmosphere of his court, his office, his embassy, and having to conform to the demands of entertainment television by over-simplifying, over-generalising, over-acting his ordinariness, has a small bit of his authority chipped away by each of his appearances.

The non-television generations, those approaching middle-age and over, will probably be only minimally affected by these demeaning displays. Having acquired their attitudes to authority — acceptance, awe, respect, subservience, fear — from the radio and the printed page, some may be dismayed or disillusioned by the differences between the television image and their previous views of those in commanding places in society. But the majority, cushioned by their pre-conceptions will either be amused, tolerant, pleased, or indifferent to these efforts on the part of authoritative institutions and persons to ingratiate themselves with the masses. This same majority has come to accept the vulgarities and dissembling of politicians in the pursuit of votes as perfectly normal.

But the impact of television — the fifth factor — may be quite different on the telly generation that was brought up on the box from birth. Their first intimation of the figures of authority will come from watching them gambol and posture in the frivolity-oriented universe of entertainment television.

Perhaps the most depressing, distressing and puzzling dilemma that faces today's older generation is the refusal of the young to accept the rules of Society which were not so long ago believed to be sacrosanct. Parental authority, which Plato and most philosophers until the nineteenth century assumed to be an imperative basis for any civilised state, is being eroded at an alarming pace. Respect for social codes and shame for transgressing them has deteriorated to a level where the former social sanctions and penalties have become ineffective and impotent deterrents.

The young arrested for hooliganism or drug-taking or rioting, display few signs of remorse when photographed in the custody of the police or seen in a courtroom. While parents mutter embarrassed and concerned explanations to television or newspaper reporters, their children wave cheerfully and defiantly to the media while being trundled off to trial or prison. Even in extreme cases of social aberration, such as the

Sharon Tate murders by the Manson cult, these young, mainly middle-class killers displayed little but indifference or contempt for the revulsion and horror of society over their crime. Amongst some young — and could defiance of American society go much further? — there are already signs of a move to make Charles Manson into some sort of Raskolnikovian hero-figure to be admired for his horrific, nihilistic gesture against authority.

Since television is dominated by sport and light entertainment, access to it for the more significant and serious aspects of society is strictly limited. Politicians, through news broadcasts and current affairs programmes, get the most telly time after actors, variety artists and sportsmen. Mr. Richard Crossman complained that their weekly ration was little more than that given to all-in wrestling.

Vying in Britain for the second most television time is the Church. One of the few statutory provisions governing programme content in Britain is the ruling that there shall be no broadcasting between 6.15 p.m. and 7.25 p.m. on Sundays, with the exception of religious programmes, appeals for charity, and programmes in the Welsh language and for the deaf.* In the draft of the 1954 Television Act these exceptions to the no-broadcasting rule were not included. The aim of this electronic vacuum was to encourage worshippers to go to evening prayer knowing that they would be missing nothing on the box by going to church. But someone thought that one day it might be desirable at this hour to broadcast a religious service — some national event might require it, such as a special visit by the Queen to a cathedral — and the words 'except for religious broadcasting' were inserted into the Act.

For a short time both the BBC and the ITV respected the godly silence rule and nothing was seen on the screen during this Sunday period. Then the ITV introduced their *Sunday Break* series of religious broadcasts and the BBC soon followed. 'The ghetto replaced the breathing space,' remarked Edwin Robertson in the *Baptist Times* of December 5th, 1968 out-

---

* Although this closed period for religious broadcasts was theoretically abandoned early in 1972, when restrictions on broadcasting hours were terminated it was still being used by ITV and BBC as a religious TV enclave at the time this book went to press.

lining the history of this peculiar aspect of British broadcasting.

Thus the Christian churches were given a privileged enclave on television to do with as they saw fit. In addition to this one hour and ten minutes of exclusive time, the commercial companies also put out about eight minutes of religious chat as their spiritual nightcap to conclude the day's broadcasting. This used to be known as the Epilogue slot. BBC-1 used to put out late on Sunday evenings a half-hour repeat of their early evening religious programmes but in 1971 this had been dropped. On Sunday mornings, too, both BBC-1 and the ITV transmitted an hour-long church service.

The total time accorded religious broadcasts on both major channels varied between two-and-a-half to three-and-a-half hours per week each. No other serious institutions in the land — Parliament, the Monarchy, the City, the Press, the universities, the Law, the armed forces — was granted a fraction of this time to put over its message and philosophy on television. Parliament, for example, as distinguished from politicians, is accorded on BBC-2 a mean ration of 20 minutes weekly during sessions to record and report on the activities of the Commons and the Lords.

Although occasionally the voices of Jews, Moslems and Humanists are heard in the Church's religious preserve on Sundays — which is its most important electronic pulpit — the area is designed primarily to propagate the views of 'the mainstream of Christian tradition'. The Chief Rabbi in a letter to *The Times* in 1968 pointed out that the Jewish community received but a fraction of its proportional share in religious broadcasting time based on the ratio of Jewish citizens in Britain.[1] And Humanists are constantly protesting to the broadcasting authorities that they, too, do not get a fair share of representation on the box.

But how did those 'mainstream Christian' religious authorities use their opportunity to proselytise, convert, teach or comfort their millions of potential viewers? In the early days the slot was overweighted with church services which eventually gave way to discussions and documentaries on religious themes. But gradually the ethos and format of television's popular programmes began to shape the look and sound of these Sunday evenings.

In order to prevent religious programmes from being isolated from 'real' programmes, they soon adopted the mannerisms and colouring of the electronic world around them. Constituting as it were an alien gap between something like a Tom and Jerry cartoon and *The Black and White Minstrel Show*, this Sunday slot tried harder and harder to imitate the kind of programmes viewers were conditioned to see on the box. Its more serious efforts took on the disguise of current affairs shows with all the over-dramatised, argumentative, non-reflective flavour of that type of programme.

Sharing the Sunday religious enclave with these inconclusive chat shows and the occasional documentary were the song shows. Originally they consisted of church choirs or massed ranks of middle-aged Welsh ladies lustily singing hymns. Then the atmosphere and the content began to lean heavily on the television variety show for its inspiration. There were *Stars on Sunday* with Harry Secombe and Anna Neagle and the Bachelors doing their melodic bit for God by associating Him with the biggest names in show-business.

The trend towards making religious programmes more and more at one with other entertainment shows reached its inevitable climax with the news that the commercial channel in 1972 would be introducing a religious soap opera called *Adam Smith* into the Sunday slot. 'Out go the hymns and low-key discussions,' said the *Sunday Mirror* announcing the series under the headline 'Television Shocker for Religious Hour'. 'In comes a no-holds-barred drama series which spotlights intimate human situations ... There is the girl who has an affair with a married man; the respectable businessman who is thinking of leaving his wife to live with his secretary.

'Explained Granada TV producer June Howson: "The series aims to be absolutely honest — about religion, about sex, about permissiveness, about any other aspect of life that needs to be aired. If we think it is necessary to deal with the subject of abortion, there will be no flinching. But there will be no need for four-letter words ..." It will be set in the village of Gifford, 19 miles from Edinburgh, with a Church of Scotland minister as its central figure.'[2]

The crunch question, of course, is whether this relatively large dose of institutional religion flavoured to suit the tastes of television viewers has increased the volume or intensity of faith in Christianity in Britain? Have fifteen years of this TV power to propagandise the nation about Christianity even halted the growth of scepticism and disinterest in either Protestantism or Roman Catholicism, particularly amongst the young? Has television, in short, done God any good?

The empty pews at church services and the reiterated pronouncements of leading church figures about the decline in religious consciousness is prima facie evidence that television has been no boon to Christianity. On the contrary, many religious thinkers view it as a positive malevolent force eroding the position and influence of the Church.

Back in 1965, Father Francis Ripley, Director of the Roman Catholic Information Centre in Liverpool, blamed the electronic media for a slump in church-going and a decline in the number of Roman Catholic converts. 'Television and radio have popularised a glib dismissal of religion,' said Father Ripley. 'It is easy for a speaker to demolish a religious conception in a one-minute remark which might take an hour to refute properly.'[3]

And more recently in 1971, a scholarly Catholic authority, John Eppstein, in his book *Has The Catholic Church Gone Mad?* wrote: 'One of the main reasons for the disorder of the Catholic Church today, in the fields of morals, faith, authority and worship alike, is not only the power of the mass-media, but the distinctive features which they have developed in the process of moulding and professing to articulate public opinion in recent years.'[4]

As to the question of whether or not television has benefited Christianity in Britain after almost 20 years of privileged broadcasting, the answer would appear to be that it has not. It is not merely the sight of tiny congregations — chiefly composed of elderly and middle-aged women — that is evidence of a declining interest in religion. There are the reports of a number of social surveys to support the view that in recent years there has been a marked deterioration in the influence of the Church.

In the decade between 1957 and 1967, Gallup Poll statistics revealed a serious increase in the number of people who believed that religious faith was on the decline. In 1957 52 per cent of British people thought religion was *losing* its influence; in 1967 this figure jumped to 67 per cent. In 1957, 17 per cent thought religion was *increasing* its influence; in 1967 only 9 per cent felt its significance was greater.

According to an Independent Television Survey on religious attitudes conducted in 1968, 22 per cent of Britons denied membership of any church. This was a leap of some 16 per cent from 1964 when a Gallup Poll for ABC Television produced an estimate that only 6 per cent of Britons would deny any church membership.[5]

It should be remembered that 1957 is the year which roughly corresponds to the advent of commercial television on a popular level and is also the year when for the first time a majority of homes — 60 per cent — possessed television sets. It is also interesting to note that these surveys showed that it was members of the Church of England — the faith that gets the biggest slice of the television religious cake — who provided the largest number of those who felt that religion was losing its influence.

On the other hand, if we examine the records of the Jews and Humanists — groups who are concerned about their lack of access to the television screen — we find no such precipitate decline (something like 17 per cent amongst Christians in a decade) in the overall adherence to the importance of their beliefs. The number of recognised Jews in Britain has remained relatively static — around the 450,000 mark — in the post-war years. The Humanists, with hardly any concessions granted them on the box, are rapidly gaining adherents with membership in the Humanist Association — although still tiny — increasing by some 20 per cent a year.

To claim that television is chiefly responsible for a fall in church-going or a decline in Christianity would be a wild generalisation. Other factors — materialism, scientific discoveries about the nature of man and the universe, cultural scepticism, affluence, the spread of atheistic ideologies like Communism — have contributed to the loss of religious faith. But one must face the fact that certain other religions like those of the Jews and Moslems who have not yet had the opportunity of proselytising in a triviality-dominated medium have been subjected to all these social factors and have not suffered so rapid a diminution in their influence. By eroding respect for authority television weakens the Church's defences against the social trends that contradict, reject or negate it.

Naturally the middle-aged and the elderly are less likely to have their religious attitudes changed by anything the Church might be seen to be doing on television. Their beliefs hardened into faith before television existed. But many of the telly generation have no such basic assumptions about the existence of a personal and supernatural God.

Professor Duncan Williams has provided an illustration of this failure of belief in the young in his book, *Trousered Apes*, which attempts to show how modern literature has contributed to the moral crisis in Western society. 'A few years ago I discussed John Robinson's *Honest To God* with a group of students at a church-related college,' writes Professor Williams. 'They were intelligent, articulate, if somewhat earnest, young people, but when we came to the passage in which Robinson alludes to Julian Huxley's sense of spiritual relief on rejecting the idea of God "as a supernatural being", I found the students did not need to reject any such belief. They had never had it. What had taken Robinson and others of his generation years of heart-searching and mental anguish to achieve, they had effortlessly assumed and had been waiting for him, or someone else, to articulate their position.'[6]

Again there are statistics to reinforce this personal evidence of the existence of a difference between old and young about religion. To a certain extent this has always been so. The young, farther away from the inevitable consequences of mortality, need religion less. But the interesting aspect of two surveys conducted by the National Opinion Polls in Britain shows that an anti-religious attitude amongst the young coincides precisely with the spread of television.

In 1960 a National Opinion Poll survey showed that in the age group between 21 and 24, 3 per cent classified themselves as atheists or agnostics. In 1970, another age group between 21 and 24, having had 10 years of exposure to the small screen, revealed in another NOP survey that 9 per cent of them were atheists or agnostics. No other age group in this survey showed such a large drift away from religious faith. It could be argued that a threefold increase in agnosticism amongst the young would probably have taken place because of social conditions that had nothing to do with television. But no such increases were recorded in the days before television. Has then the past decade been so unique in producing circumstances which create religious scepticism? Or has television, with its unique ability to display authority in a distorting mirror, been a factor in this growing renunciation of religion amongst the young?

Like all institutions in modern Britain, the Church is firmly convinced that exposure on television is more likely to do it good than harm. Yet when youngsters do get religion in an intense way, they expect it to look and feel and sound like a pop television programme. Thus the 'Jesus Revolution' which came to America in 1970, with teenagers wearing T-shirts proclaiming 'Jesus Is My Lord' and swaying to the songs of *Jesus Christ Superstar* in religious rave-ups, was just another passing fad with as much relevance to true religion as Batman or the Beatles. For many of these young people the Jesus experience was a substitute for television and drugs. Such cults are products of a drug and electronic media culture rather than any real religious revelation.

'At the heart of the Jesus Revolution is the personal experience of each individual — like that of 21-year-old Christopher Pike,' wrote George Milne in *The Sun* on June 24th, 1971. 'His father, now dead, was a Protestant Bishop. The boy was not attracted to his father's faith. Four years ago he was withdrawing as far as he could, aided by marijuana and, of all things, non-stop television watching. He says:"TV and grass, that was my god." When he did read the Bible, it was accompanied by drugs — and by this time he had graduated to LSD.'

Whether such conversions to Christ are likely to last is extremely dubious. More probably, when the fad has run its course and it has been thoroughly commercially exploited, it will leave in its wake thousands of youngsters disillusioned with Christianity and ready for some new cult, some new escape, to take its place. Amongst them, the rejection of religion is likely to be even harder and firmer than it was before.

Finally, the isolation of religion into its special weekend ghetto would seem to be counter-productive because it confirms to many the irrelevance of religion to the everyday problems of daily life. Thus although a large proportion of the Sunday programmes do concern themselves with serious contemporary issues such as housing, unemployment, marriage, a survey conducted by the Independent Television Authority in 1968 showed that most people failed to relate such discussions to religious programmes. Asked to list what television programmes they had recently seen that dealt with serious human problems, not one per cent of 1765 persons interviewed named a religious programme. Programmes like *24 Hours, Panorama, The Frost Programme, The News, This Week, World In Action* were named but, says the survey, 'religious broadcasts were not mentioned'.

Summing up their findings, the investigators report: 'The research has shown that the real audience for present religious television is composed in Britain predominantly of the more pious and elderly female viewer. It has shown that the young and the uncommitted turn away from much of the output because it is too closely associated — rightly or wrongly — with traditional religious practices. It has shown that the programmes which are thought to deal with serious human problems are not so much the religious programmes but the news, documentaries and current affairs programmes . . .'[7]

Like politicians, then, the Church has found that in the long run its regular and frequent recourse to entertainment-dominated television has resulted in a loss rather than an increase of adherents, has tended to diminish its authority rather than enhance it. It is just another victim of the positive television factor at work. And like so many other victims of the demeaning influence of show-biz television, it has been blind to what is happening.

If politicians and the Church can be said to be bit-players in the television spectacular, other authoritative institutions get little more than walk-on roles. Not only are there regular television niches for politicians and priests — part political broadcasts, *Westminster At Work,* the Sunday enclave, nightcap spots on ITV — but they are regularly seen in the news and are frequently invited to express their views on current affairs programmes and chat shows.

The rest of serious society, in its real as opposed to fictional capacity, gets only minuscule access to the box. For most viewers the image of what doctors, lawyers, businessmen, teachers and scientists are contributing to society comes from the romanticised, dramatised, superficial accounts of them in fictional television series like *Dr. Kildare, Perry Mason, Doctor At Large, The Troubleshooters, Please, Sir,* and *Doomwatch.*

It is not, however, the manner in which authoritative bodies and individuals are represented in fictional television that concerns us at this moment but how they are portrayed on the small screen in their true capacities and functions. And, even though they are seen infrequently on the box, such other branches of authority must conform to accepted television standards and conventions when they appear. The experience rarely embellishes their image or brings them much esteem.

The Monarchy is the institution that British television grants the most reverence and respect. Ceremonial occasions such as a coronation, a royal wedding, Trooping the Colour, an investiture, usher into the living-room of millions of loyal subjects the mystery and panoply of Royal ritual with discreet and hushed commentators explaining the function of Gold Stick-In-Waiting and the significance of the Ampulla and Spoon.

These events have always been great television successes. The Coronation of Elizabeth II in 1953 substantially increased the sale of television sets and the Investiture of Prince Charles in 1969 was a great boon to the colour television market. Yet for a long time organisers of these ceremonies made only the most reluctant concessions to the television public. Film and television cameras were tucked away behind shrubbery, in pillars, on roof-tops to record as unobtrusively and as obsequiously as possible from whatever vantage point they could scrounge.

The Investiture of Prince Charles in 1969 was the first serious recognition by the Crown that viewers not only deserved a front seat at these ceremonies but that the ceremony itself should be redesigned to cater not merely for the few who happened to be there but for the millions who wanted to be there. Under Lord Snowdon's imaginative guidance, the imposing Caernarvon Castle in Wales was converted into a huge television set where camera angles took precedence over guest-lists and sightlines were more important then pomp.

Instead of 11,000 guests that had come to Caernarvon for the previous Investiture in 1911, only 4,000 people were this time invited. Instead of the ceremony itself taking place in the confines of a secluded tent where only a few dozen persons could actually witness the most personal details of the ritual, an open dais, protected by an elegent, transparent canopy, gave generous access to every colour camera and zoom lens located in the stands and ramparts of the castle. This concentration on visual proximity for the cameras resulted in a simple un-cluttered panoramic picture of staggering beauty as, in long shot, the carpet of open green space, the confetti-like colouring of the crowded stands, the isolated dais with its three lonely figures, symbolised the fleeting nature of man in contrast to the grey, lichen-covered, time-resistant and man-mocking walls of Caernarvon that towered round them.

For the most intimate moments of the Investiture the close-up shots of the Queen and Prince Charles gave any sheep farmer in New South Wales or any rice-picker in Japan as good a view as the most privileged High Sheriff or Herald Extra-ordinary sitting in the very best seats. No one could deny that it was a grand show. And no one could deny that for those few hours the nation experienced the kind of wonder and awe and reverence that is the essence of the Royal image and without which no monarchy could in the long run survive.

Although the use of the zoom lens enables viewers to catch a glimpse of the Queen straightening out her skirt or a quizzical exchange of glances between Prince Philip and his son, the object of such televised ceremonies is not to show how similar the Royal Family is to the Queen's subjects, but how different. These medieval rituals with their splendour and archaic pro-cedures confirm that sense of remoteness and distance which is a basic ingredient of monarchical authority.

Because they occur so rarely — a coronation or an investiture or a Royal wedding are usually years apart — such Royal oc-casions are not likely to be diminished by familiarity. But the more frequent Royal events such as Trooping the Colour or the Opening of Parliament can lose their appeal through repetition. After all, it took only three landings on the moon to produce audiences complaining about the boredom of it all. If the greatest adventure of man's existence becomes *déjà vu* after three viewings is it likely that Trooping the Colour will have any greater ratings stamina? And if the ceremonial is switched off because it is boring, aren't its principal characters also being contemptuously dismissed from the living-room? And if the Queen frequently invites her subjects to switch her off, what price her authority then?

The dilemma that confronts royalty in terms of its image is how to retain the mystique of the Crown and still not appear to be too removed from the feelings and travails of the people. Recognising it as the most powerful communications medium in the land, the Queen's advisers have had to come to terms with television. How should the monster be handled?

It is all right for Princess Anne to be seen winning a European championship horse-jumping competition, but when she is interviewed afterwards, doesn't she sound like any breathless girl athlete modestly disclaiming her achievement? It is all right for Prince Charles to be interviewed by David Frost but when he is asked 'How would you describe yourself?' is it endearing or rash of him to answer 'Sometimes a bit of a twit'?

The question of how far the Queen should go in putting herself across on television as someone just like anyone else was raised when the BBC transmitted Richard Cawston's documentary, *Royal Family*, in June 1969. 'Unique', 'absorbing', 'engrossing', 'fascinating', 'hilarious', 'charming' were part of the repertoire of congratulatory adjectives that were showered upon this glimpse of the intimate, as opposed to the public, life of the Queen and her family. Its viewing figures were astronomical.

To some extent this success was predictable. There is an almost insatiable appetite for details about the private lives of living monarchs. This fascination about royalty is as intense in republics like America and France as it is in Britain. At one time any ex-governess, butler, chef, chauffeur with tittle-tattle about the backstairs workings of Buckingham Palace had a certain best-seller until the Queen's advisers took some strenuous steps to stop the marketing of this sort of gossip. Once the Queen had given her consent to a BBC–ITV consortium to follow her about for almost a year, recording never-before filmed activities of a British monarch at work, at play, relaxed and off-duty, the result was guaranteed an audience of hundreds of millions. Considering the narrow and sensitive path he had to tread between protocol and the technical demands of film-making, between reality and indelicacy, between intimacy and intrusion, Richard Cawston's programme was almost a miracle of taste and discretion.

In their enthusiasm for the innovation, some commentators claimed that at last the people were being brought closer to the truth about the Royal Family than ever before. What had actually happened was that an old image had been replaced by a fresh one more in keeping with what a telly democracy expected of their rulers.

Of course the attempt to refurbish the monarchical image, to decrease its remoteness, had seriously begun in the reign of George VI when official photographs showed the family in domestic surroundings, dressed in the conventional clothes of middle-class respectability. This documentary was adapting the trend to the television age.

But just as it was untrue that the Royal Family sat down to breakfast wearing coronets as they munched their corn flakes so it is untrue that they now behave in their private moments like any middle-class family in Surbiton or Croydon. Yet Cawston's film conformed perfectly to any public relations man's dream of what a British Royal Family ought to look like in the latter half of the twentieth century. A hard-working, conscientious, devoted Queen; a dynamic, handsome, smile-ever-playing-around-the-lips Prince; children untempted and unaffected by the permissive, violence-orientated, drug-taking propensities that trouble so many other parents; relatives that conveniently are doing well in the arts or industry. In other words, a splendid cast.

That they are as perfect and as amiable as Mr. Cawston's documentary suggested, they would, I am sure, be the first to deny. It is true that there were occasional hints of human failings that one might have glimpsed between the editing cuts. Prince Philip light-heartedly asking someone 'What's that tie? Alcoholics Anonymous?' might not have seemed as good a joke to the tie-wearer as it did to the Prince. The Queen describing the appearance of a visiting ambassador as someone who looked exactly like a gorilla revealed a welcome irreverence in her nature. Indeed it was these little asides — gossipy, somewhat malicious, even rather cruel — that made the family for me much more credible and sympathetic than all those cosy sequences of barbecuing, buying ice cream and watching *I Love Lucy* on the telly.

Whether such a documentary should have been made with the Queen's co-operation is less important than whether such a public relations exercise achieves its primary object of explaining and endearing the monarchy to the nation. 'Any institution that represents tradition must always be aware of the danger of appearing archaic,' wrote a *Times* leader dealing with this film. 'So there is the constant effort by royalty, in other countries as well as Britain, to keep in tune with the times without losing touch with the past. It is a difficult task: in the urge to be modern it is so easy to be folksy — and folksiness does not sit well on the throne.'

But, on the whole, *The Times* felt that Cawston's documentary had 'provided an intimate understanding of what members of the Royal Family are like as individual people without jeopardising their dignity or losing the sense of distance.'[8]

The *Sunday Telegraph*, on the other hand, had misgivings about its possible effects on the monarchy. 'Now that we have seen the Queen buying lollipops for Prince Edward,' said a leader on June 22nd, 1969, 'or helping prepare a family barbecue in the grounds of Balmoral Castle, will the next solemn procession of the Garter Knights at Windsor, with Her Majesty at the head, seem more dignified or more ludicrous?'

No one would suggest that one film of this kind could on its own have any serious effects on the monarchy — either beneficial or harmful. But is it a precedent that should be encouraged? If the monarchy is thought to be a valuable constitutional device for Britain can television by this sort of programme strengthen support for the Crown? *The Times* hailed the film as an 'historic innovation' in some ways akin to George V's first Christmas radio broadcast, which 'for many years provided the strongest bond between the sovereign and his people'. But, as we have already seen, the effects of television and radio are hardly comparable. Television is involving; radio is distancing. Regular doses of documentaries like Cawston's would soon turn the Royal Family into inhabitants of the posh end of Coronation Street.

Is it wise, too, for the Crown to commit itself to a precedent in which the nation will come to expect periodic revelations of the intimate lives of their monarchs? What will happen one day when an occupant of the Throne has a private life or an unfortunate personality that conflicts dramatically with the expectations and demands of a television-conditioned public? A hunchbacked Richard III, for example, or a gross George III? Will such programmes then become less candid, more cosmetic, more dissembling? Should the authority of the monarchy be subject to the whims and tastes of a people demanding, above all, star quality in their sovereign?

Although catering to the public's curiosity about the so-called 'real' personality behind the pomp and regalia may have unbargained-for long-term repercussions, such films as *Royal Family* are on the whole within the control of the monarch's advisers. They can decide whether they wish to co-operate, and it is unlikely that anything would appear in such a programme that might seriously disturb them. But when members of the Royal Family decide from time to time to be seen on chat shows or interview programmes in which spontaneity and seeming frankness are the essence of a 'good television show', they risk being dragged into unseemly public brawls which hardly add any dignity to their image.

Thus when the Duke of Edinburgh said on an American television interview in 1969 that the Queen was 'going into the red', not only was it resented as unconstitutional behaviour by some members of the Labour Government's Cabinet but became the centre of a heated controversy almost two years later. When the Tory Government announced the appointment of a select committee to review the Queen's financial position in May 1971, the Left-wing *New Statesman* strongly attacked the view that the Queen's private financial resources should not be taken into account when deciding what the Royal establishment should receive from public funds. 'The Queen is the beneficiary of a complex system of tax privileges and exceptions which has never been fully disclosed,' wrote the *New Statesman*, 'but whose value to her in terms of hard cash must be enormous. The only thing private about it is the element of concealment.

The Queen, in fact, is trying to get it both ways, pressured, to judge by his ill-judged utterance on this subject, by the Duke of Edinburgh.'[9]

Asked to justify this stinging criticism of Prince Philip, Mr. Richard Crossman, the editor of the *New Statesman*, replied that what had provoked his attack was the sensational American *Meet The Press* interview in which the Duke had said that the Royal Family 'was going into the red next year and might have to leave Buckingham Palace'.[10]

The repercussions of this row were that the question of the Queen's money became the centre of acrimonious debate. No doubt it could be argued that such open discussions about the monarchy are healthy. This would be true if all the facts were available and if intelligent arguments were provided by the medium that started it all — television — from which the public could make reasonable assessments of the case. But since the television channels either ignored the issue or devoted only a few minutes of partisan debate to it, the only thing generated by the whole affair was a heated and emotional atmosphere which, by raising suspicions about Royal privileges that were not allayed, could have done the sovereign little good.

Is there any evidence, then, to support the theoretical speculation that television has *not* helped cement the sovereign any more firmly in the affections of her people? If the televising of the Investiture, the high ratings of Cawston's *Royal Family*, the David Frost interview with Prince Charles, achieved their purpose from a monarchical standpoint there should be some objective statistics showing that more people wanted a Queen than they did before the transmission of such programmes. Such statistics as are available — admittedly very limited — show that the trend of public faith in the need of a monarchy is declining rather than increasing.

A National Opinion Poll survey conducted in 1969 revealed that 84 per cent of the British people thought that Britain needed a Queen. The age group between 16 and 34 was marginally less sympathetic about the monarchy with only 76 per cent believing the country needed a Queen. In 1971 NOP asked the same question. This time only 78 per cent of the people felt Britain needed a Queen — an overall fall of 6 per cent. A similar percentage fall in support of the monarchy was found in the 25 to 34 age group with only 72 per cent saying a Queen was needed. But the sharpest lack of enthusiasm was expressed among the 18 to 24s — the nearest group Britain has to a telly generation. Only 62 per cent of them thought the nation needed a sovereign — a startling fall of some 14 per cent in two years from the 76 per cent support figure for the Queen which this age group had recorded in 1969 and 10 per cent lower than even the 25 to 34 category.

Whatever else, then, television had done for the Royal Family through the intervention of an Investiture, David Frost and a popular documentary, it had not increased support for the monarchy. The same results had been experienced by the Church in spite of fifteen years of privileged television. The same results had been experienced by politicians — a similar NOP survey had revealed a decline in respect for M.P.s — in spite of more access to the box than any other section of responsible society.

More awesome than this steady decline in respect for the most authoritative institutions in the land is the precipitate increase in scepticism about them experienced by the age group under 25. When it is remembered that the time watershed dividing the telly generation from the non-telly generations is about 25 this difference in attitudes to authority is surely significant.

The Trades Union Congress meeting in Blackpool for their annual conference in September 1971, passed a resolution expressing dissatisfaction with the manner in which their affairs were being handled by the mass media. They recommended, amongst other things, a monitoring service to check broadcasts for bias, liaison facilities to enable complaints to be raised immediately and corrective action taken, and a standing committee to study and report on the handling of trade-union affairs on radio, television and the press.

The cause of the concern reflected in this resolution was a growing suspicion and resentment against trade unions amongst a large number of the British people. A series of strikes in 1970 and 1971 by workers in the public sector — municipal, power and postal workers — had caused great inconvenience and large financial loss to people not directly involved in the dispute. Mounds of uncollected rubbish in London's streets, failing electricity in hospitals, elderly people trying to collect their old age pensions from post-offices, provided a picture of callous self-interest on the part of these trade unions that angered public opinion and, in the case of the power workers, became so ugly that they had to call off their strike.

The medium that had contributed most to this explosion of resentment was undoubtedly television. Although a predominantly Right-wing British press had never been particularly friendly to trade-unionism, it had never succeeded in alienating the majority of the public from a certain sympathy and rapport with the economic and humanitarian goals of the trade union movement. But the unpopularity of trade-unionists amongst ordinary people in 1970 and 1971 was almost unprecedented in its 103-year history. The 1926 General Strike antagonised the middle class; the 1970–71 strikes antagonised the middle class and a large section of the working class. Desperately seeking for some explanation for this sudden surge of disapproval, the Trades Union Congress decided that the cause must be the 'bias' of television.

The trade union movement, like other authoritative institutions, finds its prestige and popularity sinking to fresh lows in telly democracies. It is the manner in which television reports the activities of trade-unionists, and particularly strikes and demonstrations, that turns viewers against them. And television does not do this deliberately. It does it because the techniques of news reporting, the conventions of discussion, the limitations of time, the need for visual corroboration, force the medium to be consistently superficial, dramatic, over-simplified and perfunctory.

Strikes are often complicated human affairs whose background may have more to do with personalities than the purely financial arguments that seem to be the bones of contention. Similarly they are often too technical and too involved to be grasped readily by anyone but the protagonists involved. Displayed on television as four-minute discussions between two sets of stubborn men, they come across as illustrations of the pettiness, incompetence and selfishness of leaders on both sides of industry. With the issue simplified to a few declamatory statements it becomes incomprehensible to the viewer that their differences cannot be resolved. Since the trade union leaders are usually the aggressors in these situations — they have stopped work, caused disruption, been the 'militants' or the 'wreckers' — their public image tends to come off second best in such confrontations.

It was because it felt that the power workers' dispute had been unfairly represented on television and because of its doubts about other aspects of union coverage on the box, that the Association of Cinematograph and Allied Technicians (ACTT) decided to carry out an investigation of television's handling of industrial affairs in the week of 8th to 14th January 1971. It was a period rich in labour disputes with stoppages, strikes, works-to-rule, lock-outs, go-slows or lay-offs reported at Rolls-Royce, the Hull docks, London Airport, a London school, Hawker Siddeley, Pilkington Glass, and tanker-drivers' oil depots.

Every piece of news and comment about trade-union affairs was monitored and analysed. The final report asserted that a large number of stories were neither natural in language nor balanced in content from a trade-union point of view. But the report was not inclined to accuse either the BBC or the ITN of conscious anti-trade-union bias. It concluded that the faults were less due to any deliberate intent than to the fact that industrial matters on television were treated in an erratic and superficial manner and that trivialisation of industrial news stemmed from technical limitations and programme values.

'What the ACTT report is saying is that trade-unionists feel that television news expresses too many of the deeply im-planted attitudes of the middle-class,' wrote Stuart Hood in *The Listener* of February 25th, 1971, 'and that insufficient efforts are being made to understand the reasoning and motives of those who are active and assertive in the trade union move-ment. They no longer find tolerable the BBC News Bulletin of January 10th which, after listing a number of home industrial problems, dismissed them thus — "But far more worrying is or should be a report from the Royal College of Phys-icians" — and went on to discuss the report on smoking. Smok-ing, and the deaths it causes, is a serious subject but industrial unrest is hardly a trivial one.'

It is, of course, true that television, even if only because of the limited amount of time it devotes to anything serious, treats industrial issues in a perfunctory and superficial manner. Since that is the way it treats politics, the monarchy, the Church, business, the universities, medicine, science, why should trade-unionists expect to get any special consideration?

In the television extravaganza where entertainers and sportsmen occupy the centre of the stage, with politicians, priests and princes playing only minor character parts, trade-unionists have only the status of spear-holders. They have no programmes of their own, no electronic forum from which to press or explain their point of view. From time to time, usually in bellicose postures, they are seen on the peripheral edge of the action.

The only time television in Britain accords them full and independent exposure is during the annual meeting of the Trades Union Congress. It has now become the custom to televise large chunks of this five-day conference live from some seaside town like Blackpool where the conference is held. Pioneered by Granada Television, and usually seen on the commercial channel in the mornings, these proceedings are witnessed by minuscule audiences.

It is perhaps fortunate for the trade union movement that their annual talking jamboree is not exposed to the gaze of larger viewing audiences. The image of the TUC has never been particularly dynamic or progressive. For decades it was associated in many people's eyes with the cartoonist David Low's carthorse as a plodding, stubborn, amiable, dense beast, more noted for its ability to dig in its heels than to go anywhere. The televising of this conference, because it projects the ritual rather than the reality of the movement, confirms this picture of archaic, monolithic, non-progressive thinking.

Conferences of this kind were never meant for television cameras. They no more show what the trade union movement is about than an annual shareholders' meeting reveals the workings of British Petroleum or Ford Motors. The real gritty achievements of the Trades Union Congress are the work of backroom boys poring over statistics or the private meetings of union leaders arguing and wheeling and dealing about what line to take with employers and the Government. None of this is seen on television.

It is, however, during an important industrial dispute that

television suddenly projects trade union leaders into the public consciousness for a few short days or weeks. While the opposing sides in a strike may have to argue for hours behind locked doors to sort out their entangled differences, television reduces these complicated affairs to a few quick flashes in a news bulletin or a few minutes of pugnacious discussion, on *Midweek*, *Today* or *Panorama*.

The highly dramatised, superficially told story of a strike on television rarely enhances a trade union leader's reputation or authority. But if the hardships inflicted upon the general public are seen frequently on the box during a strike, then television can become an important ingredient in resolving the dispute through the arousal of public interest and anger.

It is inevitable that in selecting what is newsworthy about a strike, television reporters will highlight its ugliest and most dramatic consequences. During the 1970 municipal workers' strike in London, the news bulletins showed us the streets where mounting piles of rubbish had reached sickening and revolting proportions. They didn't show us the thousands of streets where, as a result of concerted citizens' actions, there were no rubbish piles. During the 1970 power workers' go-slow, current affairs programmes were replete with heart-rending tales of the failure of incubators and old ladies dying of hypothermia because of the electricity stoppage, but little was shown of the efforts made by the union to see that hospitals were affected as little as possible.

Just how incensed public opinion had become by these nightly pictures of suffering reputedly caused by the power workers was vividly demonstrated in David Frost's live chat show on the night of December 12th, 1970. Five power workers — all shop stewards — turned up on this programme in the naïve belief that they would be able to explain to the country the merits of their case. They mistakenly assumed that a television show noted for its provocative and controversial atmosphere would provide a suitable forum for an objective examination of their position.

However, the mood of this so-called investigation into the rights and wrongs of the power workers' go-slow was established when the word 'Killers!' was flung at the five bewildered shop stewards from someone in the audience during David

Frost's introductory remarks. It set the tone for the kind of lynch television with which viewers of the Frost Programme were not entirely unfamiliar.

Sitting in the front row of the studio audience was a belligerent farmer whose contribution to the debate ended up with the words: 'You are filthy and your unions are filthy.' When one of the shop stewards resented being called a Communist and started to take off his jacket to indicate his disapproval, the burly farmer leaped on to the studio platform and knocked the worker flat on his back with a vicious right hook. What might have degenerated into an uncontrollable brawl or television punch-up was cooled by Frost's ever-ready facility with a quick gag. 'The Muhammad Ali fight was on Tuesday,' he quipped. 'This is a talk show.' The resultant laughter calmed everyone down.

Visibly unnerved by the thick air of menace that surrounded them, the shop stewards proceeded to make a thorough mess of explaining their position. They ducked out of responsibility for the power cuts, got involved in long-winded explanations that taxed everyone's patience, veered between pugnacious resentment and conciliatory gestures, and looked both baffled and frightened by the torrent of abuse that was hurled at them.

Their appearance on a show of this kind was a disastrous error of judgment. Although it looks deceptively easy to chat away convincingly to someone like David Frost, it actually requires professionalism of a high order. Shop stewards who find themselves on the work floor surrounded by similar-minded mates who share their language and outlook and goals can delude themselves into believing that convincing the public on television is just as simple as getting a unanimous response to down tools. The television studio, contrary to popular belief, is not a place from which sincerity and honesty will filter through in spite of every barrier.

Not only is the technique of television persuasion a subtle and complex art but as every lawyer knows, a man who chooses to act as his own advocate has a fool for a client. The aims of a chat show are to provide entertainment and not a judicial assessment of the truth. The ground rules are designed to generate excitement and conflict, not objectivity or logic. Individuals like these shop stewards, who without previous experience try

146

to defend themselves on television in such an environment, are bound to end up as sacrificial goats, destroying themselves and their cause for the greater good of entertaining the masses on a Saturday night.

Nevertheless, the assumption that appearing on television — irrespective of what kind of television — does every cause some good, dies hard. Thus Mr. Anthony Wedgwood Benn, a former Labour Postmaster-General, has been pressing for more access to the box for trade unions. In an article in the *Sunday Mirror* and a speech in Glasgow in the first week of May 1971 he spelt out his views about how the workers' case could be presented on television. He thought that a weekly programme of 15-minutes' duration was the absolute minimum for putting across the trade union case. He also thought that such a programme should be entirely controlled by trade-unionists themselves. His extraordinary assumption, coming from an experienced broadcaster like himself, was that if workers were able to speak directly to the people, without the intervention of commentators and experts, their message would come across pristine pure, intelligible and presumably beneficial to the trade union cause.

Regularly displayed in such a format with ordinary workers attempting to articulate their views under such stunted and artificial conditions, the trade union movement would inevitably give the impression of an authoritative body trying to justify itself with half-baked, ill-thought-out, superficial arguments. It would most likely end up as a disparaging exercise for all concerned.

Access by serious and important institutions to the television screen is a real and growing problem. But it can never be resolved with television entertainment-dominated and structured as it is now. Until there are more channels to provide adequate room for the discussion of the many-sided aspects of our society, coupled with the conversion of the medium to an adult communicator of information and education, the trade union movement would do well to ration severely its recourse to the small screen. There are, of course, occasions when an industrial crisis demands a worker's voice on the box. But unless trade union spokesmen make sure that the conditions are right — the right programme, the right amount of time, the right atmosphere for fair and serious discussion — television is likely to do more to damage their case than to bolster it.

The Law is the bedrock upon which any civilised society is founded. If it falls into serious disrepute, a nation will be faced with profound moral dilemmas and even violent repercussions. In a stable society the wisdom of the Law can be questioned, but never its authority.

As an institutional body the Law is rarely seen on British television. Except in television fiction, judges and lawyers appear most infrequently on the box. This is less true in America where it has now become common practice for lawyers to discuss with television reporters the merits and tactics of cases in which they are involved. Frenetic interviews on the steps of a courthouse with lawyers taking part in much-publicised trials are unheard of in Britain. I doubt that they bring much respect to the judicial process in America.

But if the processes and the practitioners of the Law are not seen on British television, there have been a few occasions when the small screen has presented, in the cause of 'good TV', a version of British justice which has been a travesty of the real thing. Investigative journalism attempting to expose social scandals and social ills has always been a tricky problem for television producers. The primarily bland and trivial nature of the medium does not encourage such hard-hitting programmes. The need for 'balance' and the severe libel laws are other restrictions on any producer eager to use television as a means of laying bare incompetence or corruption.

From time to time there have been welcome exposés of bad housing, racial persecution, dubious abortion clinics, grim mental institutions on programmes like *Panorama, Midweek, This Week* and *Man Alive*. Bernard Braden in *On the Braden Beat* established himself as a sort of electronic Ombudsman airing complaints about incompetent town councils or slick and suspect commercial practices. For the most part, the approach to such investigations has been serious, restrained and factual.

It is, however, when programmes take on an accusatory format rather than an investigative one that television begins to move on to precarious ground. Christian martyrs were hardly the recipients of the most civilised justice by having their fates determined by mobs.

It is because it has tried to blend the discussion of serious social affairs with pop music, gags, and frivolous chatter that *The Frost Programme* turns up so often in this book as an illustration of the dangers of entertainment-dominated television. We have already seen the sort of rough justice handed out to the power workers who had to face a hostile studio audience on this show. Sometimes, as in its enquiry into the collapse of the Ronan Points flats or in a fierce debate on the merits of hanging, the discussions have been less spectacular and more rewarding.

But on at least two occasions *The Frost Programme* set itself up as an electronic tribunal in which men, by their performance, could convict themselves in the eyes of the public of having committed a criminal offence. On February 3rd, 1967 Dr. Emil Savundra, chairman of the bankrupt Fire, Auto and Marine Insurance Company, appeared as Frost's guest to explain the recent collapse of his company. On January 12th, 1968 Dr. John Petro confronted Frost and a studio audience about newspaper allegations that he was illegally dispensing drugs. At the time of their appearances neither man was charged with any criminal offence. Subsequent to these appearances they were both charged and eventually convicted of crimes which had been discussed on the programme.

'It was with mixed feelings of regret and exhilaration that I switched off my set on Friday after watching *The Frost Programme*,' I wrote in my *Evening Standard* column on February 8th, 1967. 'Regret because this tingling, provocative and unpredictable show was off the air. Exhilaration because I had just witnessed a dramatic confrontation in which right seemed to have triumphed over wrong.

' "Well done, Frostie! ... Good old Frostie!" were approving cries that could be heard coming from the studio audience as David Frost, breathing heavily with indignation, dismissed the imperturbable Dr. Emil Savundra from the small screen.

'My first reaction was to share whole-heartedly the studio audiences approbation of the manner in which Savundra's dubious management of the Fire, Auto and Marine Insurance

Co. had been exposed and the subsequent humiliation he had suffered under Frost's relentless and ruthless questioning.

'But away from the emotionally charged influence of the box certain doubts about the ethics of using television in this way began to seep into my conscience. Let me put them to you.

'There are certain safeguards that the English legal system provides for any person in confrontation with the law. The most obvious is that he is presumed innocent until proved guilty. And the other is that he has the right to be represented by trained counsel.

'There are other supplementary conditions which ensure a fair hearing for any defendant. The jury is chosen from objective, uninvolved citizens. The defendant has a right to put his case in direct examination without being harried by the prosecution's questions and he has the right to cross-examine witnesses testifying against him.

'Finally, the dull, dispassionate, antiseptic quality of a British courtroom is another guarantee that the facts will be sifted in a calm atmosphere free from anger, hate or prejudice.

'This paraphernalia of objectivity may seem cumbersome and tedious to the impatient who demand instant justice. But they are the rocks upon which the rights of an Englishman's freedom from oppression and tyranny have been established for centuries.

'Now there is no doubt that in the context of last Friday's programme, Dr. Savundra was being asked to defend himself against accusations which, had they been proved, might have resulted in criminal charges. Foolishly and conceitedly, he allowed himself to take part in a mini-trial under conditions which would have horrified any British judge.

'He was not represented by counsel. He was not given an opportunity to present his full case. His jurors, the studio audience, not only indicated their lack of impartiality by heckling him from the start, but included a large number of victims of the collapse of the Fire, Auto and Marine Insurance.

'Even worse, his inquisitor, David Frost, unskilled in legal technicalities, asked questions which would have been disallowed in any courtroom as prejudicial or irrelevant . . . It will, of course, be argued that Savundra himself chose, as he says "to cross swords with England's bravest swordsman".

'Lawyers and judges are constantly warning defendants about the dangers of acting as their own counsel. Unless superbly knowledgeable, they will be unable to take advantage of the many safeguards the law provides for them. And a man who attempts to face the television cameras, confronting an experienced television performer like Frost, is likely to find himself in as exposed and baffling a position as anyone conducting his own case in a courtroom . . .

'What happened to Dr. Savundra is, in essence, little but lynch television — a phrase which implies that the rule of the mob has overruled the guarantees of the rule of law . . .'

Almost a year later on the same programme Dr. John Petro was another victim of lynch television. Dr. Petro, accused in the press of illegally dispensing drugs to addicts, had come on the programme to defend himself. Again we saw a man subjected to an atmosphere totally inimicable to the conduct of justice. He had no legal advice about what he should or should not say. He was confronted with surprise witnesses in the studio audience who accused him of illegal activities. The atmosphere was hostile and emotionally charged. He was harassed about matters that might have put his freedom in jeopardy. This was in essence a public trial in which David Frost and his producer had determined the make-up of both judge and jury.

In other words, the Law, like so many other institutional authorities, was taking on the colouring of a television programme. Real people in real jeopardy were being treated almost as if they were fictional people in fictional jeopardy. The emotional atmosphere of these confrontations was closer to what went on in a Western or a police drama when a villain was confounded than to the processes of a British courtroom.

The dangers implicit in such a programme were eventually recognised by the Law itself. In dismissing Dr. Savundra's appeal against his conviction for fraud, Lord Justice Salmon in his judgment delivered in July 1968 had this to say about what had taken place on *The Frost Programme*. 'This court hopes that no interview of this kind will ever again be televised. Trial by television cannot be tolerated in a civilised country,' were his stern words of rebuke. 'On any view, the television interview with Savundra was deplorable. He has no experience of television, and was faced with a skilled interviewer whose clear object was to establish his guilt before millions of people.'

Lord Justice Salmon quoted with approval and attribution my exact words about the essential safeguards provided to a suspect person by the English legal system: 'They are the rocks upon which the rights of an Englishman's freedom from oppression and tyranny have been established for centuries.'

In a letter to *The Times*, David Frost himself indignantly replied to Lord Justice Salmon's strictures. 'We are all concerned about individual rights in Britain today,' wrote Mr. Frost, 'but one of the most precious of the rights that the public has is the simple one of hearing the truth whenever and wherever it is available . . . Television has shown that it has a real part to play in seeking the truth about matters of public concern, and to remove television from this role seems to be doing both public and individual a positive disservice.'[11]

The basic difference separating Lord Justice Salmon and Frost was whether the methods used on *The Frost Programme* were acceptable ways for a civilised society to search out the truth. The case against such methods was not that television was intruding on the preserves of the law but that such methods were more likely to distort the truth, prejudice fair opinion, and deprive a man of some of his basic legal freedoms.

The point about English Law is that it has evolved, after centuries of argument and struggle, a procedural system which on balance favour an accused man when he is charged with a crime. Because philosophically it supports the view that it is far better that ten guilty men be set free rather than one innocent man be wrongly condemned, an accused person is offered certain safeguards to aid him in his confrontation with the State.

Trained counsel, a non-involved jury, a right not to answer questions or go into the witness box, protection against hearsay evidence and prejudicial innuendoes, a calm, reflective atmosphere, are a few of the elementary legal rights which were, for the most part, denied Savundra and Petro. The fact that they chose, out of ignorance or egotism, to appear in such a programme is irrelevant in English Law. In a courtroom both of them would have been protected from many of the questions and accusations hurled at them.

Let us examine some of the possible consequences of an extension of show-biz trials on television. In the case of Savundra, the verdict of the studio audience turned out to be the same as that of a subsequent jury. They both found Savundra guilty. But suppose a more plausible, a more likeable, a more convincing fellow than Savundra — equally guilty — had managed to turn the tables on his inquisitor? Suppose because of the ineptitude of the questioning, a guilty man convinced millions of viewers that he was innocent? Would it still be claimed that it little mattered if, in a court of law, some jurors were favourably disposed towards him because of what they had seen on a television show rather than what they had heard in a courtroom?

Even more disturbing, suppose the man subjected to this sort of inquisition was a Timothy Evans or James Hanratty — men dubiously convicted of murder? Suppose such men, because of pressures and rumours, had decided to commit themselves to trial by television before they had been charged with murder? And suppose again, because of the lack of elementary safeguards, because of their inability to parry the interrogator's thrusts in the unfamiliar setting of a television studio, millions of viewers had received the impression that they had been guilty of murder?

And if, in a subsequent trial, a jury had confirmed the impressions of the studio audience and *wrongly* convicted them of murder — although both these men were hanged, arguments still rage about their guilt — who would have been able to say what extra pressure, what unfair suspicion had been lodged in a juror's mind because of what he had seen on a television programme?

No one suggests that television should not engage in investigating the wrongs, the abuses and the doubts in our society. And when they are found, it is indeed the medium's duty to be as outspoken and vigorous in exposing evil men and evil institutions as energetically and as fearlessly as the press and Parliament. If anything, because of its preoccupation with entertainment, television does far too little of such investigative and crusading journalism.

These incidents demonstrate, however, the natural tendency of television, in its present state, to over-simplify, dramatise and sensationalise even so basic a subject as man's right to elementary justice. Just as the authority of politicians, the monarchy and the Church has been whittled away and weakened by the reflections of their image on the small screen, so is respect for the Law likely to diminish if judicial processes are seen to be as casual, as superficial, as arbitrary and as instant as a chat show.

There is one vital institution of authority in British life that has as yet not been seduced by the prospect of popularity through television. It is Parliament — the House of Commons and the House of Lords. While politicians and parties have eagerly sought the dubious benefits of being reflected in the ravenous eye, the British Parliament has barred the television cameras from its intimate proceedings. This reluctance of the Commons to allow its debates to be seen in the living-rooms of the electorate has been attacked in many quarters as evidence of Parliament's remoteness from the feelings, mood and tastes of the times.

'There is the smell of death about Parliament these days,' wrote the controversial journalist, Auberon Waugh. 'Parliament has given up trying to influence the public and has now moved to the defensive. We see it when they refuse television in the House of Commons, knowing full well that the public would be appalled by the mixture of exhibitionism and mediocrity which only a few witness nowadays.'[12]

If bringing Parliament to the people means the presence of persistent eavesdropping cameras in the same manner as television reports of the TUC Conference or the Party Conferences — relentless, unedited hours of repetitious speech-making — then, of course, the public would be 'appalled' not only by the displays of exhibitionism and mediocrity, but by the grinding boredom of it all. Since every Parliament will always have its share of exhibitionists and mediocrities, the fear of bringing the Commons into disrepute by revealing some of the clowns and nonentities in its midst would preclude the presence of television in the House forever. And, of course, if the public actually saw in action some of the specimens they had elected to represent them they might think twice before casting a vote for them again. Thus Parliament might eventually benefit from such exposure.

But the sight of individual M.P.s making fools of themselves on the Benches is one of the peripheral issues in the continuing debate about whether the Commons should be televised. As, indeed, are most of the other arguments bandied about over this matter. It was very reluctantly that the Commons finally permitted, towards the end of the eighteenth century, the taking of regular verbatim accounts of its proceedings — the daily Hansard reports. Radio has since 1945 broadcast a daily fifteen-minute summary, *Today in Parliament*, of what has been said by our legislators. The revelation on paper is as far as the Commons has been prepared to go. The microphone, the tape recorder and the camera as means of disseminating their activities to the electorate are still taboo.

The argument about the merits of televising Parliament has been bogged down in a morass of details. Its opponents particularly are not short of technical and practical objections. They express concern about the heat of the television lights, the cost of the operation, the danger of exhibitionists hogging the screen, the embarrassment of showing how sparsely attended are some of the debates and the undignified spectacle of M.P.s sprawling on the benches with their feet up; the problems facing non-photogenic M.P.s; the pitfalls of trying to preserve a fair balance if only a limited part of the debate is televised; the difficulty of trying to squeeze into a half-hour — which is about all such a programme is likely to get in current BBC or ITV schedules — a fair interpretation of a full day's debate; the unreliability of television producers seeking sensational or telegenic effects; the thorny questions of Parliamentary privilege and libel.

None of these problems is insurmountable. An experimental exercise could have revealed which of these objections were trivial and which had enough real merit to require further study about how to eliminate them. But such an experiment was precisely what the Commons rejected in a free debate in the House on November 24th, 1966. It was lost by one vote.

A private member's motion in November 1969, to bring TV cameras into the House, sought approval for an experimental period of closed-circuit broadcasts of Parliament's proceedings. This was hardly a drastic suggestion, but it might have provided some factual evidence at least about the practicability of the proposition. However only 107 M.P.s bothered to vote on the question — less than one-sixth of the House — and the motion failed to receive the necessary 100 votes (it received 75) which were needed to authorise the experiment.

What became clear during the course of an impressive and eloquent debate was that M.P.s were anxious about signs of a growing indifference and disenchantment with the image and authority of Parliament. Would television help halt that decline in prestige and influence or would it aggravate it? Would television show Parliament as an effective means of governing Britain which truly reflected the will and aspirations of the people? Or would it confirm suspicions that Parliament had become an insular, smug, inefficient, archaic governing instrument?

'Many people think that we are already becoming a kind of Augustan Senate, that we are declining in repute,' said the Conservative M.P. Mr. Julian Amery, supporting the motion for an experiment. 'If so, it is partly because the country does not know what we do and partly — let us admit it in all honesty — because we lack the discipline or the stimulus of knowing that what we say really counts.'

But for those opposing the introduction of television cameras there was a more profound fear lurking in their speeches which had nothing to do with the technical or procedural difficulties. Put bluntly, it was the fear that television would force changes on Parliament which would eventually alter its nature and substance. Would Parliament end up, as almost everything else regularly subjected to the ministrations of the box, as an appendage of the entertainment business? 'I see television as a technique which will put Parliament to *its* service,' said the Conservative, Mr. W. F. Deedes, voicing this apprehension. 'We shall not, as some hope, use television to our advantage or, more important in the Parliamentary sense, to the people's advantage. On the contrary, television will put us to its advantage.'

The implications of this remark are that the aims and purposes of television are in some measure in conflict with the aims and purposes of Parliament and the people. What is good for television is not necessarily good for the people. What, then, are the functions of television that make it so doubtful a force for the good of the state? Other M.P.s made the point. Said Labour M.P. Mr. Maurice Edelman: 'It is not the function of Parliament to entertain. We are not a peep show or a raree show.' Said Labour M.P. Mr. Peart, Leader of the House: 'Is not the temptation to treat the proceedings of the House primarily for its entertainment value so insidious as to be virtually insurmountable?'

When, three years after this debate, Parliament again was faced with the decision of allowing television to record its proceedings, nothing about the medium had fundamentally changed. Its primary purpose was still to entertain; suspicion about the impact of television on society had hardened. Nevertheless before the Commons debated the issue on October 19th, 1972, it seemed almost a foregone conclusion that this time M.P.s would not be able to resist the argument for modernising themselves by revealing their activities to every living-room in the land. Leading articles in such influential papers as *The Times* and *Guardian* urged the Commons to agree to a limited experiment which would show how it could be done. Reflecting very much a minority opinion in the press, I wrote in the *Evening Standard*, on October 18th, 1972, the day before the debate: 'The truth is that until the totality of British TV becomes a more responsible and more committed instrument of social values and education, it is essential that the major institutions of order and reflection stand aloof from television. They should disdain the temptation to conform to the box's standards and demands ... There must be somewhere in our land where the citizens' problems and future can be weighed, debated and discussed without the camera glaring to hinder reflection, and the need for instant popularity intruding to jostle contemplation and confuse objectivity ... Such bulwarks against the telly take-over should obviously be the law courts and Parliament. If, and when, television changes, we can all think again.'

To the surprise of most commentators, the Commons rejected a television experiment even more decisively than they had six years before. With many more M.P.s voting, the Commons rebuff to television was carried not by merely one vote — as in 1966 — but by 191 votes to 165. There can be little doubt that the prime motivating factor underlying this decision was suspicion and distrust of the medium.

'We shall err if we treat this decision superficially as a snub by Parliament to television,' wrote the Tory M.P., William Deedes, in the *Sunday Telegraph* on October 22nd, 1972, 'or even as a redressing of the balance of power — and this is about power. *Au fond* it is not discreditable to television but perhaps otherwise ... It marks awareness shared by many in broadcasting, as well as some in politics, that the conquest of television is not quite limitless; that until it has thought through more convincingly where it is hurrying and why it wants to get there limits may be set. Some will describe that as reaction. I prefer to regard it as the beginning of wisdom for the Box.'

Undeterred by this rebuff in 1972, the pro-TV lobby, heartened by a fresh influx of more Labour and younger M.P.s, made another attempt on February 25th, 1975, to get TV cameras into the Commons, and although the latter agreed to a limited experiment in radio broadcasts of their proceedings, they once more turned down scrutiny by television by 277 to 265.

Thus we have in Britain the curious situation that Parliament, having created through legislative action the most powerful medium in the land, now feels it would be sullied or harmed by too close an involvement with its own creation. This is how the argument runs. Television is predominantly an entertainment medium and if Parliament associates itself with it the chances are that it will be trivialised and demeaned in the process. On the other hand, if Parliament does not go on television it will be seen to be increasingly out of touch with the electorate, will be held more and more in suspicion for its remoteness, and will be increasingly condemned for its exclusiveness.

Impaled on the horns of this dilemma, the Commons has decided to cower in the safety of non-activity, opted for the cameras to be kept out, and is presumably hoping that it will still be able to communicate an image of a modern, concerned, involved legislative body without recourse to the small screen.

It has, of course, one other course open to it. It could by legislative action change the nature and direction of television in Britain. It could insist that the right to broadcast entailed a responsibility to 'inform and educate' which was at least as important as the responsibility 'to entertain'. It could lay down regulations, similar to those about early evening Sunday broadcasting, which would demand a higher proportion of serious programming at peak-time hours and a reduction of the entertainment content of television. Such regulations would be binding on *all* channels. If this meant that advertising revenue would not be so plentiful to finance such a service then the Government would have to find other means of financing it.

It is a sad state of affairs that Parliament itself is too ashamed of its own creation to use it as a means of strengthening understanding between the Commons and the people. The Commons have only themselves to blame for their dilemma. A minor effort of will and understanding could change British television so that Parliament, in the words of Mr. Deedes M.P., could make a 'profitable alliance' with it. Must Parliament continue to deny itself the one contemporary means of communication that could do most to restore its prestige and influence because it is loath to interfere with the advertising and show-business interests that now determine the direction and values of British television?

Television has conferred no particular benefit or esteem on any institution of authority — the Church, the Monarchy, the Law, the trade unions — that has had any large measure of recourse to it. Indeed, such evidence as does exist indicates that the telly generation — the under twenties — has less respect for these pillars of the Establishment than any other age group, that in the past decade such disrespect has accelerated much faster in that age group than it did in the decades before television, and that the loss of respect for authority over the past ten years is statistically much higher amongst the telly generation than it is amongst those who were only marginally influenced by the box in their most formative years.

How healthy is a society whose principle sources of authority are constantly being sapped and undermined? If there are other social factors responsible for this loss of faith in institutions that represent law, order, faith, continuity, stability, tradition — the impact of science on religion, the probability of human extinction by the H-bomb, the stark contrast between affluence and poverty, the technological advances which an older generation has been unable to control — how much has television contributed to the communication and acceleration of that loss of faith? And how far has television, by the manner in which it distorts life through its limited techniques and frivolous values, made its unique and signal contribution to the generally unwarranted and excessive disillusionment with the institutions of our society?

Of course, there are those who believe that mankind will never achieve its spiritual and cultural potential until the corrupt institutions mankind has so far devised are demolished. This tiny minority might indeed take the view that television, as it is now structured in Britain and America, is doing posterity a service by insidiously undermining the Establishment in its own particular and inadvertent fashion. The anarchist might well see in profit-motivated, entertainment-orientated television an ally which is hastening the inevitable crisis in capitalist society. But one thing is certain: whatever society some day replaces this one — Marxist, syndicalist, anarchist, Fascist — it will have the good sense not to run television as we have done.

In the name of free speech, we have allowed limited speech on television to every vital institution in our society. In their desire to communicate with the public, major sources of authority have been forced to present clownish, warped and untrue pictures of themselves. In their naïve faith that entrepreneurs and showmen can be trusted to recognise and keep a proper balance between their own rewards and the social needs of society, governments and politicians have unwittingly become the victims and prisoners of their own electronic monsters.

Authority in all its guises is, in my opinion, being influenced by a positive television factor. At the moment, this influence is contributing significantly to the growing cynicism and disrespect for all forms of authority. This need not be so. But it will continue to be so until fundamental changes are brought about in the structure and purpose of television in English-speaking, television democracies.

CHAPTER SIX

Cain's Kindergarten

There is simply no concrete evidence that television is to blame for violence. No schoolmaster would make such an error. It is largely an assertion without proof. After all, you come into contact with the human young every day, so you know that some will be up to no good whether they have been watching television the night before or not.
Lord Hill, Chairman of the BBC, speaking to a Conference of Schoolmasters, January 1st, 1969

Television entertainment based on violence may be effective merchandising, but it is an appalling way to serve a civilisation – an appalling way to fulfill the requirements of the law that broadcasting serve 'the public interest, convenience and necessity'.
United States National Commission on the Causes and Prevention of Violence, September 23rd, 1969

When the mass media are not interested in what is right or wrong, violence regrettably, will flourish.
Jo Grimond, former leader of the Liberal Party, *Guardian*, May 21st, 1968

The camera zoomed in to a close-up. The American sergeant, using a straight razor, deftly cut off the ear of a dead Vietcong. Casually, he dropped the ear in his pack and marched off with his souvenir. The television reporter explained that ear-cutting was not an unfamiliar practice among American troops in Vietnam. The incident was shown on CBS network news.

A man, terror oozing from his body, runs and stumbles through the dark city streets trying to escape from an ominous car which has him caught in its headlights. Trapped against a wall, he waits while the two cops get out of the car. The cops, coldly and casually, mow down the helpless man with their pistols. Two strangers leap into the scene, violently tussle with the police and force them to flee.

'Bogus cops,' says one of the strangers, examining something the fleeing men have left behind. Dusting himself off, the handsome stranger saunters into a luxurious flat where a luscious blonde, sprawling invitingly on a sofa, greets him with a sinuous body and a come-and-take-me smile. It is the opening of a routine American television crime drama.

Of all the suspected consequences of the fifth factor, violence is the one that generates the most controversy and gets the most publicity. Is the unprecedented rise in violence of almost every kind in countries like America, Britain and Canada which has taken place at almost the same time as the spread of television merely a coincidence? Or is there a causal link?

The incidents that I have just described illustrate the kind of television violence that is the evidence in the argument and the basis for the concern. One is the violence of reality found in newsreels and current affairs programmes; the other is the violence of fantasy that pervades most of the fictionalised series that dominate the air in America and, to a lesser extent, in Britain. Between them they make up a mosaic of a society in which acts of violence, preparations for violence and the repercussions of violence are considered normal, routine and very often admirable.

However, before considering the consequences of this surfeit of visual violence, it is important to decide whether there is any difference in the impact of programmes of real and of fictional events. Since the presentation of news is the one field in which broadcasting organisations can consistently claim they are carrying out their duty to inform the public, they are zealous in their efforts to protect their freedom in this area. In America they insist that under the First Amendment to the Constitution they are, like the press, guaranteed full freedom of speech. Said Mr. Frank Stanton, President of CBS, in his statement to the National Commission on Violence: 'We not only have the right to report the news as we see it, but the even more profound constitutional right to be wrong.'

Since news by its very nature deals chiefly with events that are transitory, sudden, extraordinary and abnormal, it tends to reveal life as a series of isolated, volatile incidents that are charged with emotional conflict and symptomatic of constant change. Inevitably the display of violence forms a large part of this news mosaic.

But life is much slower, much more tranquil, much more resistant to change than the impression given to us by the small screen. Even such a historical flashpoint as the Russian Revolution took 50 years to build up. Although most students are in their classrooms, the ones we see on television are those engaged in student demonstrations. Although most Ulstermen are peacefully in farms and factories, the ones we see are those engaged in fighting the British Army or victims of bomb blasts in Belfast. Although most aeroplanes stay in the sky, the ones we see are those that crash.

This highlighting of the quick, the dramatic and the violent has always been the tradition of news reporting. In this regard television has merely taken over the values and techniques of the newspapers. But because of the technological nature of television news — its need to illustrate each story with moving pictures and its limitations of time — events are reduced to urgent and highly selective captions. Reflective analysis of what is going on rarely accompanies the telling of the news. And such comments as are made are usually superficial and over-simplified. In Britain the total number of words spoken by BBC news readers during a day would not add up to one single page of *The Times*. Television bulletins are not merely newspapers reduced to headlines, but in America they are usually intoned as if the headlines were set in the big, bold print of crisis and disaster.

It is inevitable then that not merely will violent events receive a disproportionate amount of time on news bulletins — killings, explosions, riots, raids, punch-ups make hypnotic viewing — but that, selected and presented in the manner demanded by the medium, they will often unduly heighten and emphasise the violent nature of the occasion.

In America there was considerable pressure brought against the major networks to curtail their coverage of the horrors of the Vietnam war. During the most intense fighting phases in 1967 and 1968, television news bulletins were nightly filled with pictures of men with legs shot off, screaming in pain; sacks of dead waiting for shipment home. There were also much resented scenes of Americans cutting ears from dead Vietcong for souvenirs and American marines setting fire to village huts with their cigarette lighters.

It has been argued that the revulsion set up by these nightly demonstrations of carnage was responsible for a switch of public opinion against the continuance of the war. Having become appalled and disgusted with the blood in their living-rooms, runs the theory, millions of Americans exerted pressure on politicians to seek a negotiated settlement. There is a counter-theory that the display of so much violence eventually enured viewers to the sight of death and pain, desensitised their responses to the horrors of war, intensified their hatred of 'the enemy', and strengthened their resolve to achieve total victory.

Thus a Louis Harris Poll, reported in *Newsweek* magazine on July 10th, 1967, provided little support for the view that television had helped to turn the nation against the war. Said *Newsweek*: 'People were first asked if television made them feel more opposed to the war or not: 52 per cent said no, 31 per cent said yes. Next they were asked ... did television make them feel more like "backing the boys in Vietnam"? Here the results were 73–11 in the affirmative, and even the extreme doves shared this view by 50–21. Finally they were asked if television made them feel more like backing up the boys or opposing the war. 64 per cent said they were moved to support the boys, 26 per cent to oppose the war.'[1]

Nevertheless, even if reporting of the war on television may have had a certain important influence on American public opinion, the men in charge of American network news decisively defend their right to report events precisely as they see them. 'It's an ugly war, and we've shown just how ugly it is,' said Mr. Reuven Frank, head of NBC News. 'The Pentagon is always pressuring us to show less of the horror and do something about the pacification programme. But pacification is just a fancy word for occupation and is a total disaster. And it's also a dull story.'[2]

The issue of violence in news bulletins was raised again over the coverage of the riots during the Democratic Convention in Chicago in 1968. This time the networks were attacked not merely for transmitting these tumultuous scenes but for presenting a biased version of what had taken place. According to politicians like Mayor Daley of Chicago, the cameras failed to show the provocation the police were subjected to before they moved into violent action against the student demonstrators.

American network officials were unanimous in dismissing the charge that they had deliberately distorted the picture of what had happened in Chicago. Said Mr. Elmer Lower, President of ABC News: 'The truth is that those pictures didn't do the politicians in the Democratic Party any good. Having seen the bad news, their natural reaction was to shout "Kill the courier!" '[3]

Bias, like beauty, is in the eye of the beholder. Considering that their very existence depends upon Government licence and considering the strict surveillance to which they are subject whenever they dare comment on any serious aspect of national activity, it is unlikely that major broadcasting organisations in Britain or America would ever consciously or deliberately set out to transmit biased news. The bias is likely to be towards producing 'good' television news (i.e. dramatic and spectacular news) rather than towards any particular political, ideological or ethical point of view. Occasionally, and very rarely, some subjective or committed comment will seep through the thick net of balance and neutrality. If it does, you can be sure the broadcasters will be given an uneasy time over it.

The real fault of television news is not that it is biased but that its determined stance of objectivity makes it the perfect medium for conveying the views and attitudes of the Establishment and the status quo without comment or criticism. Most of the time it acts as a conduit pipe for orthodox voices of government and opposition. Dissenting groups that do not fall into traditional, acceptable patterns such as the Black Panthers, Communists, hippies, Weathermen, Welsh or Scottish nationalists, the IRA, only get into the news when they do something sensational or violent. The technique of violent demonstrations planned deliberately to catch the TV camera eye is already a well-established propaganda device used by 'unacceptable' minority groups to get themselves publicity and attention.

Since there is a danger that violence in the news often results in nation-wide publicity for suspect minority bodies; since it can lead to imitative acts of violence by other individuals and groups; since it can contribute to a brutalising of sensitivity to the consequences of violence, should broadcasters censor by omission unpalatable incidents that might unduly shock, disturb, frighten or pain consensus opinion?

Senior television executives in America are united in their rejection of any suggestion that they should be responsible for choosing which news is good or bad for the viewer. 'I would regret meeting the man who *did* know what was good for society,' said NBC's Reuven Frank. Supporting this attitude was CBS's President of News, Richard S. Salant, who said, 'I never ask myself whether my reporting provides a useful social service.' If the police are brutal, we have a duty to show it, said Mr. Frank. If American soldiers are cruel and inhuman, we have a duty to show it, said Mr. Salant.

'There is nothing we wouldn't show, apart from obscenity,' said CBS's Mr. Salant. But on second thought he had one reservation. 'I'm not quite sure we'd show a rape.' Thus Mr. Salant had no qualms about transmitting the execution of a Nigerian soldier during the Biafran war. 'We didn't show the whole thing,' said Mr. Salant. 'The quivering body was cut. We had a few protest letters. But Americans may not have bothered too much because they probably thought "What's Biafra?" '[4]

When the same incident was broadcast in Britain, public opinion was much more outraged than it had been in America. Could this be evidence that Americans, because of years of subjection to the sight of killing in Vietnam, have become more indifferent to displays of brutality than Britons?

'Last week's televised execution cannot be excused on the grounds that it added to public knowledge,' wrote Mr. Ronald Butt in the *Sunday Times*, voicing the concern of many. 'It added absolutely nothing. There was nothing unique about this execution except the deliberate act of policy by the Nigerian authorities concerned to have it televised. And why reduce our own painfully acquired standards by conniving at that? But the chief reason for protest is that it was one further stage in the slow build-up of cosy violence which is seeping unwanted into our homes . . .

'The passive majority is being slowly conditioned to accept violence as normal and to brush it aside — not to resist it. We take it as part of our evening's entertainment, between the Corn Flakes and the Comedy Show. We are used to burning monks and corpses over our coffee cups: the impact has a diminishing return and horror is transmuted into cow-like complacency . . .'[5]

What restraints then, if any, should there be on the depiction of real acts of violence in news and current affairs programmes? How does one balance the duty to keep a democratic electorate informed about the nature of ugly and shocking aspects of human activity against the possibility that such visual portrayals within the confines of a domestic environment will tend to create a mood of insensitivity and indifference to those very activities? The answer to that question will depend largely upon whether there is any convincing evidence that the determination of broadcasters to tell the truth as they see it has contributed in any substantial way to the escalation of violence in Britain and America. However, although there has been a great deal of investigation into the consequences of *fictional* violence on the small screen (which, in my opinion, convincingly establishes it as a major contributing factor to increasing violence), research on the effects of depicting *real* violence is much more fragmentary and insubstantial.

'Complaints are usually made about fantasy violence in the Western and thriller types of programmes,' says a report submitted by the Television Research Committee to the British Home Secretary in February 1969. 'Only recently has it been recognised that the portrayal of realistic or more generally acceptable or "legitimate" forms of violence (war, self-defence, villain getting his just deserts, etc.), or even straight news reporting, may also have detrimental effects. The portrayal of certain types of violence may have certain beneficial social effects, e.g. bringing home the horrors of war, serving as a warning or danger signal to society. Unfortunately, good intentions and even sympathetic, humane presentation do not necessarily provide a firm guarantee against detrimental effects.'[6]

167

Although it cannot be denied that real acts of violence on television will be imitated — student riots, stone-throwing in Ulster, defiance of the police have already had their band-wagon effects — it is essential, when speculating about the consequences of news programmes, to assess them in relationship to the entire mosaic of television. How much violence is really shown in news bulletins, who sees it, what is the context in which it is displayed? Put into this perspective it can be seen that real violence is only a tiny section of the total television mosaic, that it represents but a small fraction of all violence on television which is predominantly fictional, that it is not watched in large numbers by children, that it is presented in a context which is usually either neutral or antagonistic to the incidents being shown.

Any attempt to assess the impact of television violence must differentiate between its influence upon those to whom the medium has been a major environmental factor in their lives and those to whom it has been of merely marginal significance. This means distinguishing between children who have spent many hours in front of the box during their most formative years and adults who have come to television with their basic attitudes already formed. It also means distinguishing between countries where television has been present long enough and in enough density to have produced a telly generation and those countries where it has not.

Now what proportion of their time has the first telly generation devoted to watching real violence on television? Although there are few statistics on the matter, it would appear that the under-14s hardly watch the news at all. Recent research done at Leicester University into the television habits of delinquent boys indicates that the news is far down on their lists of favourite programmes. Even the non-delinquents who acted as controls in these experiments — all aged between 12 and 15 — did not watch the news very much.

Any parent knows that children drift away from the television set during the early-evening news and in Britain the main news bulletin on the commercial channel — *News At Ten* — is usually the signal for most under-15s to go to bed. But even if a small fraction of children did watch news programmes, how much violence would they actually see? Before ten o'clock in the evening in Britain there is rarely more than a half-hour of television news on any of the three channels. Even with such violent events as the bomb explosions and killings in Ulster, it is unlikely that the bulletins on most days were occupied with five minutes of actual violence. It is more likely that scenes of real shooting or carnage might fill a minute or two of screen time followed by interviews with eye-witnesses or comments from politicians or reporters.

In America where the early evening news programmes are much longer — they can range from an hour to an hour-and-a-half split between local and national news — there might be isolated days when a viewer could watch something like 15 to 20 minutes of real violence. These would probably have been days when there was particularly bloody fighting in Vietnam, when there were riots in Watts or Chicago, when the police descended upon a prison like Attica to crush a revolt. The critical scenes would be interspersed with interviews and comments on the event. But I would doubt if details of filmed violence shown in news programmes in America would average over any month anything like ten minutes per day. It should also be pointed out that news programmes, because they are transmitted when most people are eating their evening meal, probably receive less attention from viewers than the peak-time fictional and entertainment programmes that follow. It can thus be safely guessed that such children as do watch the news — an almost insignificant minority — will see in those bulletins a daily ration of violence hardly equivalent to what they get from a single *Tom and Jerry* cartoon or a few minutes of *The Virginian* or *Hawaii Five-O*.

Finally, violence in the news is never presented in the context of any moral or ethical situation that a child can easily grasp. He may watch students being beaten over the head by the police but he does not know which are the 'good' guys and which are the 'bad' guys. He can see the British Army being stoned by children in Ulster but it is unlikely that he will know whether the stone throwers are Catholic or Protestant or whose side he should be on. Accompanying such scenes is the voice of the news commentator — detached and dispassionate in Britain; urgent, earnest and commanding in America. While an adult, bringing his knowledge and prejudices to such scenes may be shocked or disturbed by what he sees, the child will see only an isolated violent act about which he has no views and which he can place in no perspective. The words of the announcer, filled with terms of reference and assumptions of pre-knowledge about the events, encourage the child's disinterest in the news because they are unintelligible to him.

Thus although television news may heighten and over-dramatise the violence of the actual event being shown, it is the drama that largely escapes the child. He is interested in violence when it is associated with a story, when he can be involved or caught up in some continuing action, when he can identify with some hero. The depiction of violence in the news gives him none of these satisfactions. It is unlikely therefore to contribute much to conditioning him to accept violence as a norm or to encourage him to use it when he is older.

If, then, we are trying to establish whether the violence we have in the 1970s is due in any substantial measure to what news programmes have been transmitting over the past 15 years, it is most unlikely that there is any real causal link. It is the young, as we shall see, who have contributed mostly to the rise in violence in Britain and America. In their impressionable years they did not see the news or understand the violence in it. Undoubtedly specific acts of violence — particularly student riots — have had an infectious effect on other similarly-minded groups of students. But, again, the news rarely adopts any moral attitude to such events. If it encourages imitation by reporting them, then there must already exist both the sympathy and the conditions to provoke similar situations. It is true that television may speed up such chain-reactions of violence. But it does not create them. While one is predisposed to finding television news, on its own, little to blame for our violent societies, one may become less complacent when it is watched — as it will be watched more and more — by individuals who have been brought up on a heavy diet of fictionalised television violence.

When one examines the incidence and influence of fantasy television violence on the young, one finds almost exactly the opposite conditions to those prevailing in regard to real television violence. Fictionalised violence in terms of volume is probably the most dominant cultural influence in most children's lives. Westerns, spy and crime thrillers, science fiction, war films and violent animated cartoons constitute by far the most popular viewing amongst the under-14s. Children are absorbed and involved in the action of these programmes and make heroes and idols of the cowboys, gangsters, policemen, bandits and private detectives that star in them. The moral context in which violence is depicted in a large majority of these programmes is not neutral or disapproving of violence. On the contrary, it approves of violence when committed by the 'good' guy; it is largely indifferent to the moral or physical consequence of violence, particularly when it is suffered by the villain; it does not often insist that a man who has committed violence, especially if he is a 'good' guy, has to give any legal or moral explanation to society for his deeds.

In examining the proposition that there is a positive television factor in the unprecedented rise in violence in English-speaking Western democracies like Britain, America and Canada, I shall concentrate initially on American statistics and experience. This is because in the field of action adventure programmes America has not only led the way but it is American production values and American taste that have been followed in most television democracies. *I Spy, The Man From UNCLE, Bonanza, Hawaii Five-O, FBI, The Untouchables, Kojak* are seen not only in Winnipeg, Melbourne and Manchester, but in Tokyo and Milan as well. The programmes that the British make with a view to overseas sales — *The Saint, The Avengers, The Persuaders, Danger Man* — adopt the same casual, obsessive, even flippant approach to violence as their American models.

It is important to repeat that televison occupies more hours of an average American's time than any previous medium in man's history. When people argue, as so many do, that its impact is little different from other media, it should be remembered that the typical, middle-income American male devotes more hours to television than he does to all other mass media — radio, newspapers, magazines, films — *put together*. The television set in his home is in use about six hours a day and he spends two-and-a-half hours daily in front of it.

The television viewing habits of the low-income adult show that he spends twice as much time watching the box as does the middle-income American — almost five hours per day. Since the low-income adult also reads less and goes less often to the cinema, the small screen in many cases acts as an almost exclusive provider of information and entertainment.

Children and adolescents are even heavier viewers of television than their parents. Depending on their social stratum, the average American child spends between one-quarter to one-half of his waking day watching television. Most children spend more time in front of the box than they do in front of their teachers in school. Lower income children watch television on an average of six hours per day; in some very poor areas, surveys have shown average figures rising to eight hours per day. A large number of small children watch exactly the same programmes as adults. A Nielsen study showed that over five million children under the age of 12 were still watching television between 10.30 and 11 p.m. at night. These viewing statistics come from the Report of the President's Commission on the Causes and Prevention of Violence issued in September 1969.

If these figures of intense viewing are taken in conjunction with the fact that by 1956 almost 80 per cent of American homes possessed television sets, it can be assumed that by 1975 the vast bulk of the teenage population had devoted almost as much attention to television as it had to its schoolteachers. By 1975 three-quarters of the under-21s had been weaned on the box and had had their most impressionable years influenced by it. The telly generation had arrived! How much violence, and in what form, had been included in their gross and continuous electronic diet?

Even in 1955, when television was in its swaddling clothes and less than 10 per cent of homes had owned sets for five years, there was already some concern expressed about the amount of violence on the box. A Senate sub-Committee investigating juvenile delinquency found that in a one-week period in 1954 almost a quarter of all transmitted television shows (22·3 per cent) were violent. In a similar week in 1961 the proportion of violent programmes had gone up to over one-third of peak-time shows, i.e. 34·2 per cent. In 1964 another Senate hearing found that violent shows now occupied almost one-half (an average of 45·6 per cent) of all prime-time hours.

Since this was an average figure, it was clear that some cities transmitted an even higher quota of mayhem and murder.[7]

The President's Commission on Violence calculated that from 1964 to 1968 between one-half and two-thirds of all programmes in the 7 to 10 p.m. prime-time span were of the action and adventure type containing some degree of violence. Late afternoon shows which children would watch on returning from school, and which are determined by local stations rather than the networks, are also dominated by Westerns, science fiction, adventure and cartoons. It is likely that in the time slot between 4 and 6 p.m. the quota of action-adventure programmes is even higher than it is in the 7 to 10 p.m. sectors.

If then we assume that during the past 18 years most American children watched television between 4 and 5 hours a day and something like 50 per cent of that viewing was concentrated on such programmes, they would have spent almost 16 hours a week in a violence-saturated environment. If we assume a waking day for most children of 13 hours, we reach the staggering fact that the average American teenager in 1974 has spent one-sixth of his conscious childhood and adolescence watching fictionalised violence on television. If we add to this dose of violence the further quota he received from going to the cinema, reading comic books and adventure and crime magazines, it is possible to guess that America's youth has been immersed for between *one-quarter* and *one-fifth* of its waking hours in some form of fictionalised or dramatic violence.

What precisely in this context does violence mean? What sort of acts of violence were transmitted on the screen which absorbed so much of children's time and attention? The monitoring of American television by independent and Governmental bodies shows a remarkable consistency over the past decade in the type of murder and assault that has been considered normal television fare.

Mr. Arnold Arnold reports the findings of a group called The National Association for Better Broadcasting which surveyed the output of all Los Angeles television stations during a random week in 1960. In this single week they found 144 murders (not counting mass murders), 143 attempted murders, 52 justifiable killings, 14 cases of drugging, 12 jail-breaks, 36 robberies, 6 thefts, 13 kidnappings, 6 burglaries, 7 cases of torture, 6 extortion cases, 5 blackmailings, 11 planned murders, 4 attempted lynchings, one massacre scene with hundreds killed, one mass murder of home-steaders, one planned mass murder by arson, three scenes of shooting between gangland posses with many killed, one other mass gun battle, one programme with over 50 women kidnapped.

As if that were not enough for one week, the Association explained that it had not included in its count 'prolonged and brutal fights, the threats to kill, the sluggings or the many times when characters in the crime programmes manhandled their victims, the forced confessions, and dynamiting to illegally destroy. Nor do these figures include incidents of crime on television daytime serials . . .'[8]

Of course no single individual would have been subjected to this gruesome total of violence. This bloody inventory was shared between a number of Los Angeles stations, and a child might have the delectable task of picking his way amongst the lurid situations he fancied best. Since there is rarely any lack of action-adventure stories at any particular time of the day, selectivity would enable him to watch programmes with violence nearly all the time if he so desired. In 1964 the *Ladies' Home Journal* estimated that the average American child between the ages of 5 and 14 had witnessed on television the violent destruction of 13,000 human beings, mostly during the 'children's hours' between 4 and 9 p.m.[9]

It is interesting that seven years later, even after the warnings about television violence given by the National Commission in 1969, Dr. Gerald Looney of the University of Arizona speaking to the annual meeting of the American Academy of Pediatrics in 1971, calculated that by the time an American child had reached 14 he would have seen no less than 18,000 people killed on television. In other words, in spite of all the concern that had been voiced on this issue, the electronic body count had gone up by almost 40 per cent.[10]

The symbolic moment that alerted a great many people to the fact that violence in America was in danger of escalating to intolerable heights was the assassination of Senator Robert Kennedy in June 1968. Following on the assassinations of John F. Kennedy, Malcolm X and Martin Luther King, this political killing demonstrated in dramatic form the direction American society was taking. These acts stimulated President Johnson into announcing his Commission on the Causes and Prevention of Violence, and their findings were published about a year later.

A few weeks before Senator Kennedy's murder a report by Richard L. Tobin appeared in the *Saturday Review* showing the results of a comprehensive monitoring of *eight hours* of network and local television output. 'We marked down 93 specific incidents involving sadistic brutality, murder, cold-blooded killing, sexual cruelty and related sadism,' wrote Mr. Tobin. 'We encountered seven different kinds of pistols and revolvers, three varieties of rifle, three distinct brands of shotgun, half a dozen assorted daggers and stilettos, two types of machete, one butcher's cleaver, a broadaxe, rapiers galore, a posse of sabres, an electric prodder and a guillotine.

'Men (and women and even children) were shot by gunpowder, burned at the stake, tortured over live coals, trussed and beaten in relays, dropped into molten sugar, cut to ribbons (in colour), repeatedly kneed in the groin, beaten while being held defenceless by other hoodlums, forcibly drowned, whipped with leather belts . . .'

When the new television schedules turned up for the autumn of 1968, one might have expected that some serious reduction in fictional violence would have taken place because of the outcry following Senator Kennedy's assassination only four months before. But according to a survey conducted by the *Christian Science Monitor*, whose staff watched 74 half-hours of evening programmes during the first week of the new schedules, there were 254 incidents of violence, including threats, and 71 murders, killings and suicides. The volume had not appreciably changed from the total amount of violence that had been monitored a year earlier, in June 1967, when during 78 half-hour TV programmes the same newspaper had found in a week's evening viewing 210 violent incidents and 81 killings.[11]

The National Commission on Violence asked its own Media Task Force to conduct an independent analysis of the dramatic television programmes being presented by the three major commercial networks (NBC, CBS and ABC) during the hours from 4 to 10 p.m. The study was designed to examine the programme content of the first week in October 1968 and compare it with the programmes transmitted the year before in October 1967. For the purpose of this monitoring exercise, violence was defined as 'the overt expression of force intended to hurt or kill.'

In 1967 and 1968 approximately *eight out of every ten* dramatic programmes contained some violence. Because there were fewer dramatic programmes transmitted by the networks in 1968, the rate of violent episodes per hour showed a slight decline over 1967. In 1967 there had been no less than 7·5 violent episodes *per hour*; in 1968 this had gone down to 6·7 per hour. This means that in dramatic programmes — 'fictional stories of all kinds' — which comprised two-thirds of the peak-hour output between 7 and 10 p.m. the networks were displaying a violent incident every nine minutes.

Examining the crime, Western, action-adventure type of programmes — which made up two-thirds of all fiction shown on the box by the networks — the episodes of violence in both years average about nine per hour — *or a display of violence every seven minutes.* Cartoons, which comprised 10 per cent of dramatic programmes and which were largely concentrated in children's viewing hours, contained violent episodes at the rate of 20 per hour in both years — a terrifying rate of a violent act *every three minutes.*

In order to discern what was the over-all ethical statement that seemed to be made by most of these action-adventure programmes, a study group at the University of Pennsylvania looked at a few typical weeks of peak-time programmes in 1968. Its findings were submitted to, and accepted by, the National Commission on Violence.

This particular study found that some violence occurred in 81 per cent of *all* programmes and 85 per cent of *all* programme hours. Since it is often claimed that television merely acts as a 'mirror of life', reflecting the conditions of society as they exist, one must pause at that statistic. Said Professor Williams in his book, *Communications*, 'If it is argued that "violence ought to appear because it is a part of real life", it is relevant to ask its proportion in real life as compared with its proportion in newspapers, films and television programmes. Any count in our society would show that the proportion in communications is much higher than the proportion in the rest of our living. We should then ask not only why this is so, but what other interests are reduced or excluded to allow this altered proportion.'[12]

Indeed, Professor Williams might have pushed his query one stage further. If the gap between what is seen on television and what happens in real life is so wide as to be bizarre, is it not likely that the community will suffer some adverse social effects from continuously watching such a gross distortion of their activities and life style? How close then is American television's dissemination of violence to what an average American might personally experience in his day-to-day living? According to Ramsey Clark, Attorney General during President Johnson's administration, it has been calculated that in the United States in 1967 an individual's chances of being in contact with criminal violence was 1 in 400 during the year. On a daily basis, the odds were one in 146,000.[13]

But on television during 1967 the violence contained in a routine Western, action-adventure, science fiction, crime programme averaged about nine episodes per hour. Assuming that a normal adolescent watched three hours of such programming per day — probably an underestimate — this would mean that his encounters with violence would number between 25 and 27 incidents per day. By my rough calculations, the picture of violence an American child gets from his small screen is exaggerated by something like 4,000,000 times over the volume of violence he is likely personally to encounter in his daily activities. By what stretch of the imagination or extension of dramatic licence can a distortion of such gargantuan dimensions be defended on the grounds that it is only 'mirroring' what life is really like in the United States?

The University of Pennsylvania study group also found that violence was not something committed primarily by 'bad guys' or even minor characters. More than half of 455 *leading* characters, during the two weeks examined, inflicted some sort of violence on others. At least one out of every ten leading characters was a killer. The initiation of violence was shared equally between 'good guys' and 'bad guys'. In their propensity for violence, there was little difference between 'good' and 'bad' characters. 'Police and other official law enforcement agents were almost as violent as criminals,' says this survey, 'but never paid with their lives. Seven out of every 10 official agents of law committed violence, 2 out of 10 with fatal results.'

What other personality characteristics distinguished hero-figures in these Western, police, spy, science-fiction, action-adventure programmes? 'Being violent or non-violent related most closely to efficiency, emotionality and logic,' the survey records. 'All violents were more efficient, unemotional and logical than all non-violents. Killers were even more efficient and unemotional. And killers who reached a happy end (mostly heroes) were, perhaps necessarily, the most calmly efficient of all.'

Indeed, in these programmes there is a strong co-relation between the exercise of violence and the achievement of success. Nearly half of all the leading characters who kill (25 of 54) and more than half of all leading characters who are violent (126 of 241) are crowned with a happy ending for their deed. 'To this extent,' says the National Commission's report, 'violence is portrayed as a successful means of attaining a desired end.'

Other moral and social values explicit or implicit in these programmes include the views that violence is an acceptable way of solving problems because it is not often condemned or discouraged; that the law rarely intervenes to demand an explanation for acts of violence (in only 2 out of 10 programmes was there an arrest or trial for major acts of violence); that physical pain is only infrequently shown as a consequence of a violent act (only 1 out of 4 violent acts resulted in any portrayed pain) and that, in general, television violence does not hurt too much and its results are not usually either 'bloody or messy'.

As far as violence is concerned, the mosaic of American television can be summarised as one in which violent programmes constitute the bulk of its output, that they are seen by the majority of Americans between two to three hours a day, that most American children for the past 18 years have spent about one-fifth of their waking life absorbing this kind of visual material, and that the general ethical statement flowing from these programmes is that violence is a socially acceptable form of behaviour usually exercised by hero figures to attain desired ends.

No other society in man's history has had most of its youth battered for so much of their conscious hours by visual stimuli

178

displaying and often glorifying the use of violence. Are there any other countries that have used television in a similar way over a similar period of time? The country that most approximates the American experience is its northern neighbour, Canada. The growth and spread of television in Canada was the second fastest in the world. If a television society can be said to exist when 60 per cent of its homes are in possession of a set then by 1958 only three countries in the world had achieved that status. In 1958, 86 per cent of American homes had television sets; 69 per cent of Canadian homes; 65 per cent of British homes. The magic figure of 90 per cent homes with sets was reached in America in 1961, in Canada in 1963, in Britain in 1964.

I intend to discuss the significance of these figures, insofar as they relate to violence, later on in this chapter, and also to compare violence in these countries with violence in countries where the spread of television has been less rapid. But at this point it is only necessary to say that these three societies are alone in the world in having acquired by 1974 an entire generation of which the vast majority was weaned on the box. It is also interesting that all three countries have much the same philosophy about broadcasting and that there has been considerable exchange of programmes between them. For all three, entertainment is considered the predominant purpose of television.

Canada, because of its proximity to the United States and because they have a language in common, is particularly vulnerable to the infiltration of American television programmes into the homes of its people. A study carried out by a Governmental Committee on Broadcasting showed that during the month of March 1964 between 57 and 74 per cent of all viewers were tuned to American programmes. Because so many large cities in Canada are close to the American border, 54 per cent of Canadian homes can receive American programmes directly. In Toronto, for example, there is a choice of six television stations, three of which transmit directly from the United States.

It is not surprising, then, that the diet of Canadian television is very similar to that of its large neighbour. At peak time between 7 and 10 p.m. a survey in 1965 showed that an average

Canadian television station transmitted 79·8 per cent entertainment shows compared with three American television stations which in the same week transmitted between 80 and 97 per cent entertainment in these hours.[14] A look at any Canadian schedule will show that it is occupied to almost the same extent with the sort of Western, spy, action-adventure series that is transmitted in America. Although there is a stiff quota system which should theoretically guarantee anything from 45 to 55 per cent of all programmes transmitted being Canadian, the peak-time hours are dominated either by the popular action shows or occasionally by a Canadian drama series like *Wojeck* which in its violence content differed very little from its American counterparts. Canada, then, subjects its youth to only marginally less violence on the box than does the United States.

What about Britain? How much violence is a child likely to see on the BBC or the ITV? Undoubtedly the over-all total is much less than in America or Canada. The British quota system only permits about 14 per cent of non-British, non-Commonwealth material to be transmitted by each channel. Although this foreign material is supposed to be divided amongst the non-Commonwealth world, in practice almost all foreign shows seen in Britain are American. The most frequently transmitted American series are either comedies like *I Love Lucy* and the *Dick Van Dyke Show,* or spy and crime adventures and Westerns like *The Man From UNCLE, The Virginian, Hawaii Five-O, The Untouchables.* At a rough guess, it can be said that over the years the major channels — BBC-1 and ITV — have shown weekly anything between three and six American action shows with a high violence content.

However, since the quota restrictions saved British television from inundation by this kind of American product — as has happened in Canada and Australia — the BBC and the ITV have made their own versions of the genre. Most of these series are designed to cater for appetites already whetted by the American action story. Some of them — *The Saint, The Baron, The Persuaders* — are specifically tailored for American audiences. Other versions of the crime genre that have a less abrasive flavour and try to take a less strident and more realistic look at the activities of the British police — *Dixon of Dock Green, Z-Cars, Softly, Softly* — are amongst the most popular programmes transmitted by the BBC.

The drama series which usually goes on week after week or is made in batches of 13 segments is the most successful format in the entire field of television entertainment. Producing a series of this kind is very costly and for those companies that make them easily accounts for the largest portion of a company's production budget. Just how much money and effort the commercial companies expend on making programmes with a high violence content can be judged by studying the British drama series transmitted by ITV during 1969.

Out of a total of 27 series listed in the 1970 Independent Television Authority Year Book, no less than 18 (two-thirds of them) were described as dealing with themes such as underworld crime, espionage, fraud, bullion robbery, special investigators, detectives, police, adventure and work of the Special Branch. Some of their titles were *The Avengers, Big Breadwinner Hog, Callan, Fraud Squad, The Saint, Special Branch, Public Eye, The Inside Man, Randall and Hopkirk (Deceased), The Gold Robbers*. Every one of them, with the exception of *Callan*, was transmitted in peak time hours before 10 p.m. *Big Breadwinner Hog* provoked a particular cry of outrage from the public because of its brutality and was specially investigated by the ITA before it was allowed to finish its run. The proportion of violent series to non-violent series made by British commercial companies has remained roughly the same since then.

To get the full measure of the amount of violence seen on British television one must add to the British and American action-adventure programmes the transmission of old films. Ever since 1965 films that had finished their normal runs in the nation's cinemas — they must be at least five years old — have become a regular feature of the schedules of each channel. Between them BBC-1 and BBC-2 show about eight old films per week and the commercial companies transmit something like five or six films per week.

The subject matter and general flavour of most of these films can be judged by reading the descriptions in the *TV Times* of the six films that were shown to London audiences during the week of 9th to 15th October, 1971. *Rio Bravo* was about 'a sheriff who must make a stand against a gang of gunmen'; *The Fastest Gun Alive* was about 'a gunfighter fleeing his own reputation'; *The Curse of the Fly* was 'the completion of the Fly horror trilogy'; *Moss Rose* was 'an atmospheric murder mystery set in Edwardian London'; *Assault On A Queen* in which 'a gang of hijackers plans to hold up the *Queen Mary*'. The only other film transmitted on the commercial channel that week was *Cat on A Hot Tin Roof*, one of Tennessee Williams' more neurotic plays with its own special brand of mental, if not physical, violence.

When one tries to calculate the number of programmes concerned with violence that an average British child is likely to see, a number of factors have to be taken into consideration. What is the total amount of hours he spends per day in front of the set, when is he likely to be viewing, what switching of channels is he likely to indulge in to get his particular viewing preferences?

Leicester University's Centre for Mass Communications Research monitored a typical week of British television in April 1970 and found that no less than 62 per cent of all programmes contained violence. There were more violent incidents during schoolchildren's peak-time viewing, i.e. before 9 p.m., than after they had gone to bed. Violence, indeed, was concentrated in those very programmes children were most likely to watch — cartoons and Westerns. There was an average of almost five violent incidents an hour — compared with about nine violent incidents an hour on American television. In almost half the programmes major characters were involved in violence. Most violence shown, the report said, was routinised and predictable. It also added that very little attention was given to the implications for social power and social values which the successful and approved use of violence may have.[15]

Although these statistics are disconcerting enough it should also be remembered that by the time a child reaches the age of seven or eight, he has become sophisticated enough to switch between channels to select his own particular programmes. Given a choice between a domestic serial and a police or science-fiction story, boys particularly will choose the latter. This exercise of discrimination enables the child to watch much more violence than might be assumed by merely examining the output of a single channel.

In the study of television and delinquency carried out at Leicester University by the Television Research Committee, both the delinquent and non-delinquent boys studied revealed an overwhelming preference for 'exciting' programmes of the crime, Western, science fiction type with a high violence content. Asked to name their favourite programmes, these boys aged between 10 and 20 listed 7 adventure-action shows amongst their top 10 programmes.[16]

Since British television makes available to any child during adolescent viewing hours something like 18 to 22 hours of violence-oriented programmes per week (excluding BBC-2) and he watches the box for something like 22 hours per week, it is not unreasonable to assume that he will devote at least half of his viewing time to the 'exciting' programmes he prefers.

It is likely then that the average British boy, exercising a reasonable amount of switching between channels, would be watching about 10 hours of violent programmes a week or about one-and-one-half hours per day. Girls, it should be added, reveal markedly less enthusiasm for this genre of programme and undoubtedly watch them much less than do boys.[17]

How then does the British child's immersion in an atmosphere of electronic violence compare with the violence witnessed on the box by the American child? An American boy (and probably a Canadian one) sees 16 hours of violence-motivated programmes per week; a British boy sees 10 hours per week. If one assumes a child also sees occasional violent films and cartoons in a cinema, and reads comic books and crime and adventure magazines (add another two hours per week), it can be calculated that the American boy spends between *one-quarter* and *one-fifth* of his waking and conscious life in an atmosphere replete with fictionalised violence; in Britain the child will spend *one-seventh* of his waking hours in such an environment.

Naturally I do not assume that everyone will accept all these figures. They can be ingeniously juggled upwards or downwards depending upon how you define the nature of violence in televised fiction. In the broadcasting organisations themselves restriction of violence is largely confined to cutting out incidents that are too explicit, too realistic, too shocking or too long. Although the ITA Code insists that 'violence, physical or mental, should never be allowed "for its own sake" ', it is very rare that an entire episode of any series — even programmes as violent as *The Untouchables* or *Big Breadwinner Hog* — will be forbidden an airing. In the two years between 1962 and 1964 when I was responsible in a supervisory capacity for the vetting of filmed material transmitted by Rediffusion Television, it was most unusual to contemplate ditching an episode because of violence once a series had been purchased.

The accepted procedure was to cut out the offensive items. I remember that hanging scenes were particularly taboo at Rediffusion. If there was a scene of a beating, it might be considered that 30 seconds was enough. If there was a realistic stabbing, the actual sight of the knife making contact with the body might be excised. The ITA Code, on the whole, supports the view that a censor can do his job effectively by judicious editing of objectionable incidents. Thus in discussing the quality of intensity of violence it says that 'a long shot of an ambush or a cavalry charge is one thing, a close-up of facial agony, though part of the whole, is another'. It warns about showing techniques of hanging or tying or locking up or submerging in water because these could be easily tried by a child. It urges care about 'scenes in which the less usual methods of inflicting injury are employed' such as rabbit punches, suffocation, booby traps. Its final admonition is 'in case of doubt, cut. The risk is not one that can decently be taken.'[18]

If violence is to be measured by a ruler or a stop-watch, it is possible to argue that there is not much of it on television. A *Times* survey of a week of British television in April 1970 counted 72 violent deaths during this period. But it concluded that the total amount of violence was not significant — less than two hours in the week. It used the stop-watch technique. If violence could be measured in this way — two seconds for a punch, one minute for a fist fight, half a second for a pistol shot — it is perfectly possible to come up with just such a meaningless statistic.

By such criteria Webster's Elizabethan blood-bath, *The Duchess of Malfi* would not be classified as a violent play since the murdering and torturing *actually seen on the stage* occupies only a fraction of the play's running time. Nor would Shakespeare's *Titus Andronicus*, considered visually minute by minute, be considered a particularly gory play since the rape of Lavinia and the cutting off of her hands and tongue take place off-stage, and since Tamora's eating of a pie made out of the flesh of her own sons only takes a few minutes of digestive action.

It is surely obvious that this piecemeal dissection of incidents is not the true measure of a programme's violent content. It is the over-all statement of a programme, the weight of its ethical values, the moral stance it adopts, the manner in which it condemns or glorifies violence that is the yardstick of its influence — not a stop-watch. The plots of most action-adventure programmes can be summarised as preparations for an act of violence, the act of violence itself, and the subsequent events that flow from that act of violence.

What is basically wrong with the stop-watch approach to the study of television violence is the assumption that imitative violence and imitative crime is the main danger; that the mere display of guns being fired, men being coshed, buildings being burned, bullion vans being hijacked, aeroplanes being sabotaged, banks being robbed, will encourage others — particularly impressionable children — to do the same.

In my view imitative violence is the least important aspect of the problem. There will always be an unstable group (larger than one suspects) who will experience this imitative urge, but this could not possibly account for the rise in violence amongst the young for which television is held to be a significant contributing factor. The case that links television with social violence is based on the hypothesis that any medium which occupies the young for so much of their time in the most formative years of their lives must eventually get its message about violence across. If parents, neighbours, teachers and priests spent the same amount of time conveying television's attitudes to violence, it would not be doubted that children would grow up into very violent adults. Why, then, should not television, which dominates many a child's mind and time more than any of these other environmental influences, also affect a child? Once we agree on that assumption, we must ask ourselves what

185

is the total mosaic, the total message that television is presenting to the adolescent, growing mind in countries like
Britain, America and Canada?

About violence the small screen generally has four things to
say. First, violence is usually done by the good man for moral
reasons. He wins his case by being better at the karate chop,
faster on the draw, more adept at the kick in the groin than his
opponent. The best man is the man who is best at violence.

Second, violence does not hurt very much. A razor slash
shows no blood. An Indian falls painlessly from a horse. A
gunshot wound — festering and ugly — is never seen. The true
physical consequences of violence are hidden or anaesthetised.

Third, there is little pity for the victims of violence, unlike
classic drama where the arousal of pity and terror — Aristotle's
Catharsis — were the means of purging violence. When Gloucester's eyes are torn out in *King Lear* we feel revulsion; when
a king is murdered in the tragedies of Euripides or Sophocles
the suffering of the wife and his children is one of the play's
dominant themes. But in television there is rarely any concern
or compassion for the relatives of the Russian spy who has been
obliterated by an X-ray gun or the offspring of the gangster
who has been dropped in a coffin of cement into the sea.

Fourth, society demands no explanation and little expiation
for an act of violence. There are few sanctions to be paid for
killing or mayhem. Only rarely does the State demand that a
killer stand trial for murder or manslaughter; how often are
private eyes or cowboys or spy hunters faced with a charge of
assault and battery? More often the reward for a vicious act of
violence — beating up a villain or shooting him dead — is the
smiling blonde who greets the hero to accompanying fade-out
music.

Now if we couple this total message of the desirability and
success of violence in the right hands with the other message
put across by the box that life is essentially trivial, greedy and
silly, we have a cast-iron ethical formula for the justification of
violence. If a society is so unworthy and yet cannot be changed
by legal and democratic means, isn't the exercise of violence a
perfectly moral way to bring about the necessary changes?
Furthermore isn't the use of violence a moral way to right a
personal wrong or get what you want?

Thus there is a formidable case for assuming that television by normalising and glorifying violence, by trivialising authority, by reflecting life as cheap, frivolous and greedy, has made some contribution to the rise of violence amongst the telly generation in those countries where television conducts itself primarily as an entertainment medium. Has that contribution been significant or minimal? Can television be fairly indicted as a major factor in the creation of increasingly violent societies? Or is television merely another media scapegoat for an inherent propensity towards greater violence in modern societies? What is the evidence?

Because countries like Britain and America have always been violent, the suggestion that television has something to do with increased violence is commonly regarded as absurd. The fact that there has been past violence has nothing to do with the argument. It would only be relevant if anyone were contending that television were responsible for *all* violence in a society. Such a contention is ludicrous and nobody is making it. All we are trying to measure is the degree of *increased* violence over a limited period of years in a limited number of countries.

'The United States is a violent country,' wrote Louis Heren in *The Times*. 'It was born in violence, and developed in violence. Foreign wars have been periods of regulated violence between the revolution and the latest race riots. Four of the 35 presidents were assassinated, and Mr. Johnson was not the first to limit his movements for fear of violence.'[19]

'There is no country in the world,' wrote a Venetian envoy to his masters about Tudor England, 'where there are so many thieves and robbers as in England; insomuch that few venture to go alone in the country excepting in the middle of the day, and fewer still in the towns at night, and least of all in London.'[20]

Since we have very limited reliable evidence to prove that a citizen in Washington in 1870 felt more or less threatened by violence than one in 1970, or that an inhabitant of London in Tudor or Victorian England felt more or less secure than one in 1970, it would be a futile exercise to attempt such comparisons. But surely after hundreds of years of increasing affluence, widespread education, growing recognition of the rights and significance of the individual, it might be expected in advanced societies that people should feel less threatened by violence than they did in the past. It is therefore small comfort when one reads about another leap in criminal statistics or encounters hooliganism in one's daily life to be assured that things aren't as bad as they were in the American West or in England during the Wars of the Roses.

If there is going to be any meaningful discussion about television's responsibility for violence it must be confined to a very limited area. We start off with the proposition that there was x amount of violence in every country when its first television set was installed. We move to the next proposition that television could only have affected the volume and degree of violence when there were enough people watching it to make its influence significant. And finally if there has been an increase in the amount of violence since the arrival of television, can one connect it with those who have been most subjected to it, namely the young?

But the initial difficulty that one faces in attempting to measure any increase or decrease in violence is to isolate and define exactly what one is measuring. What sort of violence are we talking about? Most violence never becomes a criminal statistic. How then can we know whether there is more hooliganism, more rowdyism at football games, more belligerence by striking pickets, more wife and child beatings, more fights at electoral meetings, more attacks on the police in political demonstrations, in 1970 than there were in 1960 or even in 1950 when television was in its infancy?

What about other kinds of violence? The violence governments use to maintain the status quo — the training of police to be more effective in riot control, laws that are passed to suppress dissent, stiffer sentences for activities that shock or outrage the establishment, the greater use of CS gas or rubber bullets to curb demonstrations? Does the state now threaten the individual with more or less violence than it did before the advent of television?

Rose K. Goldsen, an Associate Professor of Sociology at Cornell University, made just this point when she criticised a recent report by an NBC Research team conducting an 'Environmental Study of Television and Violence'. She complained that the use of the term 'violence' was too generalised. 'What kind of violence?' she asked. 'Physical violence, emotional violence, violence to bodily integrity, violence to sense of self, violence by direct contact, violence by remote control, violence to one's peers, violence to one's superiors, violence by authority figures, violence by the powerful, violence by the deviant, violence by the frustrated, violence as a norm, violence as pathological behaviour, violence for vengeance, violence to correct miscarriage of justice, violence by men to men, men to women, women to women, violence about sex, violence in sex, violence by animals or involving animals, violence by children or to children, violence whose consequences are shown, violence whose consequences are inferred, violence that is justified, violence in a measure appropriate to some previous injury, face-to-face acts of violence, institutional violence, violence in war . . . I could go on.'[21]

It is obvious that it would be both impracticable and pointless to attempt to measure each and every one of this bewildering array of forms of violence. Every society accepts certain acts of violence as necessary, legal and moral. The killing of an enemy in wartime, the parental chastisement of a child, therapeutic treatment like electric shocks, corporal punishment in schools and capital punishment in jails, the apprehension and incarceration of criminals, bodily conflict in games, suppression of riots and disorderly affrays — the list is endless. Sometimes a state exerts an intolerable level of violence to maintain its power or to suppress those of whom it disapproves. In police or terror states like Hitler's Germany and Stalin's Russia the preservation of so-called 'law and order' was a crushing assertion of autocratic violence over every other form of individual violence.

Having said all this, it does not mean that we must resign ourselves to the impossibility of finding a viable method of measuring violence. Since we are concerned with the more modest task of relating the growth of television to the incidence of violence in those few countries that we might call television societies, we are fortunate in that Britain, America and Canada have been relatively stable in their political, philosophical and economic structures over the past 20 years. What was deemed an act of violence in 1955 is still largely deemed an act of violence in 1975 according to the same legal and ethical criteria.

The National Commission of Violence accepted the view that violence was an exertion of unwarranted force against the norm, and it seems as reasonable a definition as any. Since what is 'unwarranted force' is usually defined by the law and classified as a crime, we have available criminal statistics which should provide some concrete information about whether, at least in legal terms, there has been a rise or fall in violence with the advent of television.

To what sources, then, can we go for evidence that the spread of television and the incidence of violence are related? In the first place, there are the personal testimonies of individuals. Secondly, there is the research done by social scientists and psychiatrists. Thirdly, there are the criminal and juvenile delinquency statistics.

First, then, what does personal testimony reveal about violence in our time? Just as G. M. Trevelyan felt that the views of a Venetian envoy provided some pertinent historical evidence about the state of violence in Tudor England, so will future historians be able to rely upon contemporary personal accounts to judge the temper, mood and feeling of the 1960s and 1970s. The gist of these accounts will show that whatever violence existed in America before — and the gangster era of the 1920s and the ugly years of the Depression of the 1930s were hardly peaceful — crime and brutality and mayhem had escalated to such a degree in the 1960s that citizens in major cities were afraid to walk the streets at nights and turned their homes into barred and bolted enclaves. This feeling of people besieged by terror in cities like Washington and New York was something unique in the modern history of America.

Nor was it merely the slum areas that harboured this atmosphere of menace, nor only the poor who existed in constant proximity to the sudden blow, the mugging, the robber, the pistol shot, the desperate heroin addict, the wail of the police siren. Citizens of the affluent middle-class spent fortunes organising themselves into protective units so that their comfortable homes could be guarded by electronic devices, private police, roaming dogs. Taxi drivers took their cabs off the streets before midnight, restaurants closed early. The bolt and heavy-iron bar and the peep-hole device on the door had become as normal a domestic appurtenance as the kitchen sink. The apprehensive face cautiously peering from behind a slim crack of open door became a normal social greeting.

In the *Sunday Express* of July 11th, 1971, Henry Fairlie talked about 'utterly senseless and meaningless violence that had become the habit of a society'. He described a weekend in Washington during which a woman had been raped and murdered in the early evening outside a respectable restaurant, during which five men burst into a young man's flat and held him at gunpoint while they raped two young women who had been visiting him, during which a naval commander and his son were shot dead on a crowded, busy road because of a traffic dispute. All in one weekend! 'What is the meaning of it all, this recurrent violence?' wrote Mr. Fairlie. 'Day after day it happens, and evening after evening when the streets are crowded, when neighbours are wide awake, when the highways are busy.'

And a month later on August 26th, 1971, the *Evening Standard* carried a similar account of pointless and aimless violence. This time the city was New York. 'A rash of wanton killings committed within the space of less than a week has shocked New York,' said this report. 'All the murders had one feature in common: they were committed mindlessly, in cold blood, and to no purpose, not even to avoid arrest . . . In one case a human life was sacrificed apparently because someone wanted a piece of apple pie. In another, death was the outcome of a petty argument between a hotel manager and a guest. The motive in a third case may never be known unless the killer is caught and can explain why he fired point blank at an out-of-town visitor he had never before set eyes on . . .'

The observations of these professional journalists were merely confirmations of the findings of the National Commission on the Causes and Prevention of Violence issued two years earlier in November 1969. This report (its investigation of television and violence was the basis of a separate report) was based upon studies of the 17 largest American cities. It showed that the most frequent offender was a male between 15 and 24; that in 10 years there had been a 300 per cent increase in the arrests of children between 10 and 14 for assault, and a 200 per cent increase in their arrests for robbery.

The Commission envisaged that, if crime continued to rise at the rate that it had in the decade 1960–70, the central cities of the United States would in a few years time become 'fortresses' in which the wealthy would live in privately guarded compounds; people would travel on high-speed patrolled expressways connecting safe areas; private automobiles, taxi-cabs and commercial vehicles would be routinely equipped with unbreakable glass and light armour; armed guards would ride shot-gun on all forms of public transportation; and 'the ghetto and slum neighbourhoods will be places of terror with widespread crime, perhaps out of police control during night time'.[22]

It is clear then that America in a single decade has witnessed an increase in violence unprecedented since the aftermath of the Civil War. Much of that violence was motiveless and unconnected with such accepted causes of violence as poverty, organised crime, corruption, racism, unemployment and political ideology. Most of that violence was committed by the age group between 15 and 24. The largest increase in the commission of crimes of violence was amongst the very young. In short, this unprecedented decade of violence occurred in the immediate years after America had become a television society and the largest contributors to that rise in violence was the first generation weaned on and conditioned by the box. Was it merely a coincidence?

Now let us examine the testimony of individuals in Britain about violence in that country during the 1960s. It is obvious that Britain has not remotely reached the terrifying state of menace and fear that pervades so many American communities. Yet this is small consolation when it is realised that the same escalation of violence is occurring in the 1960s in Britain and at an *even faster* rate than in America. This is the view of Professor Marvin Wolfgang, an American criminologist acting as a consultant for the Home Office on a crime-research project at Cambridge University.

Professor Wolfgang pointed out that while the murder rate and other types of robberies and assaults are 'enormously lower' in Britain than in the United States, 'all crimes of violence, when you knock them all together, are growing there [in Britain] at a more rapid rate than in America.'[23]

It is only necessary to scan one's morning newspaper to re-alise that a society with a deep reverence for the law is being subjected to more and more strange and alien convulsions of violence and disorder, particularly amongst the young. Student unrest has resulted in violent clashes with the police at some of the most respectable and revered universities. Hooliganism in the streets and in trains and buses has become a disturbing and unsettling feature of urban life. Rowdyism at football games has at times reached such serious proportions as to threaten the closure of some of the most famous football grounds in the country. The traditional awe, respect and affection the British have had in the past for their police has shown a sharp deter-ioration.

In spite of years of television programmes like *Dixon of Dock Green* and *Z Cars*, which have generally provided an endearing, flattering and sympathetic picture of policemen, we have a Police Superintendent saying, 'I do the job and I still like it. But less and less. More and more we are baited, abused and reviled. Youngsters have spat at me — sometimes straight in the face.' Said a Midlands police constable: 'It's a funny feeling being called a pig ... particularly by a 14-year-old. What do you do? You can't pull in every teenage kid who uses that word.'[24]

On the question of hooliganism and contempt for authority amongst the young, there is a growing volume of testimony from teachers of secondary schools. A report by a group of teachers in February 1970 claimed that hooliganism in class-rooms had reached such proportions as to threaten a break-down of the entire State education system. The teachers estimated that about 5 per cent of secondary school pupils could be classified as 'trouble-makers'[25] Five years later, on December 30th, 1974, the Assistant Masters' Association was so concerned with the problem of teachers assaulted by pupils that they passed a resolution demanding more effective mea-sures to treat this serious state of affairs.

There is even testimony that the quality of violence amongst the young has changed. Games have become less playful, more ruthless, more vicious. Mr. Matthew McGarvey, headmaster of a 500-pupil secondary modern school in Liverpool, said the traditional games like Cowboys and Indians are now likely to end with the boot or the knee being used. 'Boys have never been noted for their gentility when playing, but over the past few years, I, like many other people, have noted how their play has got more ruthless. I am convinced that the constant exposure to violence when they watch television is having its effect and unless something is done quickly we are going to produce a generation of people to whom distorted sex and violence are quite acceptable.'[26]

Perhaps the most ironic piece of evidence about the way in which television has directed children's minds into unusually violent channels came from the BBC itself. In June of 1971 a BBC's children's programme ran a competition to find the best film made by children between the ages of 9 and 15. They received 112 entries. But what surprised the sponsors of the contest was the amount of violence and blood that was spattered through the entries. Said a BBC spokesman rather naïvely: 'Most of them were dramas and a lot were surprisingly bloodthirsty. Quite a few had unhappy endings. The children had obviously been inspired by what they had seen on television and at the cinema and it is rather disturbing that they should reflect the violence which they see on the screen.'[27]

One of the most telling indications of the apprehension the average man feels about the atmosphere of violence in Britain came from a reader's survey conducted by the *Sun* newspaper late in 1971. To the question 'Do you feel you can walk about on your own at night', 62 per cent of readers said no and 38 per cent said yes. Asked whether they felt apprehensive if a crowd of youths approached them, 75 per cent said yes and 25 per cent said no. When asked 'Can you rest easily when your children go out?' an astonishing 90 per cent said no, only 10 per cent said yes. Had a similar survey been conducted in Britain in the middle 1950s, it is likely that these percentages would have been reversed.

We must, however, at this stage examine what social scientists have been saying in this field because it has been their findings that have largely accounted for the unwillingness of governments to make any radical changes in the structure and direction of television and have reinforced broadcasting authorities in their claims that their programmes are not doing any identifiable harm to society. Since sociology is as yet a most inexact science and mass communication research is still in its infancy, it is not surprising that these practitioners have not yet come up with tools that will measure the reactions of such complex material as human beings with the exactitude that physicists can trace the movement of light beams and chemists can predict the behaviour of molecular bodies.

In their contributions to the debate about television and violence sociologists have been somewhat similar to the Delphic oracle who, when asked difficult questions by powerful rulers, replied in ambiguous riddles which the recipients could interpret in any way that best suited their desires and ambitions. Small wonder that laymen seeking specific answers to questions about the influence of the media are driven to despair when confronted by findings of prominent sociologists like B. Berelson, which solemnly testify: 'Some kinds of *communication*, on some kinds of *issues*, brought to the attention of some kinds of *people*, under some kinds of *conditions*, have some kinds of *effects*.'[28]

The more confusion there is in the ranks of the experts, the more contradictory the arguments that are flung about, the more doubts that are cast on any form of research technique, the more likely will it be that nothing will be done to change the nature and direction of television. So long as the experts remain divided, so long will the status quo in broadcasting flourish.

'It is interesting to note the reaction of the television industry to any research which purports to show that watching violence, or any other television experience, may have undesirable consequences for the viewer or society at large,' says the Television Research Committee in its Report, *Television and Delinquency*. 'One sometimes gets the impression that in the United States the media men have "experts" on hand whose main task is to counter the statements and look for weaknesses in the work of any other "expert" whose work may be interpreted as an attack on television.'[29]

Naturally, the men who run broadcasting do not want to have it proved that what they have been doing in the past has had serious deleterious effects on their viewers. In that case they might have to make way for other men prepared to run broadcasting by different standards and different values. Similarly governments would not only be embarrassed by any definitive findings that they have negligently allowed television to harm society, but they would be at a loss to know how to correct such a situation.

The social scientists have therefore been a great comfort to broadcasters and politicians. Their general verdict about television and violence is 'Not Proven'. They never state baldly that there is no connection between the small screen and violence; they merely assert that they have been unable to establish such a connection. And when one examines the many experiments on the subject — confined primarily as they are to small groups of children in limited laboratory conditions, to questionnaire and interview methods for adolescents, to the examination of very short-term effects — it is clear that the reason so many of these experiments produce negative findings is not that there is nothing to find but simply that researchers are using the wrong tools or that the tools at their disposal are inadequate for the task in hand. In some ways they are like medical researchers who tried to find a connection between cigarette smoking and lung cancer before the discovery of the X-ray and the microscope. The relationship between smoking and cancer was obvious to anyone who cared to look long before the experts could prove it. Many millions had to die before the case was established. Similarly the coughings and splutterings and spasms of violence in television societies will no doubt be allowed to get worse before the social scientists acquire the tools to establish the obvious.

One of the more popular theories advanced by the sociologists to decry any relationship between television and violence is the view that television merely reinforces existing attitudes. Based primarily on studies of political attitudes showing that election campaigns have little effect on voter's intentions, the theory has been pushed into the violence argument where it has neither logic nor relevance. Thus J. T. Klapper, writing in 1960, said, 'Communications research strongly indicates that media depictions of crime and violence are not prime movers to such conduct. The content seems rather to reinforce or implement existing and otherwise induced behavioural tendencies.'[30]

But surely the question of conditioning or cultivation of aggressive behaviour in children between the ages of three and eight cannot be merely a matter of reinforcing violent tendencies they had before they were three! Where did they acquire these behavioural tendencies that the box only implemented or strengthened? The womb? The Television Research Committee, writing nine years after Dr. Klapper, confessed the misgivings of other social scientists about this dubious generalisation.

'In assessing the generalisations about the effects of mass communication,' said the Committee's Report, 'it needs to be appreciated that very little work has been carried out on the role of television in the early stages of the child's development. It may be true that television has relatively little influence when attitudes and values are well formed, but what about when they are not well formed, but are actually in the process of formation?'[31]

Catharsis, is, of course, another favourite defence for subjecting children to a constant bombardment of media violence. When Aristotle argued that through experiencing pity and terror by an occasional visit to a tragedy by Euripides or Sophocles, an individual might be purged of some of his violent instincts, he hardly foresaw that one day his words would be used to justify American children seeing television programmes like *Gunsmoke, The Untouchables, Hawaii Five-O* for about one-fifth of their conscious life.

It may be true that an occasional Western seen at the local cinema might have had, in the days before television, some minimal effect in draining off inherent violent instincts and rendering them harmless. But the sheer volume of television violence obviously makes it operate as a conditioning rather than a cathartic influence. If it could be argued that the display of violence, no matter how much or of what type, or under what circumstances, drains away violence, then broadcasting organisations would be doing a service to society by getting rid of all their violence codes and showing even more of the genre than they already do. I doubt if even Lord Hill who, in a speech in 1969 to teachers at Southampton indicated some support for the catharsis theory, would give the BBC *carte blanche* to raise its level of violent programmes by way of a contribution to public-service broadcasting.

As the psychiatrist Dr. Fredric Wertham has written, 'to use the term *catharsis* as a justification for media mayhem is at best a misunderstanding. Neither Aristotle nor Franz Fenon meant it that way . . . Do you give a child an erector set so that he will get rid of his interest in real construction, or a chemistry set so that he gets out of his system his natural bent for science?'[32]

Dr. Wilbur H. Schramm of Stanford University, whose views on the media tend to exonerate television as a basic cause of either violence or delinquency, is another authority who has turned sour on the catharsis theory. Speaking to a Senate Sub-committee on Juvenile Delinquency in 1961, he said: 'Now, there was quite a long time when we thought that perhaps it [children's viewing of violent television] might act as a cath-arsis for these aggressive behaviours. This might possibly reduce aggression. But at the present time, that is not held, because the last six good experiments, well controlled scientific ones, have indicated that it does not reduce it and actually has made more likely the fact that there will be some violent be-haviour by the persons who have seen it afterwards.'[33]

Finally, the National Commission on the Causes of Viol-ence, with all available research evidence before it, would have none of the catharsis theory. 'Some defenders of violence on television contend that viewers "drain off" aggressive ten-dencies by their vicarious participation in violent media pro-grammes,' says its statement of September 23rd, 1969, '. . . Laboratory experiments on the reactions of adults and teen-agers to violent film content provide little support for this theory. In fact, the vast majority of experimental studies on this question have found that observed violence stimulates ag-gressive behaviour, rather than the opposite.'

In an already long book it is impractical to examine all the data provided by the social scientists about media and attempt intelligently to thread one's way through the maze of conflicting opinions and conclusions. But there are some gen-eral observations that occur to a layman confronted with the task of sorting out the validity of much of this material and trying to assess the overall drift and direction expert opinion seems to be taking.

The way in which limited evidence is used to build up a pyramid of accepted opinion can be seen by the manner in which the Himmelweit study has been handled. Between 1954 and 1956, a team of researchers led by Dr. Hilde T. Himmelweit interviewed some 4,500 children about the effects of television in Britain. On the whole, the survey was reassuring about the consequences of television, finding that the medium was 'not as black as it is painted' and that as a window on the world 'it gives a view not very different from that provided in books, comics, films and radio programmes'.

Neither was the survey over-concerned about the effects of violent programmes. It believed that since the violence in Westerns was stylised and stereotyped, it would not particularly affect children, except for the very young, the immature, and those predisposed to delinquency. Only those under 7 were likely to be frightened by the violence in Westerns. Dr. Himmelweit was not, however, entirely complacent about such programmes. 'There is a great deal of talk about the need for research into the effects of showing so much violence,' she wrote. 'We feel that the need for research is used too readily as an excuse. There is no need to prove that such programmes do harm . . . the strongest reason for criticising them is their reiteration that life is cheap and that conflict is to be solved by violence.'[34]

Now, valid as the Himmelweit findings may have been about the effects of British television on children between 1954 and 1956, the situation prevailing in broadcasting at that time has very little in common, particularly in so far as violent programmes are concerned, with the kind and quantity of programmes most children saw on television after 1956. Nor did it ever have anything in common with the kind of programmes seen in America. Nevertheless Himmelweit still gets reverential mention in any list of surveys dealing with media violence years later.

What the Himmelweit survey was measuring was what television — largely modelled on Reithian broadcasting standards — was doing to British children aged primarily 10 to 11 years old and 13 to 14 years old. It is probable that not a single child out of the entire sample of 4,500 had been brought up from infancy on the box. Practically none of them had watched television in their pre-school years. In 1949 when the youngest of this group was 4 years old, less than 2 per cent of British homes had television sets.

Thus not a single child of this entire group was a television creature in the sense in which we would define such an indevidual in 1975. The television seen by these children was monopolised by the BBC on one channel, did no transmitting between 6 and 7 p.m. so that children could be sent to bed or encouraged to do homework without being distracted by the demands of the set, and was usually off the air by 10.30 p.m. Most of its content was of the amiable family kind taken over from radio such as *Life with the Lyons, The Brains Trust, Asian Club*. The BBC's chief purpose at that time was to inform; its second purpose was to entertain. The number of transmissions of violent programmes of the type we have been discussing in this chapter was minimal. In other words, in its relevance to the debate about the media and violence in the 1970s, the Himmelweit study is largely out of date.

Even when it was published it had little relevance to the American scene where a diet of violent programmes had been fed to children on a variety of channels ever since 1948. Nevertheless Dr. Schramm and other American sociologists have used the Himmelweit report to support their own views that American television was not a significant instigator of aggression amongst American children. 'The Himmelweit study, pruned and carefully excerpted, is the bible of the U.S. television industry,' wrote Arnold Arnold in 1969. 'The Television Information Office, an "educational" foundation set up by the networks, has reprinted portions of the Himmelweit study. But the TIO excerpt glosses over or fails to mention most of the limitations peculiar to British television at the time in which this survey was made. And without all these qualifications, such an excerpted reprint is misleading, to put it mildly.'[35]

It is also clear that one of the greatest stumbling blocks confronting sociologists ready to decry any serious connection between violence and television is the evidence supplied by many psychiatrists. Leading the battle for over 20 years has been the American psychiatrist Frederic Wertham, who has consistently argued that children's comics, the cinema and television have all contributed significantly to aggressive behaviour in the young. The brutalising content of these media, he contends, has 'immunised a whole generation against pity and against recognition of cruelty and violence', has made children indifferent to the sufferings of other people, has subtly distorted human values.

'Whether crime and violence programmes arouse a lust for violence, reinforce it when it is present, show a way to carry it out, teach the best methods to get away with it, or merely blunt the child's (and adult's) awareness of its wrongness, television has become a school for violence,' writes Wertham.[36]

But the great difference of opinion amongst experts can be deduced from Halloran's survey of the research position in *Television and Delinquency*. 'Wertham shows little respect for the work of Himmelweit, Schramm and their colleagues,' says Halloran, a sociologist, 'often regarded as classics in this field. Wertham claims that in the questionnaire or survey approach the whole child is not examined and the essence of the television-child relationship is not touched. He writes of the "dubious scientific value" of such work . . . Wertham, although undoubtedly one of the most outspoken, is not alone amongst psychiatrists in holding that television has detrimental effects. It is worth noting that of all those professionally concerned with the problem it is from the psychiatrists that we have the most unequivocal statements about the damage caused by television.'[37]

With the experts in such a state of disarray, how can one ever hope to get a concrete answer to the relationship between television and violence? If governments or broadcasters are going to wait for any wide consensus between social scientists and psychiatrists on this issue before doing anything, it is clear that nothing is likely to be done for a very long time. But should there be any further delay? Even the most confirmed disciple of the view that television does no serious harm will concede the fact that it is likely to affect the disturbed, abnormal, maladjusted and delinquency-prone child. The assumption, however, is that there are not enough of such children about to produce a major social problem.

'The abundance of this noxious material in the mass media is beyond dispute,' said the sociologist Dr. Mark Abrams. 'But does it lead to direct, imitative behaviour on the part of ordinary average children? . . . Does it create among them a general climate of undesirable values? The available evidence from research on these points among children is slight and often negative. It appears that when maladjusted and well-adjusted children are exposed to identical amounts of violent mass-media content, the former, unlike the latter, show a marked preference for such material, derive distinctive satisfactions from it, and, in the process of consumption, their problems are sustained rather than resolved. Since media violence, in some way as yet unknown to us, apparently intensified the difficulties of maladjusted and frustrated children, a strong case can be made out for removing such material. The strength of the case, however, depends very largely on two considerations: first, how large is the proportion of our children who are maladjusted and frustrated? If it is very low, e.g. 1 or 2 per cent, then the introduction of censorship could hardly be justified; while if it is high, e.g. 20 or 25 per cent, then the case would seem to be unanswerable. Unfortunately, this is yet another area where, in spite of the abundance of debate, we lack any reliable, relevant facts. We do not know whether it is 2 per cent or 22 per cent.'[38]

Since that statement was made in the middle 1960s, evidence of what television does to normal children has become available which indicates that its influence is neither as 'negative' nor as 'slight' as Dr. Abrams suggests. But if we merely confine ourselves to the problem of television's impact upon the unstable, there is undoubtedly grave cause for concern. Assuming that there is some statistical relationship between the number of maladjusted children and maladjusted adults, then we may already have reached the position where 20 per cent of the child population falls within the categories of the unstable or disturbed or delinquency-prone. In Britain in 1970 almost half of the hospital beds were occupied by the mentally ill. It has been calculated that 1 in 9 women and 1 in 14 men will at some time enter a mental hospital. If this is the number that have reached such a critical stage that institutional treatment is advisable, how many more are there whose disturbances are never diagnosed or are just not severe enough to qualify for some sort of confinement?

If these figures make awesome reading, there are some even more worrying findings about mental health in America. In 1961 a team of Cornell University sociologists and psychiatrists studied a representative sample of the population of mid-town

Manhattan in New York. They came to the startling conclusion that only 18·5 per cent of New York city dwellers could be considered mentally 'well'. They found that 58·1 per cent of their sample suffered 'mild' or 'moderate' mental disturbance and that no less than 23·4 per cent suffered from mental symptoms which could be called 'marked', 'severe', or 'incapacitating'.[39]

Even though the report's conclusions were cautious and hedged with qualifications, one can assume that they were more accurate in identifying the extreme mental cases — the 23·4 per cent — than the cases teetering on the verge between normality and moderate instability. Another report in the *New York State Journal of Medicine* of July 1st, 1971 stated that 'at least ten million of our young people under 25 are thought to suffer from mental and emotional disturbances'. Is, then, America not close to reaching the figure of 20 per cent maladjusted children which Dr. Mark Abrams considered sufficient to make an unanswerable case for censoring the violence content of mass media?

What then, can one conclude about the state of social science research on this subject? The impression one gets from reading the literature is that those who persist in denying any connection between television and increased violence are being pushed more and more on the defensive. In spite of all their reassurances, the public is not convinced. Each fresh study, based increasingly on children who have been brought up on television rather than those who have not, finds new evidence pointing towards a relationship between television and aggression.

The Television Research Committee, for example, in its study of British delinquents in 1966, while still leaning to the view that the mass media play only a minor, contributory role in delinquent behaviour, admitted that no such survey as their's could offer 'proof or disproof about the suggested causal relationships between media content and deviant or law-breaking behaviour. If such relationships exist they may well be of a more subtle sort than is commonly imagined.' Nevertheless their investigations turned up certain differences between the way in which delinquents and non-delinquents used television which they thought were significant and warranted further study.

Although both delinquents and non-delinquents watched the same amount of television and the same amount of programmes, delinquents significantly preferred the exciting and aggressive programme and liked hero figures more than did the control groups. Delinquents, too, didn't think of television as a means of relaxation which could mean they use television as a source of short-term stimulation to an unusual degree. Also delinquents talked less with their friends and family about what they saw on television than non-delinquents. This bottling-up of their electronic experiences, without a chance of having them aired or explained or contradicted by their peers or adults, could clearly have unpredictable effects.[40]

This latest statement on the subject of television and violence in Britain has, however, been over-shadowed by the findings of the American Commission on the Causes and Prevention of Violence. The particular merit of this Commission was that it was able to stand outside the internecine bickerings of the experts and reach conclusions untarnished by the demands of previously committed positions. Composed of a number of distinguished laymen — jurists, diplomats, politicians — under the Chairmanship of Dr. Milton S. Eisenhower, this Commission could be said to be a kind of Grand Jury surveying the available evidence and reaching its verdict on the basis of logic and common sense.

Having heard all the arguments of the broadcasters, having been provided with all the conflicting research studies of the social scientists, having commissioned its own Media Task Force to produce certain evidence that was unavailable elsewhere, it reached unequivocal and decisive conclusions that clearly connected fictionalised television with violence in America. Here are some of its findings:

'The preponderance of the available research evidence strongly suggests that violence in television programmes can and does have adverse effects upon audiences — particularly child audiences.'

'Television enters powerfully into the learning process of children and teaches them a set of moral and social values about violence which are inconsistent with the standards of a civilised society.'

'Younger children, between the ages of 3 and 8, are particularly susceptible to observational learning when the material portrayed is new to them and therefore absorbs their attention.'

'Young children and a large proportion of teenagers from low income families believe that people behave in the real world the way they do in the fictional world of television.'

'Television is a particularly potent force in families where parental influences and primary group ties are weak or completely lacking, notably in low-income areas or where violent life-styles are common. In these instances, television does not displace parental influence: it fills a vacuum. The strong preference of low-income teenagers for crime, action, and adventure stories means that they are constantly exposed to the values of violent television programmes without the ameliorating influence of their parents . . . The television experience of these children and adolescents reinforces a distorted, pathological view of society.'

'We believe it is reasonable to conclude that a constant diet of violent behaviour on television has an adverse effect on human character and attitudes. Violence on television encourages violent forms of behaviour, and fosters moral and social values about violence in family life which are unacceptable in a civilised society.'

There was only one crumb of comfort in this vigorous denunciation of American broadcasting. 'We do not suggest that television is a principal cause of violence in society,' it said. 'We do suggest that it is a contributing factor.'

A 'major' contributing factor or a 'minor' contributing factor? The Commission must have decided it was a 'major' contributing factor. 'Television entertainment based on violence,' concluded the Commission, 'may be effective merchandising, but it is an appalling way to serve a civilisation — an appalling way to fulfil the requirements of the law that broadcasting serve "the public interest, convenience and necessity".'

What would seem to have been almost the final word on the subject was the US Surgeon General's Report which after almost three years' work at the cost of a million dollars revealed its findings early in 1972. When a summary of the Report was first announced it became the subject of a minor Government scandal. It turned out that the networks had been given the

205

right of veto over members of the committee, and NBC and ABC had duly blackballed seven of the proposed experts, who had previously published studies claiming there was a causal relationship between television and adolescent aggression. Of the 12 Committee members, 5 were network officials or social scientists, according to *Newsweek*, with close ties with the industry.[41]

In the event, the first report of the Committee's study gave the impression that violence on the box did not have adverse effects. But this suspect optimism was considerably modified in the subsequent row that followed. 'Parents all over the country may be lulled into complacency by the committee's summary,' said clinical psychologist Robert M. Liebert, who contributed to the study. 'But what has been found is that the violence a child watches on TV is directly related to the amount of violence he does afterwards.'

And when in March 1972 Senator Pastore's Committee held four days of hearings on the Surgeon General's Report, *Variety* summarised the occasion in these words: 'It soon became obvious that the days when an industry spokesman could argue before a Congressional committee that the impact of televised violence isn't really known are over ... The controversy was more or less rendered moot by the unanimity of opinion that what now exists is harmful and must be changed at once.'[42]

Having surveyed the personal testimonies and scientific research about violence and television, we are left finally to examine whether the criminal statistics in any way bear out the fears of those who see in television a unique medium stimulant towards more violent societies. If we take the only three countries in the world that have had television long enough in sufficient volume to provide a telly generation — Britain, American and Canada — is there anything statistically similar about their crime rate and their violence ratio? Since they transmit in a large measure the same sort of entertainment-dominated programme mix, they should, if violence on the box can be blamed, reveal the same sort of trends in the growth of violence amongst the same age groups. Should there be any similarity in these trends and statistics, we must ask if there are any other common national and social conditions, apart from the fact that they are primarily English-speaking societies with similar legal and governmental institutions, that would account for conformity in their violence profile. And, finally, can it be said that if such similarity in violence trends exists that this merely reflects universal movements and influences? For example how do the crime statistics of the last 20 years in Russia, Hungary, Chile, Yugoslavia, Sweden, France, Holland — where there is a different philosophy of broadcasting or where television has appeared only recently — compare with those of America, Britain and Canada?

The chief difficulty with crime statistics is that changes in legislation and methods of computation are constantly shifting both the definition of crime and the manner in which crimes are counted. But however you look at the figures, qualifying and slicing them as you will, they show that in those three countries that have had television in a majority of homes for 15 years or more the crime rate has gone up significantly.

Since we are trying to establish if there is any relationship between television and violence, it is clearly crimes of violence that will interest us most. In Britain this category, known as 'violence against the person', includes murder, attempted murder, manslaughter, assault and wounding. By far the largest category of crimes in this group is 'malicious wounding and other like offences'.

A summary of the general history of crime in Britain since the beginning of the century was provided by Norman Fowler in an article published in *The Times* on April 6th, 1970. 'After a period of stability at the beginning of the century crime rose at an average rate of 5 per cent a year between 1915 and 1930; and at about 7 per cent a year between 1931 and 1948,' wrote Mr. Fowler. 'Though it showed an overall decrease between 1949 and 1954 hopes that this might be a permanent trend were disappointed. From 1955 to 1965 crime increased by about 10 per cent a year and, although it seemed to be levelling out in 1967, now seems to be continuing this steep climb. In 1968 figures went up by 7 per cent and all the indications are that last year the rise was over 10 per cent which will bring the total of crimes to nearly 1,500,000.'

Between 1949 and 1954, the years when television was mon-opolised by the paternalistic, Reithian BBC the total amount of crime in Britain *actually went down*. But since 1955 when commercial television came on the scene, 50 per cent of homes possessed sets, and broadcasting became more and more dominated by an entertainment ethos, the crime rate has increased at a rate higher than that at any other period in this century. From 1955 to 1970 overall crime has increased by about 250 per cent. The figures show that in 1955 there were 7,884 crimes of violence against the person 'known to the police'. In 1970, there were 41,088 crimes in this category, and in 1971 there were 47,036 an increase between 1955 and 1971 of 500 per cent! Thus crimes of violence had accelerated at a rate almost twice as fast as all crimes. 'Spectacular' was the adjective used by the criminologist Nigel Walker, in the *Sunday Telegraph* of December 5th, 1971, to describe this rise in criminal violence. It has been even more 'spectacular' since 1971. In 1973 crimes of violence had escalated to 61,277, an increase of 17 per cent over the previous year, and a rise since 1955 of almost 700 per cent.

For those who might assume that these statistics had something to do with Britain's increased population, the relative population growth between 1951 and 1972 (the last census) was about 10 per cent. For those who still console themselves that Britain is not a very violent country it is salutary to note that in 1931 Britain's record of violent crime per head of population was roughly one in 22,000; in 1961 one in 3,000; and in 1970 one in 1,300.

Just as we find a disproportionate increase in violent crimes as compared to all crimes between 1955 and 1973 so we see a disproportionate increase in the number of violent crimes committed by the under 21s (the telly generation) and those committed by the over 21s. The number of people over 21 found guilty of violent crimes in this period has gone up by about 400 per cent; the increase in convictions for those in the age group between 14 and 21 has been no less than 12 times or 1100 per cent. If one compares 1950 to 1973 the figures are even more horrendous. In 1950 only 783 persons under 21 were convicted of crimes of violence. In 1973 it had rocketed to 14,115 — a rise of 1700 per cent! There may be other explanations for such a staggering discrepancy between the rise in violent crimes committed by the telly generation and the non-telly generation other than the existence of the small screen, but it would be interesting for some politician or broadcaster to suggest what they are.

Let us now look at similar statistics in America. Oddly enough, considering its preoccupation with crime, the crime count in America is not very satisfactory. The former Attorney General, Ramsey Clark, has indicated some of the fallacies and errors in America's crime statistics. 'Most crime is never reported to police,' he writes. 'And much crime is inaccurately reported ... Crimes in America are so many and varied that we endeavour to count only those defined as serious for national reporting purposes. Millions of serious crimes are unreported each year. Tens of millions of lesser crimes such as minor thefts and larcenies are not counted, though they differ little — often only in the value of the property wrongfully taken — from serious crimes of the same nature.'[43]

Because each state has its own responsibility for law enforcement such national statistics as are available should best be judged as guidance to trends rather than an accurate statement of crime in America. It is the Federal Bureau of Investigation that has centralised the data which is now accepted as a reasonably fair picture of crime in America. By 1968 its records covered 92 per cent of the nation's total population. But, as Ramsey Clark points out, this is just 'the beginning of an accurate, comprehensive crime report'.

It is therefore obvious that the farther back we go in seeking comparative crime figures, the less reliable will these comparisons be. We will therefore confine ourselves to the crime trends as reported by the FBI for the decade from 1960 to 1969. Since over 50 per cent of American homes possessed television sets as far back as 1953, it will be impossible to fully assess the contiguity of television's appearance and the rise in crime.

Since the FBI statistics are confined to seven classes of 'index' crimes — murder, rape, assault, robbery, burglary, larceny and car theft — they provide us with the same offences as the British include amongst crimes of violence against the person. Such 'index' crimes are split into two classes. Violent crime includes murder, rape, aggravated assault and robbery. The other three categories — burglary, larceny and car theft — are listed as crimes against property. Aggravated assault is defined as 'an unlawful attack by one person on another for the purpose of inflicting severe bodily injury usually accompanied by the use of a weapon or other means likely to produce death or serious bodily harm.' If we confine ourselves to 'violent crime' we can compare the figures to British crimes of 'violence against the person', except that rape in Britain is treated separately as a sexual crime.

According to the FBI, violent crime between 1960 and 1969 has increased by 130 per cent. During this decade arrests of adults for violent crimes were up by 54 per cent. Juvenile arrests (persons under 18 years of age) for violent crimes increased by 148 per cent. Although the population of this age group in these ten years had risen by 27 per cent, the arrests of under 18s had gone up 100 per cent. 'It is apparent,' says the 1969 FBI Crime Report, 'that the involvement of young persons as measured by police arrests is escalating at a pace almost four times their percentage increase in the national population.'[44]

Commenting on these figures, Ramsey Clark said 'Nearly the entire increase in arrests for the commission of serious crimes during the 1960s is accounted for by minors ... The one clear fact is that more young people are being arrested, whatever the charge.'[45]

Before we go on to examine Canadian crime statistics, we might compare the crime profile in Britain and America. The rise in crimes of violence since TV became a mass medium has been taking place at about 11 per cent per year in Britain and at almost the same rate in America. In Britain there have been three times as many convictions for violence amongst the under 21s as amongst older age groups. In America arrests for violent crimes amongst the under 18s have risen at just about three times the rate of the over 18s. Considering the basic historic and social differences between the two countries, this similarity on the issue of criminal violence is, to put it mildly, striking.

Now how does the pattern of crime in Canada compare with that of the other two television societies? As we have seen, over half of Canadian homes had television sets in 1955 and their programme fare is much the same as that in America. Because of revisions in Canadian statistics our statistics must begin with the year 1962. Murders and attempted murders have risen between 1962 and 1970 from 300 to 698 — an increase of almost 150 per cent. Assaults (not indecent) have risen from 27,818 to 76,997 — an increase of 176 per cent. Robbery has gone up 134 per cent. Possessing offensive weapons has risen 147 per cent. Thus the overall *annual* increase in crimes of violence has been about 11 per cent — almost the same figure as in Britain and America. Canada's population during this nine-year period has only gone up by one-tenth.

What contribution do the young make to this escalation of crime figures? Since young offenders in Canada are bracketed in the 16 to 24 age group, in Britain in the under 21s, and in America in the under 18s, comparable statistics are difficult to come by. It is unlikely, for example, that those between 21 and 24 in 1968 in Canada would have had their formative years influenced by television. Even so, it is significant that indictable offences committed by the 16 to 24 age group is going up at about twice the rate of older age groups. The juvenile delinquency figures show a rise from 1957 to 1969 of almost 200 per cent — from 9,679 to 27,197 cases. And juvenile delinquency may be rising even faster than this, since the figures do not include informal cases dealt with by the police, social agencies, schools and youth-serving agencies. 'The young men and women in the age group between 16 and 24 account for 22·0 per cent of the total population 16 years and over,' said the *Canada Year Book for 1970*, 'but they form over half of the criminal population committing indictable offences [in 1967].'

It is evident, then, that in spite of the variations in statistical data, violent crime had been going up by at least 10 per cent a year during the 1960s in Britain, America and Canada; that the telly generation has made an unprecedented and disproportionate contribution to that crime rate; and that there is at present no sign that this rate of increase in crime is either diminishing or levelling off.

We must now ask ourselves whether this explosion of crime during the 1960s is symptomatic of conditions everywhere. Have countries without television or those who have run television along different lines experienced the same phenomenon? The answer is no. If we discount revolutionary and political violence which may erupt for short periods in any country, there is no evidence of such precipitate increases in criminal violence throughout the world.

In Western Germany there were 103,456 crimes of violence, including sex crimes, committed in 1962; in 1968 the figure was 94,531. This indicates an overall *reduction* in seven years of almost 10 per cent. Dutch figures show a similar *reduction* in violent crimes with the figure for 1958 standing at 12,424 and for 1968 only 10,902. Although Eastern European countries are not very forthcoming about criminal statistics, official spokesmen insist that on the whole they seem to be going down. Independent observers who have spent some time in countries like Russia, Rumania and Yugoslavia confirm the official view that there has been no undue increase in crimes of violence amongst the young. The Hungarians claim that their juvenile delinquency statistics have remained constant between 1964 and 1969. In 1969 the figure given for those between 14 and 18 in Hungary who had broken the law was only 1·1 per cent.

Although countries like Sweden and Japan now have television sets in over 90 per cent of homes, it is too soon to say what effect this may have had upon their young since it was not until the early 1960s that television had reached 50 per cent of the population. Even as late as 1967 countries like France and Italy had television in less than 50 per cent of homes. An interesting latecomer on the television scene is Australia which did not acquire 50 per cent coverage until 1964. However, since it transmits a large proportion of American action-adventure series and since its broadcasting philosophy is as entertainment-oriented as that of Canada and America, it will be interesting to see if its crime statistics begin to develop in the next five years or so along the lines we have seen in those two countries.

What we have, then, is a unique similarity in the rise of violent crimes in those three countries with a high degree of action-adventure programmes in their schedules and with the entertainment of viewers as television's dominant objective. Are there any other environmental or social conditions that those three countries have shared over the past 15 years, other than television, that might account for this simultaneous escalation in violent crimes?

The causes of crime are numerous. Ramsey Clark has produced his list of basic causes. 'If we are to deal meaningfully with crime, what must be seen is the dehumanising effect on the individual of slums, racism, ignorance and violence, of corruption and impotence to fulfil rights, of poverty and unemployment and idleness, of generations of malnutrition, of congenital brain damage and prenatal neglect, of sickness and disease, of pollution, of decrepit, dirty, ugly, unsafe, overcrowded housing, of alcoholism and narcotics addiction, of avarice, anxiety, fear, hatred, hopelessness and injustice. These are the fountainheads of crime.'[46]

It is no doubt true that such incentives to crime are common to every advanced society. They stimulate crime in Holland as well as Britain; in Hungary as well as Canada. Why, then, has crime increased so markedly in certain countries in the 1960s but not in others? Indeed, it could be argued that in the television societies there was less racism, less poverty, fewer slums, less ignorance, better housing, less sickness and disease in 1970 than there had been in 1955. But in spite of the alleviation of the economic and physical lot of the underprivileged and criminally-prone, in spite of more education and a wider spread of literacy, three of the richest and most humane and most legally-conscious countries in the world witnessed a rise in crime of unprecedented proportions and saw their young corrupted by a cult of violence.

It may be, of course, that crime feeds more on frustrated expectations than on chronic inequalities. Raise hopes too high and when they crash, violence usually has the last word. It may be that the American dream offered too much too soon to the educationally underprivileged, the racially oppressed, the economically downtrodden of the United States. It was not because they were poor and overcrowded and ignorant that they took to violence, but because they had been brought up to believe that they would escape the lot of their fathers. It was television that had brought a fresh dimension to the impossible American illusion that equality and affluence were available to all. The power of the commercial with its promise of success through the use of the right hair oil or shaving cream was far more potent than the Horatio Alger myth of the shoeshine boy becoming a millionaire that had sustained earlier generations of

Americans. For blacks and poor Puerto Ricans the difference between what the box had told them was their natural right compared to the reality of their slum-existence and the let-down when they reached maturity and social rejection might possibly have stimulated more violence in this generation than had the frustration of past generations.

By its example, television had also taught the poor and the bitter and the discontented that violence was a moral way of righting such wrongs, of dealing with a society that had raised false hopes and was callous and indifferent about what it had done. To some extent the same hopes and expectations of a better life through material acquisition had been raised by tele-vision in Canada and Britain. It seems only on this speculative level that there is any common ground for explaining why crimes of violence rose in Britain and America and Canada in the same years and roughly in the same dimensions.

If one seeks other reasons for the rise in violence, it is difficult to find any factor that applies to all three countries. It has been said that the special circumstances that brought about extra violence in America in the 1960s were its frontier history, the liberal gun laws, the Vietnam war, the new militancy of the blacks. Even the frontier myth, as Louis Heren pointed out, is largely a product of the media — and again mainly television. 'The frontier myth is nonsense, literally bloody nonsense, be-cause it can still excuse and glorify personal violence,' wrote Mr. Heren. 'The southern planters and poor whites, the presi-dents of great corporations and special deputies never walked the street of some frontier town at high noon . . . The frontier myth, with its lonely hero triumphant in a hostile world, [has been] perpetuated not only by films and television but by authors ranging from Fenimore Cooper and Ernest Heming-way to Micky Spillane. It is about time America grew up.'[47]

But if its frontier history inspired Americans to violence, if guns were easy to come by, if the Vietnam war had disgusted or brutalised the young, if the blacks took to crime against an oppressive society, that might theoretically explain what had been happening in the United States. But why did Britain and Canada go the same way? None of these explanations has any relevance for these societies. Instead of a tradition of violence, Canada has had a tradition of God-fearing respectability and

"modest connection" between screen violence and violence in society. But the interaction between television and society is two-way, subtle, complex and cannot be reduced to black and white arguments supported by the simplistic use of statistics.

'It was certainly not the purpose of my previous letter to belittle the educational effect of television. Rather it was to poke some gentle fun at those who hold an *idée fixe* that there is a direct and instantly measurable relationship between rising crime rates and television (and before television — films) . . .'

This obviously called for a further letter from me which *The Times* duly printed on August 15th, 1974.

'While Mr. Denis Forman belittles "the simplistic use of statistics" to establish a link between TV and violent crime in the United Kingdom, he offers as an alternative explanation for our rising crimes of violence, wild generalisations about the prevalence of violence in Africa, Latin America, Northern Ireland and even Vietnam.

'To answer a statistical case with speculation, surmise and no statistics or facts of any kind is hardly the way to win an argument.

'The fact is that countries that provide a large amount of TV violence i.e. Britain, America, Canada, show a consistent pattern of rising violence among the young. Countries that do not provide such a steady diet of violent TV programmes may show some rise in youthful violence but nothing like the drastic escalation in the countries I have mentioned.

'I challenge Mr. Forman to produce one single country not involved in violent political strife, i.e. Ulster, the Middle East, Vietnam, that has reproduced or surpassed Britain's sevenfold increase in violent crime in the 17 years since Granada TV came on the air.

'In any case all Mr. Forman's arguments and stonewalling tactics were used by his American counterparts when they presented their evidence to the Surgeon General's Advisory Committee. But after spending one million dollars and sifting through three years of research and five volumes of technical reports, the committee decisively rejected Mr. Forman's case by finding a positive and meaningful link between TV violence and social violence.

'Said Senator Pastore, Chairman of the Senate Committee

that received the Surgeon General's Report: "We now know that there is a causal relation between televised violence and antisocial behaviour which is sufficient to warrant *immediate remedial action.* It is this certainty which has eluded men of good will for so long."

'As Chairman of Granada TV, Mr. Forman would be better advised contemplating what "immediate remedial action" should be taken by TV companies in this country rather than persisting in a campaign to dissociate himself and his colleagues from sharing some of the blame for this nation's appalling crime rate among the young.'

CHAPTER SEVEN

The Great Divider

If you ask a member of this generation two simple questions: 'How do you want the world to be in fifty years?' and 'What do you want your life to be like five years from now?' the answers are often preceded by 'Provided there is still a world,' and 'Provided I am still alive.'

Hannah Arendt, *On Violence*

The trouble today is that the younger generation will take anything valuable they find in the toilet. You wouldn't find the older generation cheating you in the toilets.
Stanley McNamara, 55-year-old Birmingham lavatory attendant, *Guardian*, April 15th, 1971

I am a drop-out because I believe that most of America lives in a world of myths.

American hippie

There is nothing new about the generation gap. The impatience of youth to take on the tasks of their elders and prove that they can do better provokes resentment and fear amongst the older generation about the presumptions and aspirations of the young. This power struggle is deeply imbedded in the nature of man. Almost 2000 years ago Pliny the Elder was petulantly complaining about the Roman youth of his day. 'Which of them pays submission as an inferior to age or authority?' he wrote in his *Letters*. 'These young gentlemen begin life as sages, and know everything from the first; there is no one they revere or imitate, as they are their own models.'

Man has learnt to live with this constant conflict between the young and the old. Indeed changes and progress through the ages have been brought about largely because of the pressures caused by such differences. The young, unfettered by custom and experience, have often seen more clearly the misguided direction being taken by their elders. But it is self-evident that the generation gap must never become so wide as to discourage communication and understanding. If the opportunities for a meaningful dialogue between generations become too limited then many of the young will either refuse to co-operate with a society they distrust or react violently against it.

'One of the fashionable fallacies, widely prevalent today, is that the problems confronting mankind in the latter half of the 20th century differ only in degree from those faced by previous generations,' writes Professor Duncan Williams in *Trousered Apes*. 'They are, on the contrary, totally unprecedented and, until this is generally realised and accepted, no move towards their solution will be possible. The sources of the contemporary crisis can be summarised as: an almost total loss of religious faith — a denial of any ultimate reference; a majority of the world's peoples under the age of 25; a population explosion which threatens to engulf mankind; and finally a nuclear ability to destroy the species ... The Red Guard in China and the student demonstrations in Europe and the United States appear to share certain common characteristics: a hatred of anything which commands the allegiance and respect of the older generation, including a contempt for traditional ethical and moral values; a passionate need to be active; and above all a total rejection of authority, both secular and sacred.'[1]

The trouble with this analysis is that it is far too generalised and far too global. It is tempting to assume that a generation brought up under the shadow of atomic annihilation would react in a similar fashion to such an awesome eventuality. But the Chinese Red Guard, for example, were not rebelling against authority and the older generation. They were, on the contrary, demanding that the precepts and dictates of an elderly and revered leader, Mao Tse-tung, be obeyed without question. They were insisting upon more discipline, more order, more faith in authority, not less.

Although there was undoubtedly an element of rejection of their parent's world in the philosophy of the French students involved in the 1968 May Revolution, they were motivated much more by such hoary revolutionary figures as Trotsky, Liebknecht and Rosa Luxemburg than by such counter-culture heroes as Timothy Leary, Allen Ginsberg, Alan Watt or Abbie Hoffman. A revolutionary movement that relies upon the workers' support for its successful fruition can have very little to do with the generation gap.

If, then, we are going to examine what influence television may have had upon the widening of differences between the young and their elders, it is essential that we do not get misled by trying to find some cosmic common denominator like the loss of religious faith or the prospect of atomic annihilation. Manifestations of youthful dissent and protest have been varied and multitudinous in the 1950s and the 1960s. Television, obviously, could not have had much effect on many of these in certain countries — France, for example — simply because television had played no part in shaping the attitudes and values of most of the protesters and revolutionaries. But where television has existed long enough and in sufficient volume to have made an impact upon a generation, can we detect anything in the quality and nature of certain types of youthful protest that can be attributed to the way television has been used in that society? In other words, has the small screen made any special contribution in America and Britain to the gulf that separates so many young from the world of their parents?

At the outset, it is probably prudent to assure those readers whose own children are emerging as recognisable replicas of themselves, ready to undertake the responsibilities and tasks of the immediate past, that they are not part of the dissident and alienated youth we are now discussing. In spite of the shadow of atomic extinction, the pressures of technocracy, the values of a consumer society, the menace of a population explosion, the decline in religious faith, the existence of entertainment-dominated, violence-saturated television, most young people will strive to make a success of their lives as orthodox farmers, craftsmen, lawyers, salesmen, executives, doctors, miners, dock workers, communicators and the rest. But majorities never changed anything very much. They have invariably been stimulated, provoked, inspired and led by provocative, persistent, aggressive, passionate minorities. The committed, involved and non-orthodox sector of youth — even if only a minority — are more likely to determine the shape of future society than the bulk of young people who placidly accept the status quo.

'Throughout the West it is the young who find themselves cast as the only effective radical opposition within their societies,' writes Theodore Roszak in *The Making of a Counter Culture*. 'Not all the young, of course: perhaps only a minority of the university campus population. Yet no analysis seems to make sense of the major political upheavals of the decade other than that which pits a militant minority of dissenting youth against the sluggish consensus-and-coalition politics of their middle-class elders.'[2]

Confining, then, our attention to Britain and America in the 1950s and 1960s, what were the broad categories of youthful dissent and alienation? Richard Neville in *Play Power* has classified the radical international youth movement into three divisions. While it may be difficult to squeeze every manifestation of youth protest into these three groups — the Chinese Red Guard, for instance, hardly fit — they are reasonable enough classifications for America and Britain.

'The terms *New Left Underground* and "*militant poor*" are loosely applicable through the wide and scattered domain of youthful insurgency,' says Neville. 'Sometimes these categories generously overlap, at other times, less generously, they conflict. The *New Left* is comprised largely of the "alphabet soup" of student protest (S.D.S., S.N.C.C., N.A.C.L.A., R.S.A., B.L.F., R.S.S.F, etc) with just occasionally a dash of L.S.D.

'That unpopular label, *Underground*, embraces hippies, mystics, madmen, freaks, yippies, crazies, crackpots, communards and anyone who rejects rigid political ideology ("it's a brain disease") and believes that once you have blown your own mind, the Bastille will blow up itself. The *militant poor*, whose struggles require a separate book, include Europe's radical young workers, blacks and assorted ethnic communities emerging in the United States.

'In different areas, at different times, a different compound of these categories becomes the agency of disruption. The actions of the *New Left* are said to be "political". The antics of the *Underground* are said to be "cultural". In fact, both sociological manifestations are part of the behaviour pattern of a single discontented body.'[3]

But whether their actions are 'political' or 'cultural', the root cause that unites these protest movements is a disappointment, disillusionment or disgust with the spiritual and environmental heritage handed down to them by their elders. Students, of course, have been the shock troops of social upheaval since the days of the French Revolution, if not before. What distinguishes these political manifestations of the young — particularly in entertainment-oriented, telly democracies — is the way in which they increasingly reflect those other consequences of the positive television factor I had discussed earlier — the growing disrespect for authority and the growing acceptance of violence as a normal or moral act.

The random and generalised nature of this resentment against authority has few, if any, precedents in modern history. In the past, dissident youth has pin-pointed its particular authoritarian bogies with a certain amount of precision. Individuals may have hated their parents, loathed certain politicians, rejected priests or generals or philosophers. But the alienated youth of today lump father, President, Monarch, Prime Minister, Pope, politician, policeman, priest, professor, teacher, publisher, executive, scientist, together as an army of obsolete and discredited relics of the past.

The political fringe of the protest movement still bears banners flaunting portraits of Marx, Mao, Trotsky and Marcuse, but these revered icons represent less a true link with historical dialectic than images designed to frighten the wits out of the bourgeoisie and established authority. The Underground and non-political wing of alienated youth do not make even these obeisances to the contributions of other generations. With them, authority must be totally rejected. Such wisdom as reposes in the past they prefer to seek in the East rather than the West — in Zen, Taoism, Hinduism and mystic Christianity.

In America, Britain and Canada the magnitude and intensity of this generational conflict began to reach startling proportions in 1966 and 1967. Resentment and rejection of the acquisitive, technological and hypocritical values of the immediate post-war ruling generation were already evident amongst the young of the middle 1950s. British youth began to look back in anger as they read John Osborne and marched from Aldermaston on C.N.D. demonstrations. American youth were taking to the open roads and opting-out according to the beatnik philosophy of Allen Ginsberg and Jack Kerouac. But the numbers were always relatively small and their significance exaggerated by the media. It was not until a decade later that this small trickle of youthful protest against the life-style of their elders turned into a flood which shook the ruling Establishments in the West and sent them into a state of shock from which they have not yet recovered.

Who were these additional recruits who joined in their hundreds of thousands the ranks of hippiedom and student protest? Why was there a sudden and startling increase beginning about 1965 in the number of young people who simultaneously found drugs, sexual freedom, anarchic political protest, violent rejection of authority, active alienation from social norms, an attractive alternative way of life? The beatniks had been around since the middle 1950s. There had been an Underground press in America as early as 1955 when *The Village Voice* was first published. There were political and social causes which roused student protest in the 1950s and early 1960s such as the Campaign for Nuclear Disarmament and the Freedom Fighters campaigning against racial segregation in America.

But why from 1965 on did thousands of beatniks proliferate into hundreds of thousands of hippies? Why was there a phenomenal eruption of Underground newspapers and magazines — the *International Times* and *Oz* in Britain, the *Los Angeles Free Press*, *Other Scenes*, *East Village Other*, *The Berkeley Barb*, *Rat* in America, the *Vancouver Free Press*, *Octopus*, *Tribal Village* in Canada — and why did the older Underground papers see their circulation rise from hundreds to tens of thousands? Why did the tone and mood of political demonstrations escalate from relatively orderly demonstrations to the vicious confrontations we began to see in the latter half of the 1960s?

And, finally, why were these manifestations of youthful protest and rejection so much more in evidence, so much larger in the sheer numbers of those involved in them, in the frivolity-dominated telly democracies than in other countries in the world? Of course, there were hippies and Underground papers and student demonstrators in Italy, Holland, Sweden, West Germany and most European countries. But they never flourished to anything like the degree that they did in Britain and America, with few magazines surviving for any lengthy period of time.

As far as political activists amongst the young were concerned, the Rudi Dutschkes and Cohn-Bendits were following a tradition of student involvement in politics in Europe going back to the French Revolution. Except for such romantic revolutionaries as Byron and Shelley, it cannot be said that social upheaval in Britain has been marked by any large-scale involvement of the young. From the Chartists until the General Strike of 1926, it was the workers and middle-class intellectuals who were primarily engaged in active political dissent. Not until the Spanish Civil War could one detect a true revolutionary fervour amongst a substantial number of students. When in 1933 the Oxford Union voted against fighting for King and Country a shudder of disbelief ran through the nation. Similarly in America, there was relatively little participation by students in either revolutionary events or movements from the founding of the Republic to the end of the Second World War.

What happened, then, in the middle 1960s to activate these disparate groups of young people into such violent or alienating gestures against the entire mainstream of their parents' culture? The cynicism about religion, the fear of over-population, the prospects of man's atomic extinction, the stifling demands of technocracy, were all apocalyptic shadows hovering over mankind in the 1950s. Why did we not get the young practising 'total rejection' in that decade?

Again, as we asked over the question of violence, was this merely a bizarre coincidence? According to Charles Reich in *The Greening of America,* the new Consciousness amongst the American young originated with the impoverishment of life, the irrationality, violence and claustrophobia of the American Corporate State. 'The new consciousness is the product of two interacting forces: the promise of life that is made to young Americans by all our affluence, technology, liberation and ideals, and the threat to that promise posed by everything from

227

neon ugliness and boring jobs to the Vietnam War and the shadow of the nuclear holocaust. Neither the promise nor the threat is the cause by itself; but the two together have done it,' writes Reich.[4]

The trouble with this analysis is that most of its factors — with the exception of the Vietnam War and atomic annihilation — could have been said to have been influencing American youth in the 1930s, let alone the '40s or '50s. Then how is it that dissident British youth, without the violent and irrational accoutrements of the Corporate State and without a promise of affluence and liberation or a threat of the Vietnam War, have moved in the very same direction and speak much the same language of rejection as America in almost the *very same years?*

Could it be that by the middle 1960s our societies through the medium of television had presented to an entire generation a vivid and convincing microcosm of everything that was said to be wrong with life in America and Britain? We have already seen in earlier chapters how the representatives of authority — politicians, churchmen, trade union leaders — have steadily demeaned themselves and their functions by readily cavorting as bit part players in the show-biz spectacular of television. By 1966 there had arrived on the social scene the first generation who had from their earliest formative years watched daily a mosaic of their country's life-style on television. It was a mosaic primarily dedicated to the quick sell, the easy laugh and the fast buck. It portrayed no concept of social responsibility other than faith in the status quo; no promise of spiritual enrichment other than through commercial success; no consistent ethical message other than the right to use force as a means to a moral end. It was a mosaic in which the leaders of men could be seen adopting the make-up and the mannerisms and the techniques of the entertainer to gain public favour. It reflected life as primarily disorganised, frivolous and, to a large extent, pointless. The total mosaic of life as seen on the small screen was *not* concerned, *not* serious, *not* logical, *not* involved.

Is it any wonder, then, that the idealistic young should react with intensity and revulsion against this picture of the life-style of their elders and their country? Of course, it will be argued that television's version of society was not the only one the

228

young experienced. They had their own home life, their communal activities, their schools, their newspapers and books, against which to check the validity and veracity of the total television image. The majority of the young obviously do not accept television's image of British and American societies or we would have our streets and universities filled with hippies and protesters. But the dissidents have always been a minority. For those amongst the young who would naturally rebel, who wanted to change things as they saw them in their immediate environment, who were frustrated by poverty and a mean education, who had an unhappy home life, who were visionaries or idealists, who were mentally unstable, who were bitter about racial discrimination — and it is from their ranks that the challenge to the status quo and the older generation has always come — there was nightly offered to them in their living rooms evidence to justify their discontent with society.

Television did not originate their dissatisfactions but it confirmed and intensified them. The telly generation, bolstered with that evidence, needed little persuasion to be convinced that social institutions were corrupt and dehumanising and that authority was incompetent, insensitive and hypocritical. By the mid-1960s there had been produced, through the inadvertent efforts of television an unprecedented number of young people under the age of 21 ready to oppose and defy authority or drop out of any involvement with institutionalised, traditional society. It was the tapping of this reservoir of discontent that transformed the normal pools of rebellion amongst the young into the floodtide of alienation and rejection that has not yet seriously receded.

At this stage I must concede that any theory that attempts to associate television with the extraordinary volume of youthful dissent and alienation in Britain and America can only be speculative. Direct statistical evidence such as we have when establishing a link between television and criminal violence does not exist to vindicate such a theory. If young people were asked to name the factors that had provoked them into rebellion or rejection they would probably answer that they 'don't dig society', 'couldn't stand society's ideals', wanted to 'do their own thing', were sickened by the hypocrisy and materialism of society, wanted to find sexual and spiritual freedom, were in search of universal love. Few of them would list television.

This is not surprising. Television's influence is much too subtle to be detected by its victims. The easiest trick in the world to debunk the influence of television is one used by David Frost. He asks an audience: 'Is there anyone in this room who would say that television has brainwashed them into believing what they do not really believe?' Naturally, no one puts up his hand. That for Mr. Frost is convincing evidence that television has little influence in changing or forming people's attitudes or values.[5] As an experiment it is as conclusive as asking a sexual deviant if it is breast starvation that is responsible for his tastes, or an aggressive paranoic if it is brain damage that stimulated him to violence. How could they possibly know?

There is little doubt, however, that particularly amongst hippies and drop-outs the vision of the 'plastic' or 'straight' society they most vehemently deride is the one presented to them on the small screen. The Underground press regularly vilifies the box. Ridiculing it is one of the favourite sports of the so-called counter-culture. Television is considered to be the super-salesman of the system peddling myths and dreams that will lull the people into a willing acceptance of their boring, consumer-motivated, God-haunted, culturally deprived, spiritually empty, treadmill existence. The picture of a middle-aged man drinking beer watching a Western on the box is the image of the older generation most frequently conjured up by the alienated young.

The proper stance to take about television is to laugh it out of existence. This is the view of Charles Reich laying down some methods by which the new Consciousness amongst the young can subvert and change the false culture that flows from the medium. 'One can watch television, the news, the ads, the commentators, the dramas, and just laugh and laugh; all the power of television turns impotent and absurd,' he writes.[6]

When, in London in November 1970, a group of yippies took over *The Frost Programme* and forced Frost to continue his programme from a different studio, Jerry Rubin, the American yippie leader, just had time to make a few pungent remarks about television. 'We stand for the disruption of a society demented by money, we want to put judges in jail, make war against pigs, destroy narcissistic television like this,' said Rubin, when asked by Frost to describe his ideological position. 'In our society, we would stuff you and put you in a people's museum as a remnant of the last culture.'

The ability of television to present itself as a true and convincing reflection of the society in which it operates is perhaps the greatest confidence trick yet achieved by any medium. The avowed aim of television is to provide entertainment or, in other words, escape from reality. An escape from reality cannot be reality. It must be an illusion, a fantasy, a distortion, a lie.

And yet because of its peculiar visual properties and its association with the private environment of the home, it is not deemed to be a liar in the living-room. On the contrary, it is trusted and believed in a way in which no other medium before it has been trusted or believed. For the sensitive and deprived young, particularly, it turns out to be the greatest deceiver of all.

'Our society insists that children first be taught the prescribed mythology, in school, in films and, earliest and most universally, on television,' writes Charles Reich. 'The television world is what our society claims itself to be, what it demands we believe. But when the television child finally encounters the real world, he does not find families like Ozzie, Harriet, David and Ricky, "Father Knows Best", or "My Three Sons". He does not find the clean suburbs of television but the sordid slums of reality. He does not find the high-minded statesman of the screen, but politicians who are mediocre, small-minded and corrupt. He does not find perpetual smiles or the effervescent high spirits of a Coke ad, but anxieties and monotony. And when he stops believing in this mythical world, the breach in his credulity is irreparable. Society and television ask total belief; when their picture of the world is unmasked, the result is total disbelief. The child of an earlier generation could get some unsettling shocks without coming to disbelieve everything, but the faith that is now taught is so complete it cannot survive a shock. The child becomes a sceptic of everything. He sees right through every form of posture and pretence; he believes nothing he is told; he experiences that crucial feeling of the new generation, betrayal.'[7]

Before television, a child grew to maturity within the confines of the relatively narrow child's world. It was a slow, gradual development in which the child could adjust reasonably leisurely to a limited area of experience as his senses acquired the abilities to understand or enjoy them. If, as he grew older, he became disillusioned, bored or impatient with the world within his immediate, direct experience, he could always hope for something better around the corner, something more exciting over the hill, something more worthwhile or more testing or more satisfying in the next town or city or country. Television, however, denies him an escape route. He soon learns that things around the corner, places over the hill are likely to be as unrewarding and frustrating as where he is.

There can be no generation of children — at least in modern times — that has been expected to select, without intelligent supervision or guidance, from amongst myriads of concepts and images (most of them directed at adults) the ones that will be good for it and reject those that are bad for it and society. The belief that this selective process will be wisely carried out by children from infancy to adolescence is a touching demonstration of man's inherent faith in his own ability to survive. But is there any real evidence that such trust in a child's instinctive moral geiger-counter has been justified?

All the signs indicate that instead of choosing amongst the multitude of values and standards and concepts offered them on television those which their parents and the Establishment would prefer them to choose, a large section of the young have either perversely selected other values or rejected the whole bumper package *in toto*. Because television acts as total environment, its picture of life is accepted by the very young as a picture of real life. It is also an extension of their home lives, their neighbourhoods, their dream lives.

By the time children have moved into adolescence some will have begun to question the rightness of the values and standards of the adult world. The initial impulse to resent or reject adult values will probably be triggered off, as it always has been, by direct experience. Resentment or hatred of parents; frustration due to poverty or lack of opportunity; boredom with the immediate environment; mental or physical illness; failure or non-acceptance at school or amongst colleagues; inability to cope with expectations of parents, teachers or neighbours; eagerness to keep up with the members of a rebellious or anti-conformist peer group — these are merely some of the reasons that motivate children to turn away from the accepted attitudes of an older generation. When, coupled with this disillusionment and disappointment in their personal lives, they also discover at about 14 or 15 that they have been nurtured through television with a vision of life that is also illusory and unattainable, their sense of betrayal is, as Charles Reich says, painful and acute. They identify the failure in their own lives with the failure of the dream they had for escaping or eradicating it. Somewhere, sometime, television had promised them that things would be better. But the big world on the small screen has turned out in reality to be as monotonous, frustrating and hurtful as the private world they want to reject. Television has confirmed and reinforced their disillusionment not only with their own lives but with the total life that has been offered them by the older generation.

Thus the manner in which television acts as a positive factor in demeaning authority appears to be bearing fruit amongst the dissident young. Are they also affected by that other positive message of the medium — the normality and morality of violence? We have already seen how there is a clear statistical link between the telly generations in Britain, America and Canada and the growth of criminal acts of violence. Is there any evidence that violence has also increased amongst the young seeking political and cultural ways of changing society? On this question, one must make a distinction between the political or revolutionary wing of dissident youth and the hippie drop-outs or proponents of a counter-culture.

In the late 1950s and early 1960s, the philosophy of the New Left and the beatnik disciples of Allen Ginsberg were both permeated with a deeply felt conviction that love and tenderness could be effectively harnessed to bring about a beneficial change in man's condition. The 'flower people' convinced themselves that if their vibrations were right they could even come to love 'the cops'. A 1962 statement of a New Left student group reads: 'We regard *man* as infinitely precious and possessed of unfulfilled capacities for reason, freedom and love . . . We oppose the depersonalisation that reduces human beings to the status of things. If anything, the brutalities of the twentieth century teach that means and ends are intimately related, that vague appeals to "posterity" cannot justify the mutilations of the present . . .'⁸

But by 1969, the New Left had spawned revolutionary groups whose crucial tactic for social change was violence. The most fanatical of these groups, the Weathermen, came into being as a direct splinter movement from the Students for a Democratic Society which was responsible for the pacific sentiments in the 1962 manifesto I have just quoted.

'The Weathermen do not simply talk about violence, they act it out,' wrote Jeremy Campbell in the London *Evening Standard* on November 5th, 1969. 'Last month, they rampaged through the streets of Chicago armed with clubs and wearing motorcycle helmets, smashing the windows of parked cars and department stores and injuring 40 policemen. In September, five Weathermen invaded a classroom at a girls' school in Boston, manacled an English teacher, cut off the telephone and handed out revolutionary leaflets. In another incident they gate-crashed a Harvard examination hall and when two students attempted to leave, knocked them unconscious with karate blows . . . It is easy, and tempting, to dismiss the Weathermen as club-swinging buffoons, capering on the fringes of anarchy . . . But the Weathermen do stand for something significant and disturbing in the student radical movement: a mounting sense of frustration and a growing acceptance of violence as an instrument of political change.'

This same recognition of the increasing prevalence and justification of violence amongst the disaffected and idealistic young was voiced by Theodore Roszak, whose views are on the whole sympathetic to the aims of the counter-culture. 'I am bleakly aware that an ideological drift towards righteous violence is on the increase among the young, primarily under the influence of the extremist Black Powerites and a romanticised conception of guerilla warfare,' says Roszak '. . . The tragic search may be on again among radical dissenters for ways to "make murder legitimate", as Camus phrased it — and with this tendency the New Left runs the risk of losing its original soulfulness. For the beauty of the New Left has always lain in its eagerness to give political dignity to the tenderer emotions, in its readiness to talk openly of love, and non-violence, and pity. It is, therefore, depressing in the extreme when, on behalf of a self-congratulatory militancy, this humane spirit threatens to give way to the age-old politics of hatred, vindictiveness, and windy indignation. At this point, things do not simply become ugly; they become stupid. Suddenly the measure of conviction the efficiency with which one can get into a fistfight with the nearest cop at hand.'[9]

Nor is it only the extreme fringe of the radical young that has embraced violence as a necessary and moral attribute of political action. Replying to a Gallup poll conducted in late 1970, 44 per cent of college students thought that violence was justified to bring about social change in the United States (compared to 14 per cent of the public at large); 48 per cent believed that personal freedom and the right to dissent were being curbed in the United States; and 37 per cent described themselves as 'far left' or 'left' politically, compared with 17 per cent who called themselves 'right' or 'far right'.[10]

This readiness to challenge the Establishment with overt demonstrations of violence is also a feature of the more extreme radical student groups in Britain. Although the massive anti-Vietnam parade in October 1968 was, on the whole, designed to be an orderly and peaceful protest, the organisers could not control a small minority of the marchers determined to provoke a confrontation with the police by storming the American Embassy. The rampage in a Cambridge hotel by students protesting against the Greek Colonels' regime provoked fierce prison sentences for the young men who had been convicted of taking part. And the activities of the Angry Brigade, another manifestation of youthful revolt, has included the planting of bombs in public places and in the homes of public figures whose views they oppose.

But if the criminal young and the politically rebellious young have taken to violence in this unprecedented way, surely there is one section of the telly generation that is more aggressively pacific than ever their fathers were — the beatniks, the hippies, the flower people. It might even logically be argued that the very intensity of the proclaimed passivity of the hippies is a positive rejection of the violent world of their parents as they have seen it manifested on television. In other words, the conditioning effect of television has not only produced more violence amongst the criminally-prone and the political dissidents, but it has also induced amongst the culturally alienated a revulsion against the violent way of life they have seen on the box.

Whether society can afford to derive much satisfaction from a medium that might be encouraging the young to become non-violent purely as a gesture of disgust and rejection of that whole society, is doubtful. But, alas, there is a good deal of evidence that even amongst those who loudly proclaim that it is better 'to make love not war', there is a disturbing acceptance of violence which too often belies and contradicts their noble slogans and intentions.

The Underground press, for example, is replete with comic book imagery that revels in grotesque bestiality beyond the wildest dreams of *Tom and Jerry* animators. Its typography has the crude, jagged immediacy of a high-pitched yell. Its illustrations seem inspired by mind-bursting psychedelic visions and the crudest forms of *graffiti*. Its campaigns eschew understatement and concentrate on the outraged shriek. Its language generally rails, thumps and shocks rather than reasons or elucidates.

'There are manifestations around the fringe of the counter-culture that one cannot but regard as worrisomely unhealthy,' writes Theodore Roszak. 'Elements of pornographic grotesquery and bloodcurdling sadomasochism emerge again and again in the art and theatre of our youth culture and intrude themselves constantly into the Underground press. Many of the Underground newspapers seem to work on the assumption that talking about anything frankly means talking about it as crudely and as savagely as possible ... Even where such crudity is meant to satirise or reply in kind to the corruptions of the dominant culture, there is bound to come a point were sardonic imitation destroys the sensibilities and produces simple callousness.'[11]

When a feud develops between conflicting groups in the Underground, they do not pelt each other with flowers but adopt techniques reminiscent of the manner in which quarrels are settled in a television Western. The *International Times* of December 30th, 1971 carried this account of dissension between way-out pop addicts and the American *Rolling Stone* magazine which in 1968 Richard Neville praised for its crusading zeal, its wit and imagination, and its 'inherent libertarianism'.[12]

'A bunch of freaks under the aegis of the *Rock Liberation Front* recently forcibly invaded and occupied the offices of *Rolling Stone* for several hours,' read the story, carrying a New York dateline. 'The occupation followed several hours of demonstrations in front of a townhouse owned by Paul McCartney's manager and father-in-law, John Eastman. The McCartney demonstration was to protest against "McCartneyism" which was defined as the apolitical songs and apolitical life style which has consciously been projected by the former Beatle . . . Marching to the Rolling Stone Offices, they found the place locked up, but an infiltrator threw open the door, and about 60 people stormed in and sat down on the floor . . . While confusion reigned in the office, several members of the crowd, said to be members of the "Magic Christian Collective", systematically rifled the files in search of something incriminating. When a large bundle of liberated files were carried towards the door, three Rolling Stone thugs jumped the perpetrators and a 20 minute free-for-all ensued, like a scene from a John Wayne movie.'

It is this alienation from authority and the acceptance of violence that so often bewilders the older generation about their young. These attitudes have undoubtedly played a significant part in widening the generation gap. While there may be disagreement about how significant television's responsibility has been in creating that gap, it is quite evident that it has done precious little to narrow it.

Entertainment-oriented television caters predominantly for mature and elderly audiences. Even children's programmes are largely designed to relieve parents of the chore of educating or entertaining their offspring. Every survey of viewing habits indicated that the age group between 16 and 21 watches less than other age groups. During these years teenagers are making social contacts outside the home, studying, courting, going to the cinema, attending university, playing outdoor games or taking part in other group activities with people of their own age. These activities take them away from the box and they do not return to it as heavy viewers until they marry and become more homebound.

Since this kind of television is largely financed by advertising, there is a natural tendency to provide programmes which will appeal to the groups that not only have the greatest spending power but also watch it most. With the very young tucked away in bed and with the teenagers outside the house, the bulk of viewers at peak time are composed of young parents, the middle-aged and the elderly. Since their purchasing power is what the commercials are aimed at, great care is taken that the small screen does not offend them. Said an important advertising executive to an American Governmental committee: 'A programme that displeases any substantial segment of the population is a misuse of the advertising dollar.'[13] It is the fear of irritating or disturbing even a minute proportion of this mass of potential customers that accounts for the bland, non-controversial, predictable quality of almost all television financed by advertising money.

It is not surprising, then, that spokesmen for the dissident young or the views of the counter-culture are rarely given any exposure on television. The sight of long-haired hippies advocating free love or demanding liberalisation of the drug laws in a peak-time programme would not only outrage many middle-aged viewers but would provoke fierce protest from politicians determined to maintain television as a castrated social force. Television executives, always eager for a quiet life and sensitive to any whiff of public disapproval, see to it that the box only rarely acknowledges the existence of a social phenomenon that captured the imagination of an entire generation and that dominated the lives of a substantial section of young people in the late 1960s.

When, for example, the BBC in 1968, following on the events of the May uprisings in France, decided to invite to Britain certain student leaders of the European Left to discuss their aims and policies, protests against their being heard on British television echoed loudly in newspapers and Parliament. The foundations of British society would apparently be threatened, according to some of these voices, if such students as Daniel Cohn-Bendit were to be allowed to transmit subversive ideas to the British public. One single programme called *Students in*

Revolt, because it contained anarchic and revolutionary students from countries like France, Yugoslavia and Germany, was denounced as a dangerous exercise of irresponsible judgment on the part of the Corporation.

Just as political dissidents are, except for token gestures, banned from the small screen in Britain so is the hippie movement denied access on television. From time to time young people who have opted out of conventional society are invited to take part in a talk programme — usually in the Sunday religious slot where their views can be balanced or nullified by a parson or a middle-aged social worker — but such appearances are extremely rare. Indeed, the rigid format of the talk show with its polite ping-pong of views limited to a few minutes from each speaker is no place in which hippies can convincingly present their case. Their rejection of forms and conventions, their contempt for the logic of established authority, their tendency to ramble and declaim rather than debate along orthodox lines, makes them appear particularly alien and frightening to the average viewer who is embarrassed and disturbed by untoward behaviour on the box. Television has cultivated its own brand of genteel etiquette — no bad language or insulting behaviour — which rouses much indignation when it is transgressed. Hippies are not likely to respect such rules. The television executive, more concerned with protecting his audience from shock than disseminating information, is naturally reluctant to take risks with hippie appearances.

Thus when Jerry Rubin, the American Yippie leader, was invited on *The Frost Programme,* he would not give the producers of the show a positive assurance that his language would be acceptable or that he would vacate the rostrum when his appearance was over. To cover any untoward event, an alternative studio was set up by the producers to which David Frost could retreat in case things got out of hand on the night. Their precautions proved necessary. Rubin not only attacked Frost for having 'debated with a mass murderer — Spiro Agnew', but claimed to be smoking hash on the programme and urged 15 of his followers to take over the studio floor. Their simian antics, shouts and obscenities hogged the screen for a few minutes until the television commercials came to Frost's rescue. Naturally there were outraged calls the next morning for an investigation into such an insult and affront to viewers. Retractions were called for and assurances demanded that such people as yippies be banned from television.

In America, too, broadcasting authorities are bothered by the problem of wanting to give hippies occasional, fleeting appearances on television and at the same time needing to guarantee that they do not unduly offend their viewers. Following the Chicago conspiracy trial, the defendants were invited to appear on almost every major talk show. But just as Jerry Rubin caused trouble for the Frost show in Britain, so did the appearance of Abbie Hoffman prove a headache for the Merv Griffin show in America.

'The Chicago Seven, the engaging crowd of radical eccentrics who starred in the winter's marathon trial, have the Establishment here demonstrably rattled,' wrote Michael Leapman from New York in *The Times*, on April 6th, 1970. 'Proof of this came last weekend when one of them, Abbie Hoffman, appeared on Merv Griffin's late-night television talk show wearing a shirt made out of the American flag.

'Or, rather, he did not appear wearing the shirt. For senior executives of the Columbia Broadcasting System (which counts as part of the Establishment by most reckonings) blacked out all the shots of it, although they allowed Mr. Hoffman's verbal message to get through to the viewers.

'People who phoned to complain about the mess this made of their screens pointed out that Roy Rogers, the singing cowboy, was allowed to wear a similar shirt in a variety show earlier in the year and that a current commercial for a new car includes a man dressed as Uncle Sam.

'The television people replied that if Mr. Hoffman, a self-confessed revolutionary, were seen wearing the flag some viewers might be offended. Yet they knew before inviting him that his stock-in-trade is to offend just those people who hold the flag dear and who are certain to be angered anyway by what he had to say . . .'

It would, of course, be unrealistic to expect that any broadcasting organisation relying upon advertising income and the goodwill of the Establishment would turn television into a ready platform for ideas that it considered dangerous and subversive. But surely it should be possible for television to present from time to time a fair and unbiased account of the opinions of the young without this being interpreted as incitement to revolution.

Yet such a reasonable and essential service to the community is precisely what television cannot do with its present priorities. Since the bulk of available time must be devoted to amusement and entertainment, there is a jostling queue of interests trying to squeeze into the remaining few hours. With so many sections of society already denied access to the box, it is hardly surprising that students, dissidents, revolutionaries, find the doors of broadcasting studios shut to them.

Thus the present structure of television in Britain and America distorts or stifles any dialogue between the generations. There is no place on television, except for pop music programmes, where the young can feel free to do and say things in their own way. The television hierarchy acknowledges only in a token and perfunctory manner the existence of a significant social phenomenon. Their justification for indulging in this reassuring lie is that exposure on television will merely encourage the spread of anti-social activities such as drug-taking, permissiveness and anarchy.

Now there is not a tittle of evidence that being banned from the small screen has in any way deterred hundreds of thousands of young people from joining the ranks of the disillusioned, the alienated, the dropped-out and the rebellious. Indeed, the more restrictive television has become the more determined have the dissident young become to find other means of spreading their gospel. The very fact that the most powerful medium is afraid to transmit their views convinced them that those views must be right. Otherwise 'straight' society would be able to face up to the argument and the challenge. Thus they retreat into their own underground where they organise their own press, cultivate their own life-style, communicate chiefly with their own generation, insulate themselves against the reason and values of their elders.

It is, of course, not only television that averts its eyes from a recognition of the so-called alternative society. The other media — radio, the press, magazines — only fitfully and gingerly recognise its existence. Even if some of these organs of opinion were ready to risk offending their regular audiences, they would find that a whole phalanx of legal limitations would prevent them from adopting the tone of the counter-culture.

'The Underground press is a goldmine (or gravel pit) of news and opinions that can never find its way into straight media because it transcends the self-imposed bounds of good taste or infringes covenants of libel, blasphemy, obscenity, sedition or veracity,' wrote Richard Neville, explaining the difficulties that would beset ordinary newspapers if they tried to ape the ways of the alternative press.[14]

Serious newspapers and magazines, however, do report and comment upon the issues that interest the alienated young — drugs, Vietnam, student unrest, police corruption, Black Power — far more often and far more deeply than does television. It is true that the straight press is usually critical about such issues as drugs and permissiveness, but at least in the columns of newspapers there is a recognition that such practices exist and that large numbers of young people take part in them.

But television is under relentless pressure to avoid such issues, to bury them under a discreet carpet of neglect, to permit them on the screen only with the utmost trepidation and then to ensure that when they are aired they are unlikely to be taken seriously.

Since we are building up a society in which most people get most of their facts about the outside world from television and not from the printed media, the inability or refusal of the television hierarchy to comment adequately on the counter-culture means that large sections of the population remain ignorant about what it is that has caused such alien and baffling behaviour in their children. With little to guide them about what is happening, they react with anger, fury, fear or resignation to the activities of the dissident youth movement. Unable to provide the necessary facilities for programmes that might bridge the chasm of misunderstanding between the young and the old, television exacerbates the situation by its neglect of the problem or its distortion of the truth. It thus has acted as a positive factor in maintaining and widening the ugly generation gap that has plagued Britain and America in the late 1960s and early 1970s.

CHAPTER EIGHT

The Telly Trip

Current models of social adjustment – mechanised,
computerised, socialised, intellectualised, televised,
Sanforised – make no sense to the new LSD generation,
who see clearly that American society is becoming an
air-conditioned anthill.
> Timothy Leary, *The Politics of Ecstasy*

The youth versus age factor is a particular charac-
teristic of the drug problem. One of the more famous
saying in the cannabis coteries is 'don't trust anyone
over thirty'.
> Michael Schofield, *The Strange Case of Pot*

The literature on drug abuse is extensive and contradictory.
There have been almost 2,000 books and serious articles published on cannabis alone. Although there is a certain amount of
agreement on *how* drugs affect the human body and *who* takes
them, there is very little that is either convincing or authoritative about *why* people begin taking drugs in the first place.
In a book of this kind it would be presumptuous to make any
categorical assertions about a link between television and the
terrifying rise in illicit drug consumption amongst the young.

'In many ways we are closer here to the art of the novelist
than that of the social scientist. We can only offer hypothesis
. . .' said a Canadian Government Commission report, discussing the motivation of drug taking. 'It is idle to seek a single,
unifying explanation or theory. This whole area is character-
ised by bewildering diversity and conflicting impressions . . .'[1]

Nevertheless, when one examines the array of explanations
for drug use, there is a striking similarity between many of
them and the causes that have been advanced for the widening

243

of the generation gap. Indeed, although I recognise the speculative nature of the claim, I think there is already enough available evidence to suggest that television is a probable — as distinct from a positive — factor in the widespread increase of drug use, particularly amongst the young.

What is unusual about the global picture of the drug phenomenon in the middle 1960s is that its severest outbreaks should have occurred in three Western societies with practically no previous history of large-scale illegal drug consumption amongst those populations. Although other countries have also had an increase in drug taking, the rise has been neither so widespread nor as concentrated amongst adolescents as in America, Britain and Canada. In France, for example, the authorities became acutely concerned about drug consumption in the late 1960s. In 1969 it was estimated that there were 35,000 French taking drugs mostly cannabis. But in that same year Canada, with half of France's population, could count almost ten times that number of drug-users. Britain, with a slightly larger population than France, was considered by some sources to have 8 or 9 times France's total of drug users. And in America, heroin takers alone numbered hundreds of thousands, and cannabis users could be counted in the tens of millions.[2]

Other countries in Western Europe — Italy, Sweden, West Germany — have also had an upsurge in drug abuse but at nothing like the rate of escalation in Canada, America and Britain. A report by the World Health Organisation issued in 1971 notes the rapid acceleration of cannabis consumption in Canada and America in the late 1960s. It quotes surveys showing that one-third of American college students had taken cannabis at some time; up to 10 per cent of British university students had tried it, while only 1 per cent of students in Brazil had taken it at least once. 'There is no evidence of more than occasional use in most Eastern European countries,' notes this Report. 'In some North African countries with a long-established pattern of use among lower-class males, there appears to be no upsurge among youth or middle-class groups. In Morocco there are indications of an overall decline in cannabis use, associated with an increase in the use of alcohol.'[3]

It is thus clear that the rise in drug taking in the late 1960s

244

was not a world-wide phenomenon. Certain countries were hardly affected at all; others had relatively large increases; only a very few found that illegal drug use had become a serious national problem. While the reasons for the taking and craving for drugs would be varied and obscure, it is fair to assume that the rapid spread of the habit would be in some measure due to the speed and pervasiveness of contemporary communications media. As more people learn to read, as more people acquire radios and television sets, the customs and fads of one corner of the earth are noted and observed wherever the media are free to report them and feel that they are newsworthy. And the speed with which such information is transmitted and picked up is unprecedented in man's history.

But it is extremely unlikely that such a direct imitative response to a television programme would occur in any but a limited number of viewers. Inadvertently, the reporting of drugs on television, whether in the news, documentaries or current affairs programmes, probably creates an aura of acceptability about the activity. If admired pop singers like Mick Jagger and John Lennon are charged with drug offences teenagers are more likely to suspect the workings of the law than the morality of their idols. Their first experiences with cannabis also make young people dubious about the veracity of the terror tales they have heard from the older generation about pot smoking. The more television and the press discuss the subject, the more familiar it becomes. And with familiarity, the fear and awe surrounding the question of drug taking diminishes and eventually disappears altogether. With little ethical revulsion against illegal drug use amongst the young, the narcotics peddler is less likely to have his activities reported to the police than if his customers or victims truly felt they were being deliberately exploited for some evil design.

Programmes which discuss or display the use of drugs — documentaries, news bulletins, discussion shows or fictional drama — are not, in my opinion, those that encourage drug taking in any serious form or volume. Certainly a few people will be tempted to imitate what they see on the small screen in defiance of any warnings that usually accompany such programmes. But such cases are, I believe, relatively few and do not constitute the main argument for suspecting that the television experience and the desire for drugs are in some way linked.

However before one can advance any theory on the matter, it is necessary to differentiate between the various drugs that are being illegally consumed and the physiological and psychological reactions that are experienced by those who take them. Although there are a bewildering variety of drugs, the ones that will concern us here — and which constitute the vast bulk of illegal drugs — are the amphetamines, L.S.D., the opiates and especially heroin, and cannabis.

A brief run-through of the properties of the most popular illegal drugs reveals the diversity of psychological needs that they satisfy. Cannabis for repose, conviviality, creative extension; amphetamines for energy, excitement and 'kicks'; L.S.D. for adventure, mystical revelation, heightened awareness; heroin for a sexual spasm, social withdrawal, drowsy oblivion. Some drug takers test all these sensations; most drug users are content with only one. But there is no common denominator of tastes or desires that links them together. The escalation theory that there is a direct route from soft drugs like cannabis to hard drugs like heroin is clearly belied by the statistics. Millions try cannabis; relatively few end up taking heroin. It is clear that there can be no single explanation or theory that would account for all forms of illegal drug use.

What, then, has all this to do with television? It is curious that when one reads the explanations advanced by experts as to why people start taking drugs — particularly the young — many of those explanations seem to have some relevance to the television experience described in these pages. The three main conundrums that must be answered about the contemporary drug phenomenon are: why does anyone start taking illegal drugs in the first place; why do they continue to take them; and why did all this reach unprecedented proportions in the late 1960s?

Trying to solve the mystery of why individuals start taking drugs, the authorities fall back on such generalisations as a search for pleasure, curiosity, a desire to experiment, a longing for spiritual revelation, a desire to conform to what others in the peer group are doing. As to why so many youngsters should all be doing this at the same time in widely-separated countries, the experts suggest a bewildering range of causes which include technological change, increased affluence, the undermining of the nuclear family, scepticism about conventional religion, the ominous threats of nuclear power, overpopulation, environmental pollution, changes in attitudes to individual freedom and authority, rejection of material success and the work ethos, an alienation from existing values and norms.

Since the increase in drug-taking has taken place predominantly amongst the young, it is interesting to note how these explanations of the drug explosion are so very similar to the causes usually advanced for the generation gap. If then television has in some ways helped widen the generation gap, might it not also be playing some significant role in the encouragement of a recourse to drugs amongst the young?

When a mature adult — someone in their early twenties and over — decides to take an illegal drug for the first time, he or she has usually worked out some personal rationale for taking that decision. They are seeking relaxation from tensions, a break from reality, an exploration of oneself, an assertion of individual freedom, a desire to be convivial, a more sensitive appreciation of music and the arts, a desire for experimentation or adventure, a hope of better sexual awareness or performance, an exploration of consciousness, a desire to keep up with the young or their children. These are only some of the varied explanations adults advance for starting to take drugs in the first place. There are many more.

But when one examines the reasons given by teenagers for their initial drug experience, they tend to be far less sophisticated and far less complex than those advanced by adults. It is true that after they have been on L.S.D. or cannabis or heroin for any length of time, they begin to rationalise their reasons for drug taking along much the same lines as those used by older consumers. There appear to be three recurrent explanations that turn up over and over again as the trigger that propelled them into the drug scene. They wanted to gain the respect of their peers by doing what everybody else in their social group was doing. They were bored. They resented or resisted the lifestyle and values of their parents and/or society. Sometimes these motives existed in isolation; often they were jumbled together as one cause.

247

Here are some examples taken from a variety of sources investigating the drug phenomenon:

'I don't know if I would have been accepted by my friends if I hadn't used drugs. My feelings are that I wouldn't have been. I wanted to be like them. They were all using drugs because they got bored with things.' (A 14-year-old girl addict.)[4]

'Sure, I use pot. It feels good. My God, my dad really thinks that makes me an addict. He's a scared man. When I tell him he smokes, drinks, and uses tranks (tranquillizers), he says "Two wrongs don't make a right." But all the time he's running around. He says he has to support a family and pay the bills, but man, he runs just to run.' (A 19-year-old boy.)[5]

'I couldn't stand the ideals of society, its customs and traditions. And my damned parents.' (A 15-year-old hippie.)[6]

'I got sick of L.B.J.'s society — I just don't see how what he is doing is of any use. My father is a sergeant in the Army and fought in Vietnam. That's not for me — definitely.' (A 16-year-old drop-out.)[7]

'Mr. Jones (the average American) is basically not a happy person. Mr. Jones comes home at night, he's tired — he has a beer, he watches television, and goes to bed. He gets up the next morning and goes through the same thing. Mr. Jones is caught up in a very depressing sort of life and he knows that his children would say that he is not basically a happy man.' (A 22-year-old hippie justifying pot and L.S.D.)[8]

Although these statements are from American drug takers, they are echoed in almost the same words by British and Canadian youngsters. If they do not start to take drugs simply because someone in their group is doing so, it will probably be because they are bored or because they are reacting against the life-style of their parents. In other words, drug taking is a positive defiant gesture against the older generation, which is made either by rejecting their values or by adopting the values of their own group. 'Doing one's own thing' in many cases merely means 'not doing the orthodox or expected thing'.

We have seen how television acts as a positive factor in undermining authority. We have also examined television's probable responsibility for widening the generation gap. Television assures the sceptical young that the straight or plastic society is everywhere — in Montreal as well as Moose Jaw, in

New York as well as Akron, in London as well as Hereford. It is inescapable. The true drop-outs and true addicts reject it totally.

Most young people, of course, when they try cannabis or amphetamines for the first time have no intention of adopting a hippie life, nor do the vast bulk of them ever become drop-outs or addicts. What they probably recognise — and what gives them their initial thrill — is the knowledge that they are engaging in an illegal act. Coupled with the excitement of illegality is the awareness that what they are doing is the gesture most likely to shock, anger or frighten their parents. They know that most parents would view with benign tolerance a first cigarette or a first drunken experience. But illegal drug taking constitutes a particularly aggressive and deliberate act of defiance against authority. And if television has tarnished the substance or justification for that authority, more and more young people will be prepared to thumb their noses at it by smoking a joint or swallowing amphetamines.

This connection between drug taking and the rejection of accepted norms and life-styles — the picture of life television executives boast so often they are mirroring — is recognised by every serious authority as one of the major causes of drug taking amongst the young in Britain, America and Canada. Said the Canadian Commission on drugs: 'Because cannabis is illicit and the object of strong disapproval from those who are, by and large, opposed to social change, it is a symbol of protest . . . This Commission has very often been told by young people that they reject all that is traditional, conventional and stereotyped, because they consider it to be hypocritical, phony, dehumanising, threatening and ugly. As a result, they may become alienated and some may be plunged into a frantic search for an identity which may be accepted to them by their own standards.'[9]

Said Dr. Norman Zinberg, an American authority on drugs: 'By choosing the very drugs damned as harmful and evil by their middle-class parents, and used traditionally by the people their parents most wish to stand apart from — the blacks, the outcasts, the apathetic — the cannabis-using generation rebels against its parents' more and does so in an aggressive and painful way.'[10]

Said Professor Lewis Yabolonsky in *The Hippie Trip*:

'Most youths who drop out into the hippie movement have access to and usually can have all the cultural prizes of American society. Their condemnation and rejection is total. They reject the American family, religion, education, government, and the economic and materialistic prizes of American society . . .'[11]

Thus there seems to be a united front on the part of authorities, on the anti-authoritarian motives for drug taking. Yet in other countries where cannabis has had a longer history of heavy use — India, North Africa, Mexico, Thailand — the causes of cannabis consumption tend to be either purely social, medicinal, religious, ritualistic or aphrodisiacal. In these countries usage is much more evenly distributed amongst all age groups. The idea of taking drugs as a symbol of authority-rejection is rarely heard or expressed.[12]

What, then, has caused this disillusionment with authority in Western telly societies that provokes many adolescents into their first drug experience? If the small screen plays a positive role in helping to create that disillusionment and disenchantment with the life-style of their elders is it not valid to assume that in this respect there exists a direct link between drugs and the box?

Again, as on the question of drug-taking and authority-rejection, there is a measure of agreement that the frustrations attendant on trying to reach goals that are pitched too high may be a cause of illegal drug consumption. But all societies have had goals which some people have rejected because achieving them was unattainable. Why in the late 1960s did so many of them turn up in the telly societies? It is true that the post-war generation has been confronted with unprecedented technological innovations, educational demands, wider opportunities which offer mirages of greater happiness in return for more work and more ability. But these ascending aspirations and expectations were experienced by the young of the 1940s, 1950s and early 1960s. Why did they erupt into drugs and delinquency on such a large scale amongst the telly generation?

If one examines the output of the box in countries that transmit primarily entertainment, it is clear that the total mosaic of television functions either as an escape from reality or as a stimulant for material aspirations. The commercials promise instant success, glamour and popularity if one buys the right soap, perfume and deodorant. It is not just the products themselves that are held out as fairy wands to easy acclaim, but the backgrounds in which they are consumed project a vision of domestic, social and sexual achievement which is unattainable for most people. The true environmental norm in which the blacks of Harlem, the poor of Glasgow's Gorbals, the deprived of Montreal, eat their Corn Flakes, wash in Lux and Hoover their carpets, consists of frayed furniture, peeling wallpaper, cracked walls and decrepit plumbing. The environmental norm of the commercials consists of gleaming kitchens, neat living-rooms, sparkling bathrooms, tasteful wall-paper, green gardens, pleasing furniture. Most viewers' real world is peopled with tired mothers, rumpled fathers, demanding children, pimply boy-friends and plain girl-friends. Only the advertising man's world is filled with smiling mothers, energetic fathers, bonny children, virile males and seductive females.

Advertising has, of course, offered a creature-comfort Elysium to the consumer for almost a century. But the special quality of television has brought a persuasive power to the visions of the huckster which no newspaper advertisement, no outside hoarding or billboard, no radio commercial ever had. The glowing, ordered, product-rich, handsomely peopled universe in which goods are consumed takes on a cumulative pattern of reality. A child may be able to reject the claim that a certain chocolate is the crunchiest, the chewiest, the tastiest mankind has ever devised, but it is less easy to reject the illusion that out there, in the television world which he assumes mirrors the real world, everyone has a natural right to eat chocolates in gadget-filled, pleasant homes and in the company of exciting beautiful people. As adulthood approaches, particularly amongst the poor and deprived, it is soon discovered that the promises of television — and not only commercials proffer a euphoric, glistening vision of contemporary existence — have turned out to be a cruel deception.

Amongst those who have speculated as to whether or not this television experience has anything to do with drug taking is Professor S. I. Hayakawa of San Francisco State College. 'All too soon,' said the Professor, 'young people learn that the maps

251

of reality given them by television do not correspond to the actualities. Material possessions and the consumption of all approved national brands do not bring happiness or peace of mind. The world, they discover as they approach adulthood, is far more complicated than they ever suspected. Getting along with other people is not easy; you have to adjust to them as much as they have to adjust to you. The world makes all sorts of demands the television set never told you about, such as study, patience, hard work, and a long apprenticeship in a trade or profession, before you may enjoy what the world has to offer. Disillusioned young people may at this point reject or rebel against the culture and its "materialism", — not realising that what they are rejecting is not the culture as such, but merely the culture as depicted by Madison Avenue and the networks.

'Even as they reject the culture as they understood it through television, they miss the pleasant fantasies they enjoyed as children when they turned on the set. So they "turn on" in other ways. Having scornfully rejected the notion that they can achieve instant beauty and radiance with Clairol, they espouse the alternative view that they can achieve instant spiritual insight and salvation with L.S.D. The kinship of the L.S.D. and other drug experiences with television is glaringly obvious: both depend upon "turning on" and passively waiting for something beautiful to happen.'[13]

Thus if a rejection of society's norms may be a motive for illegal drug taking what specifically has pitched those norms so high in the 1960s as to make so many young people reject them as unattainable? Is it not probable that television plays some part in the creation of aspirations which are so high that only drugs can compensate those who feel themselves failures and outsiders because they have been unable to satisfy them?

Although there has been a considerable amount of investigation into the causes of drug taking by psychiatrists, doctors and government bodies, there has been little professional examination of the part, if any, that television plays in the sudden narcotics explosion in the West. One of the few authorities who has given this possibility some serious thought is Dr. Norman E. Zinberg of Harvard University. His views on the subject were contained in a paper delivered to an international conference in Aspen, Colorado, under the auspices of the International Association for Cultural Freedom and the Aspen Institute for Humanistic studies. They might usefully conclude this collection of theories linking drugs and television.

Having interviewed over a thousand drug takers, Dr. Zinberg and his associates were struck by the fact that a number of historical, economic and political events recurred again and again as explanations for the mood and philosophy of the generation that had grown up during the 1960s. He examined such a diverse group of events as the Great Depression of the 1930s, the Second World War, the increase after the war of legitimate drug consumption in America, the generation gap, technological changes, and the evolution of the nuclear family as contributing to a climate of social change and a breakdown of old structures. This variety of social forces coalesced, according to Dr. Zinberg, to create a climate where non-medical drug use could flourish.

But most of these conditions existed in the late 1940s, the 1950s and the early 1960s. Why did not the American young of those years adopt a drug culture to meet their problems of adjustment? And, although Dr. Zinberg does not ask the question, why did the young of Canada and Britain also take to drugs in the latter half of the 1960s even though much of their historical and economic and technological background was quite different from the social milieu in which American children were raised? 'Why now?' asks Zinberg. His answer is that 'the advent of television in the late forties, combined with two decades of unusually rapid social and psychological changes, produced a generation for whom the patterns of sensations and thought associated with the drug experience were particularly apt'.

Dr. Zinberg, of course, did not profess to find any simple correlation between drugs and television but listed a number of ways in which the cognitive experiences derived from a constant viewing of the box when young could lead individuals to behave in adolescence and maturity in quite a different manner from that of the non-television generations. I shall attempt to provide the gist of his argument.

During his investigations, Zinberg noted that while some middle-aged people had adverse and unpleasant reactions to their first cannabis experience, young people who had been brought up on the box rarely did so. He was also impressed by how frequently visual imagery pervaded the descriptions of the effects of cannabis and other psychedelic drugs. From these observations, he developed an hypothesis that television could be subtly changing peoples' modes of perception and feeling so that eventually it brought about changes in behaviour. For example, he traced the non-intellectual response to cultural experiences by many drug users — their desire to be 'washed over' by sensation, to be lost in them without needing any analytical or logical vindication of their feelings — to the learning processes inculcated by the small screen. Radio and print forced children to structure words into logical patterns in order to make them meaningful as a mode of communication. Nouns, for instance, had to be distinguished from verbs. Words had to be constructed into phrases, sentences, paragraphs. While concentrating and focusing on this task so that they could make better contact with the outside world, their inner feelings and sensory impressions were in some way inhibited. And the development of such inhibitions was encouraged so that the child could better master the external content of print and the significance of words which were accomplishments to be praised and rewarded.

'But in the homes of the generation now reaching the age of 20, television was far more widespread than radio,' said Dr. Zinberg, 'and the child could participate in the experience it offered without the intellectual structures which radio demanded. The screen acts in a pacifying way because the flickering images utterly absorb the infant. If the developing child's first task is to differentiate between the self — what is me — and the outside world — what is not me — it seems possible that television permits and encourages a oneness with the screen, a sense of total participation, that does not emphasise that difference. The set is switched on and everything is there. The outside world is forcefully and completely brought into the room without his needing to prepare at all. The boundaries between inside and outside imperceptibly diffuse. When a field or some other outside scene is shown on the small screen, a two-year-old tries to walk into it.

'. . . The encouragement to participate, combined with the screen's insistence that you watch it — try ignoring a turned-on screen as you might a phonograph or a radio — gives rise to a situation where the viewer must use his own inner processes to complete an external situation. Inhibiting sensations cause an interference with this experience. Rather than setting the task of separating ourselves from external reality, television insists on diminishing such boundaries.

'Many of the current crop of drug users describe this melting away of boundaries between their internal and external worlds as their most important reaction to cannabis use. They insist that the rush to organise sensory impressions cognitively is less important than to be "in" them. They wish to participate, experience, get with what is happening intuitively and emotionally, rather than to organise thoughtfully and intellectually.'

I leave the question about whether or not a drug culture would be ultimately detrimental to mankind's development and future to other authorities. Just as it is impossible to make assertive value judgments about whether scepticism about authority is healthier than respect for it, or whether individual violence is more acceptable than state violence, so is it impossible to weigh up in any concrete way any of the social consequences of television in the long run. Every society has to decide what sort of activities it either wants to encourage or agrees to tolerate in its citizens. But if a society is blind or indifferent to the impact of a major conditioning factor which is shifting individuals in directions that it considers undesirable, then it will suffer unnecessary stresses, anxieties and disruptions. It would, therefore, appear to be prudent — to say the least — for any society concerned with the drug problem to investigate the possibilities of a connection between its television system and drug consumption.

CHAPTER NINE

The Half-Truth Machine

It may be that the broad reaches of the American public have become so inured to falsity in wide areas of the advertising and mass entertainment media that they are incapable of discrimination.
                    Robert MacNeil, *The People Machine*

This medium is bound to deceive. Even if you put the truth into it, it comes out a deception.
                    Malcolm Muggeridge in *The New Priesthood*

As an executive at Granada Television in 1961, it was part of my duties to survey any original film offered to the company with a view to its possible transmission. One day a young man named Peter Watkins turned up in my office with a remarkable piece of film. I hadn't listened too carefully about the details of how he had come to shoot the film and it wasn't with very much optimism that I joined him in the company's viewing theatre to see it being run off. Watkins was an amateur film-maker and my experience with the kind of film usually shot by amateurs had not been very encouraging.

But hardly had the first images begun to flicker on the screen when I found myself riveted by this extraordinary example of documentary filming. It dealt with the last ten days of the Hungarian uprising against the Russians in 1956. In a corner of Budapest a small group of students and workers were seen defying the tanks and the artillery of the Russians until most of them were either killed or captured.

The startling dramatic quality of the film was achieved by the utter realism with which it depicted the violence, the agony, the despair and the courage of those involved in this microcosm of a revolution. The shuddering film frames during moments of violent action indicated the use of a hand-held camera. The rough camera work, the crude lighting, the texture of the celluloid, the chaotic shots of fighting, tussling men had that quality of immediacy and involvement reminiscent of the work of cameramen covering the front-line fighting during the Second World War at places like Stalingrad and Arnhem. It could only have been shot on the spot.

When the film was over — it was just under an hour in length and called *Forgotten Faces* — I asked Watkins how he had managed to be in Budapest in 1956 and how he had contrived to get such a record of the fighting out of the country.

'But I have already explained that to you,' said Watkins, patiently. 'It wasn't made in Budapest. It was shot in Canterbury and all the actors are English amateurs. That location is not very far from Canterbury Cathedral.'

My first reaction was incredulity. The faces, which I had seen in such lingering close-ups, seemed so utterly un-English and the locale so thoroughly Balkan that I found it very difficult to accept my own self-deception. Would other people find this re-creation of those real events as convincing as I had?

Before showing it to any one else at Granada — and to test whether or not my own reaction had been merely one of gullibility — I decided to work with Watkins on getting the film into better shape. The commentary was, in my opinion, too strident and too anti-Russian and gave the film a heavy propagandist flavour which I thought needed toning down. There was also some technical work on the sound track and some re-editing that Watkins himself wanted to do.

An intense, handsome, non-smiling young man of about 25, Peter Watkins was not someone whose views about his own work could be easily shifted. After a number of letters and meetings, I finally thought the film was in a reasonable enough shape to be shown to two senior Granada executives who would make the final decision about whether or not we should try to find a slot for it in the company's schedule. The commentary was still not to my liking but Watkins and I had agreed to differ about it.

I had decided not to tell my two colleagues — both very experienced film men — anything about how the film was made to see if their views of its authenticity would be the same as mine.

They sat through the film in absorbed silence. When the lights went up, one of them turned to me with exactly the reaction I'd expected.

'How did that boy shoot such a film in Budapest during the fighting?' he asked.

'But it wasn't made in Budapest,' I replied triumphantly. 'That's the remarkable thing about it. It had me fooled, too. It was made in Canterbury and all those people in it are amateur actors . . . English amateurs.'

There was a long silence.

'Oh, we couldn't possibly show it then,' said the other executive, very quietly but firmly.

'Why not?' I asked.

'If we show a film like that,' he replied, with impeccable logic, 'no one will believe our newsreels.'

In the event, *Forgotten Faces*, although some extracts of it were shown on a BBC programme about amateur film makers, was never transmitted in its entirety on television. Peter Watkins, however, went on to use the same realistic techniques in his prize winning film for the BBC reconstructing the battle of Culloden and in *The War Game*, his fierce, imaginative account of what England would be like after an H-bomb attack. Indeed *The War Game* so vividly and convincingly depicted the horrific consequences of nuclear destruction that the BBC, who had financed its production, did not have the courage to transmit it. Its stark and brutal scenes were considered too upsetting and gruesome for television viewers. It was seen, however, in cinemas throughout the world.

The Granada executive who expressed his unease about what Peter Watkins' film might do to the faith of the viewer in the authenticity of the television newsreel, was unintentionally recognising television's vulnerability as an instrument for conveying the truth. While the verbal lie is as old as man's ability to speak or write, the visual lie is something that still runs counter to most people's conception of the natural order of things. The stage magician earns his livelihood because the audience stubbornly clings to its notion that the eye cannot be fooled. The eyewitness is accepted as more reliable evidence of the truth of a happening than the touch, hear or smell witness. Because of this faith in the infallible recording ability of the eye most people are prepared to trust more readily what they see on the box than what they hear on the radio or read on the printed page. This readiness to believe in the veracity of television as compared with other media has been repeatedly confirmed by social science research. A survey in the late 1960s showed that 45 per cent of the public named television as 'the most impartial and most trustworthy' of media on political news with only 18 per cent preferring the press and radio.

Yet the distortion of the visual image has become one of the commonplace techniques of the cameraman and the film editor. The faked photograph is already a familiar ingredient of espionage and blackmail. How far away are we from the faked newsreel, the faked reconstruction of a past event (suppose someone turned up with an 'authentic' film of an unsolved murder or an attempted assassination?), the faked documentary?

In the hands of someone like Peter Watkins the technique can be used to provide a compelling insight into human behaviour or to give us a fresh perspective on a historical event. But in less scrupulous hands, what are its potentialities?

In free societies like America and Britain it is most unlikely that deception as thorough as that perpetrated in the notorious anti-Semitic Protocols of Zion, Clifford Irving's sensational biography of Howard Hughes or van Meegeren's fakes of Vermeer could take place on television without soon being detected and exposed. There are just too many people involved in the making of a television programme. The chances of success of a good forgery or fake exist in inverse proportion to the number of people involved in its production. But the possibilities of making a short-term impact through the transmission of a faked incident — a contrived visual incident to discredit an individual or a group during an election campaign, for example — cannot entirely be discounted as something that one day might be attempted.

In less free societies the use of television to provide visual evidence of something the state wants to establish is already taking place. The obvious blunt instrument that a government can use to disguise or bend the truth is the negative one of censorship. In any society where television has become the main source of news for most people, the simple device of not showing or mentioning the event on the small screen means that for large sections of the population the event has not actually happened. In one-party states or dictatorships the use of television to reinforce the propaganda apparatus of radio and the press has provided the central authority with an awesome instrument for thought control. But television, to be effective as a restrictive instrument of the state, must be run in harness with the ideological aims and attitudes fostered by radio, the press, the schools and the universities. When de Gaulle tried to use broadcasting as the voice of the French state while leaving the press and the universities free to contradict and dissent from that voice, it was television that was discredited as the 'liar' in the living-room. The Russians and the Chinese do not make such an elementary mistake in their approach to television.

We take for granted verbal and printed propaganda since the use of words and drawings to produce distortions of the truth and one-sided interpretations of events has always been with us. We have therefore developed a natural scepticism about facts and views conveyed in this way. The more educated and sophisticated we are, the more refined is our ability to sift the true from the implausible, the logical from the illogical. But most people have not yet cultivated the same wariness about such relatively new communications phenomena as the photograph and the moving picture. While ignorance persists about the ease with which celluloid and electronic tape can be tampered with and counterfeited, the television medium is likely to be believed even when it distorts and misrepresents — intentionally or not.

Thus when the Russian army marched into Czechoslovakia in August 1968, the world was able to witness the event as it happened through the existence of a land-line link which permitted television pictures to be transmitted to Austria and which the Soviet authorities inexplicably failed to close for almost 48 hours after the invasion. This visual story was supplemented by film shot by Czechs and foreign cameramen and smuggled out of the country. The total impression conveyed by these film and television pictures was one of a people courageously standing up to massive military force as they vilified, harangued and derided the invading army. We saw Russian troops being shouted at by angry students; tanks being greeted by fist-waving, sullen crowds; men and women sitting in front of Russian tanks in passive resistance; blood-spattered statues and bullet-ridden buildings; dead bodies in the doorways. These scenes, with their accompanying commentaries outlining the fierce resentment of the Czechs against this Russian action, roused world opinion to passionate protest against this aggressive act.

A few months after the invasion the BBC-2 programme *Europa* showed British viewers how the Russian invasion of Czechoslovakia had been seen on television screens in Russia and some of the Eastern European countries. There were almost the *same pictures* as those transmitted in Britain. But the commentary accompanying them had completely reversed their message and significance. The gesticulating and fist-waving crowds were now evidence of the Czech people waving enthusiastic greetings to the advancing tanks. The bullet-spattered buildings and dead bodies were evidence of the existence of subversive Czech elements who were threatening the Socialist state and who had to be put down by 'loyalist' Czechs and 'peace-loving' Russian troops.

Inevitably, time will pile up more and more of these dubious bits of celluloid and electronic tape, recording events that never happened and distorting events that did. One shudders to think of the task confronting future historians faced with this heap of manipulated visual evidence purporting to be primary source material. With the perpetrators of the forgery long since dead, who would know what did or did not take place?

Artists, of course, have never been restrained by the demands of accuracy in giving their versions of the past. We are not expected to take literally the details of the Battle of Borodino in Tolstoy's *War and Peace* or the vision of the American Civil War in M.G.M.'s *Gone With the Wind*. But the television historical documentary is a fresh development — still in its infancy — that is bound to bring perspectives of the past to millions who would normally never have read an historical account of such events. Yet compared with the standards of written history, work in this field is usually superficial, slovenly, badly researched, naïve and over-dramatised. This is probably inevitable due to the limited programme time into which a historical episode or era has to be compressed; the lack of trained historians to help organise it; the temptations to use dramatic reconstructions; the need to keep the programme visually exciting in order to hold audiences.

The obvious exception in this field was the BBC's gigantic account of *The Great War*. It required no less than 26 one-hour episodes to produce a visual record of that cataclysmic event, and in its way the series was something of a TV masterpiece. It was impressive not only for the treasure-trove of rarely seen cinematic material of the period, but for the restrained, factual, objective, historically verifiable nature of its commentary. But television rarely ventures on a project of such scope and expense. When the BBC tried to repeat the success of *The Great War* with its *British Empire* series of 13 programmes it singularly failed to please those with knowledge of the subject and was bombarded with epistolary abuse in the letter column of *The Times* by dons, editors and civil servants. 'The current series on the British Empire has had little research and less thought,' was typical of the complaints of its critics, 'and is even more lacking in sympathy either for those who were ruled or for those who ruled them.'[1]

Yet the *British Empire* took two years to prepare and each episode was given a budget of about £50,000 which must make it the most expensive documentary series in British broadcasting history. The more routine attempts to portray history on the box do not have such effort and money lavished upon them. The results rarely stand up to serious historical scrutiny.

An illustration of how fictionalised film can be used to give a false impression of a historical fact was seen in Granada TV's account of the Russian Revolution, transmitted to commemorate the 50th anniversary of that event. Called *Ten Days That Shook The World*, it was made with the assistance of the Russian agency, Novosit, and a Soviet director, and it is therefore not surprising that the end product did not overly offend the official Russian interpretation of those times.

Inevitably — since the documentary was only an hour long — the final result turned out to be a digested, over-simplified, child's eye-view of the Revolution. But its more objectionable feature was its constant use of clips from old Eisenstein films to illustrate vital incidents of the revolt. Although sub-titles were occasionally flashed on the screen to indicate a fictional reconstruction — some valid film of the past was arbitrarily linked with the Eisenstein montages — it would have needed a very acute viewer indeed to have worked out what was meant to be true and what was false.

Thus for the storming of the Winter Palace we were shown huge waves of Red Guard fighters streaming their way in thousands against a fierce resistance of government troops who had barricaded themselves inside the Palace. This is Eisenstein's highly romanticised interpretation of the event. The truth, of course, was that the taking of the Winter Palace was a desultory, almost absurd affair, with a women's battalion offering the most persistent resistance to the mob outside. Occasionally there was a slight skirmish with officer cadets.

Fifty years after the event, one might have expected that a British television programme purporting to be an historical analysis of what actually happened would have done more than repeat Eisenstein's official version of a heroic battle of gargantuan proportions instead of the comic-opera incident objective historians say it was.

Now it may have no great bearing on the ultimate happiness of mankind whether the masses acquire a false or true impression of the past. History's usefulness as a guide to human affairs has been disparaged by many — from Henry Ford, who said history was bunk, to Hegel, who thought that peoples and governments had never learned anything from history or acted on principles deduced from it. Indeed, it might be argued that the myths and fables of religion and nationalism have been far more compelling social forces than facts ever were. What difference, then, does it make if television merely perpetuates in its own way the lies and distortions of the past? If television confined its application of its distortion techniques to the past alone, it would probably only be philosophers and historians who would be seriously concerned about the matter. But if the public accepts misrepresentations of the past as harmless and normal on the television screen, will it in time become just as indifferent to misrepresentations of the present?

Every serious journalist who has worked in television news or current affairs recognises that there is inherent in the medium — even when it is used with no intention to misrepresent — a basic dishonesty.

263

Said Malcolm Muggeridge: 'The villain of the piece is the camera, the enemy is the camera. We who are accustomed to working with it know that it is capable of infinite deception, probably the greatest of all deception, and yet is accepted as having some sort of objective truth in it. And since the camera dominates the thing more and more, so the possibility of deception grows greater and greater.'[2]

Said Philip Whitehead, a Labour M.P., who was editor of ITV's *This Week* and worked on BBC's *Panorama*: 'Television is the only profession in which the word "cheat" is an inseparable part of the vocabulary. I think it's alarming that so often, in order to preserve a smooth visual flow and in order to re-create an assumed sequence of events or to prepare a visual montage which approximates to an idea, you do dishonest things.'[3]

There are a number of ways in which the quality of truth is reshaped and restructured when it is subjected to the attentions of the camera. The mere presence of the cameraman and the paraphernalia of his art divides an occasion into performers and audience. What the viewer sees, selected for him by the cameraman and the producer, is often significantly different from the atmosphere and mood being experienced by those actually on the spot. The camera eye transmits a contrived image of the event, not its reality. Thus, comparing what actually happened during the burial service of Senator Robert Kennedy in 1968 with what was actually seen throughout the world on television, Sophy Burnham of *New York Magazine*, reported: 'To anyone watching on television, the funeral service at St. Patrick's Cathedral was a solemn, moving moment ... the rest of the Cathedral was a jungle of cameras, cables, mikes, wires, lights and monitors, with the TV technicians climbing in the scaffolding and the still photographers hanging like children on a jungle gym ... Incredibly, one bored technician was reading a paper high above, while the audience sat perspiring under the hot lights, watching the photographers gathered like gargoyles round the altar. The only feeling of solemnity you got inside the cathedral was by watching one of the TV monitors mounted on a pillar.'

It may, of course, not be very serious if one electronic layer of artifice is superimposed on an already staged occasion like a

264

funeral or a ceremonial. In time it will probably change the very nature of the ceremonial itself so that formalities and practices will be subtly altered to meet the demands of the TV watchers. State funerals, inaugurations, coronations and even political conventions will no doubt undergo structural and procedural changes to make it easier for the viewer to see and understand what is going on. The way we look at these things will thus shape the way they actually happen. But such adjustments will never entirely close the gap between the true experience and its reflected image.

The presence of cameras, however, does not only change the nature of a formal occasion. They can heighten, intensify, and even create spontaneous events by their mere existence. During the racial riots in Detroit and Cleveland in 1967, there was substantial evidence that the reporting of the looting and the violence on television escalated that very looting and violence. The fact that the small screen can act as an unwitting agent provocateur was recognised by President Johnson's Commission on Civil Disorders which recommended that there should be a delay of at least thirty minutes before the transmission of TV news about a civil disorder. This moratorium on immediacy is designed to enable police to reach the spot before news of the riot encourages others to join in.

The propaganda uses to which cameras can be put, especially if there is live coverage, has not been lost on the organisers of demonstrations and protest marches. Not only are the banners most vigorously flaunted and slogans most loudly chanted where TV cameras are known to be taking pictures but it has not been unknown for police to be deliberately provoked to retaliatory reaction in the hope that some nasty piece of police brutality will catch the camera eye.

'In all sorts of areas, the presence of television, I think, significantly alters events,' said Philip Whitehead M.P. talking of his work as a British TV producer. 'I was very shaken six or seven years ago when I went to one of the first Trafalgar Square punch ups, where Colin Jordan [a Right-wing racist] and his mob were holding a meeting, and the massive saturation coverage of that by television turned it into a riot with people actually staging their own battles in front of the television screen.'[4]

The producer, of course, can claim that if people insist on behaving differently because TV cameras are focused on them, it is something that can hardly be blamed on him. If cameras were completely hidden wouldn't he be often accused of invasion of privacy or voyeurism or unfair spying? It may, indeed, be impossible to sort out the ethical considerations that ought to govern the transmission of material that has in some way been affected by the presence of cameras. The problem is less about the use of such telly activated events than about the way in which the viewer can be protected from believing them to be the whole truth.

But if the public ought to be warned about what the innocent placings of cameras can do to the news, they should also be aware that occasionally the creation of events is not so accidental or guileless. Where it is difficult or inconvenient to film an actual happening, producers or cameraman sometimes feel justified in reconstructing it or staging it. In Chicago in 1961 a local station owned by the Columbia Broadcasting System transmitted a programme purporting to show 'a marijuana party' taking place in a student's room. The F.C.C., the Federal Government's supervisory body regulating American television, investigated the programme and found that the party had been deliberately set up for the benefit of the station's TV cameras. Their findings not only condemned the programme, but declared that it was the duty of the TV journalist to have reported the crime of illegal drug taking to the police if he knew it was taking place, and that the reporter should have disclosed the identity of the participants in the party even though he had promised not to.

Because of the ease with which it can be censored, delayed and faked, television has come to play a central role in the propaganda struggle in every modern war. While the written word still has some reasonable chance of evading the tight censorship net cast over objective reporting during a war, the TV journalist has very little chance of getting through what he wants to say in the way in which he wants to say it. Conscious of the power of television, the censors not only supervise exactly what the cameras are allowed to take but also insist on seeing the filmed material before it leaves the battle zone. The result is that during the Six Day Israeli-Arab War, and during

266

the 1971 Indo-Pakistan War, television was sometimes three to four days behind the newspapers in showing pictures of what had taken place.

In Vietnam the American broadcasting organisations were powerful enough to show aspects of that war which did not please the American authorities. The sight of American Marines in a Vietnamese village setting alight huts with cigarette lighters, and American soldiers cutting off the ears of dead Vietcong with straight razors, and putting the ears in their packs for souvenirs, was hardly likely to give the folks back home the vision of a humane, civilised army that the Pentagon insisted their forces were. With the country divided about an undeclared war, it was possible for American television to get such anti-war scenes on the small screen. But such toleration has not existed in other wars.

The problems of taking unauthorised pictures in a war zone were graphically described by Murray Sayle in the *Sunday Times*. Sayle had covered the Indo-Pakistan War for that paper. 'All my television colleagues wanted was for the Pakistanis (and the Indians) to leave them alone so that they could go up to the fighting and get on with their job of reporting the war,' he wrote. 'However, news managers see the television crews very differently — as a way of getting their propaganda across with all the illusion that what you see is the whole story ... The threat to TV men is always the same: play ball or you will get nothing, while your more compliant rival gets our guided tour — but of course he need not explain to his viewers and the official will step out of shot just before you say "roll it" and will stay out until you say "cut".'[5]

Sometimes the frustrations of not getting any action shots either because no fighting is going on or because the authorities do not want cameras near some particular phase of fighting, leads TV crews to desperate straights in order to get a story. Edward Behr of *Newsweek*, commenting on Sayle's article in the *Sunday Times*, described in a letter to the paper what happened to him when he was in a forward position on the South Bank of the Munnawa Tawi River in the Chhumb sector of the Pakistani Western front.

'All was quiet, until suddenly a hail of shells sent us scampering into bunkers, rudely interrupting the "As I stand on the banks of the Tawi River" piece to camera by a CBS reporter,' said Behr. 'The shelling continued for some time, and it was only two weeks later, in Rawalpindi, that I discovered that it had been caused — not, as I suspected at the time, by the irridescent baby-blue outfit of a dashing Italian cameramen — but by *another* CBS crew, on the other side of the Munnawa Tawi River. Intent on shooting war scenes, they charmed the local artillery commander into having a go. The shells obligingly loosed off for CBS had to land somewhere — in this case, in the very near vicinity of CBS crew number one.

'For the record, I should admit our side was just as guilty. We too stopped by the Indian artillery positions, and asked them to loose off a few rounds. "I'm sorry, you should have come earlier," said their colonel, "these shells cost £45 apiece, you know." '6

Like so much else in our style of television, war, too, has become an aspect of entertainment. If its a dull war — nobody much being killed — the viewer will get bored and the executives back home will be tempted to cut costs and bring the crews out of the war zone. To justify their existence, TV newsmen will be tempted to find something exciting or dramatic to film. Thus an isolated bit of action, caught by some enterprising reporter, can give millions of viewers an impression of wide-spread bloody fighting when in reality the front is relatively quiet and uneventful.

'With a typical television crowd at work,' reflected Murray Sayle, 'with lamps and clapper boards, no one would any longer doubt that this is at least in part show business, with a powerful effect on the audience. When massacres are staged, and hostages coached for the media, the convention that our presence does not make some of these things happen is getting impossible to swallow.'7

Although politicians, as we have seen in earlier chapters, have few scruples about using television to provide flattering and biased versions of themselves and their activities to the viewers, the small screen is now generously used as an adjunct of diplomacy. Undoubtedly the most significant diplomatic occasion ever made into a television spectacular was President Nixon's visit to China in February 1972. Whether the trip resulted in the 'normalisation' of relations and the easing of tension between the two powers cannot be known until some time after these words are written. But undoubtedly it brought a fresh dimension to the manner in which television can be manipulated for purposes of state.

Both sides in the discussions used the small screen as skilfully as they could to advance their own particular positions. This was not always as mutually altruistic and idealistic as the toasting and bowing and hand-shaking indicated. Nixon was obviously out to enhance his prospects for the 1972 Presidential elections. The Chinese were determined to use the box for furthering their special approach to Communism and to establish their claims to being a power of equal status with America. Indeed, because Mao was to be seen only for a few brief moments, giving a gratified Nixon a special audience, it was Mao's remoteness and inaccessibility that won him these particular propaganda stakes. Compared with the grinning, constantly ingratiating figure of Nixon, Mao emerged as the Olympian personality with almost God-like status.

There was much heart-searching amongst journalists about the manner in which the Chinese had stage-managed the whole affair — no crowds to greet the President either on his arrival or departure from China — and about the tight restrictions placed on American TV crews so that only occasional glimpses of the country and its people were transmitted. Most of the coverage was on the level of a glossy travel brochure highlighting attractions like the Great Wall, tombs of the Ming Dynasty and the opera, with relatively brief references to slum areas and military preparedness.

Some reporters were convinced that even shots of so-called ordinary people, and those who actually said a few words on television, had been specifically planted by the Chinese authorities for American cameramen. Thus Philip Potter in the *Daily Telegraph* on February 25th, 1972 was most suspicious about the authenticity of Chinese people enjoying a 'spontaneous' day out in the leafy gardens near the tombs of the Ming emperors. 'Little girls with slightly rouged faces and pink and green ribbons played skipping games,' wrote Mr. Potter, 'but rouge and ribbons other than red are seldom seen in China. Family groups strolled about, listening with exaggerated concentration to transistor radios, all tuned to the same station playing revolutionary themes. Transistor sets are not common in China. Pretty teenage girls in bright jackets and gay chiffon scarves never seen in Peking's streets strolled among the trees . . . One American TV commentator commented to his colleagues: "The New Hampshire primary [election] is so near, and I've a feeling we are being used." '

The reactions of Stanley Karnow of the *Guardian* echoed this scepticism. 'For the most part,' he wrote on February 25th, 1972, 'the Chinese being displayed to the Presidential party and the foreign press have apparently been selected and programmed to behave according to a scenario prepared in advance. At the athletic exhibition, for instance, sections of the crowd applauded on cue. The "average" citizens being encountered by Mr. and Mrs. Nixon on their sightseeing tours have evidently been stationed at their positions beforehand.'

This same awareness that viewers were being manipulated according to a prescribed script was recorded in a diary kept of the visit by two *Time* correspondents, Hugh Sidey and Jerome Schecter. 'There is the feeling that Henry Kissinger and Chou En-lai put it all down on paper months ago, then stamped their chops on the agreement, shook hands and just waited for the actors to come onstage and do their parts,' they wrote. '. . . The President and Mrs. Nixon seem more interested in posing for pictures than in actually walking on the wall . . . There is the vague feeling in the banquet hall that everybody has been part of some gigantic hoax, or maybe not quite that, but some kind of staging.'[8]

As in every trick of legerdemain, the more the viewer saw the less he saw. Even as knowledgeable a political observer as Henry Fairlie of the *Sunday Express* found what he saw on the screen a 'scarey' experience. 'One has felt close to madness: not the madness of the American people or of those who try to govern America, for they are relatively calm, but the madness of American journalism and of American television when they decide to make something seem to happen,' wrote Fairlie. '. . . Personally and professionally, everyone has spent the past seven days reading and watching and listening to what they know is drivel about Richard Nixon's visit to China. No one believes the drivel . . . It is so obviously unreal. But, as the newspapers and as television press on them, they cannot help wondering if their instincts are wrong. They feel that their own wisdom is being called into question.'9

Although Fairlie shares out the responsibility for this mass-ive dose of 'drivel' between the press and television, it was evident that the predominant impressions for most people arrived via the electronic tube and not the printed page. For every single individual who read about the visit, I would guess a hundred or more relied exclusively on the small screen for their information about it. This was pre-eminently a tele-vision event — plotted and planned as such — during which the press always played a minor subsidiary role. In view of the meagreness of the diplomatic achievements listed in the joint communiqué, it is difficult to believe that they could not have been reached by some determined efforts on the part of Henry Kissinger and the State Department without the President ever setting foot on Chinese soil.

But an agreement along these lines reached by secret dip-lomacy would not have brought about what both sides — Nixon and Mao — were seeking. Each was after a public relations vic-tory for their own particular ends. And the main armoury in that struggle was the TV camera. Without television, there would probably have been no Presidential visit.

Nixon, facing a tough electoral battle in November, needed concrete evidence that his regime was heading towards peace even if his promise to end the war in Vietnam had not been accomplished. After watching Nixon grinning and drinking with the Chinese, could any viewer accuse him of being a man not doing his utmost for world peace? The Chinese saw in Nixon's dilemma a fine opportunity for displaying to the world their new-found strength and their ability to force the world's greatest power to treat them as equals. To achieve these diverse ends, both sides conspired to throw electronic dust into the eyes of the viewers, knowing that they had at their behest the finest instrument man has yet devised for fooling most of the people most of the time.

There is, however, a far more prevalent and commonplace distortion factor in television's handling of news and current affairs. Since TV journalism is the offspring of a mating of show business and the press, it has running deep in its electro-nic psyche the fear of boring the viewer. At all costs, dullness must be banished. Instinctively, the TV producer selects for transmission the highlights, the critical moments, the drastic conflicts, the exciting visuals of any event. Even at their most responsible best, TV news bulletins give an urgency, tension, pace to the incidents they are reporting that is different from the mood of the actual occasion.

'When a reporter and camera team go out to cover any story involving action, they are looking for the best of the action,' wrote Robert MacNeil. 'I have covered demonstrations and riots and street fighting for television in many cities. The point for television is always the same: to extract the most extreme scenes . . . The editors will obviously select the scenes of peak violence and the television audience will see the very worst of what happened. In a ghetto riot, they will not see that 75 per cent of the Negroes were staying in their homes with the doors locked . . . Television conveys such an intensity of emotion in a few scenes, and is so much more powerful a kindler of emotional reactions in the audience, that its responsibility to society, in this case, is greater than that of print journalism.'[10]

Considering the inherent pressures television news faces because of the philosophy of the medium and its technical limitations, it is surprising how objective and fair most news bulletins manage to be in Britain and America. Although there are occasional complaints about biased news, such charges are rarely substantiated. There is a tradition of impartiality and honesty which is zealously guarded by TV newsmen. But in spite of all their noble intentions, the demands of competitive broadcasting and the mechanics of the medium produce distortions in the news which are dangerous purely because the audience takes TV news at its face value and rarely questions its authenticity. It is the innocence of the viewer rather than the intentions of the broadcaster that is the most disturbing aspect of television news.

Now, in spite of the medium's predisposition towards superficiality and misrepresentation, it is one of television's fondest boasts that its cumulative effect has been to create a society that is better informed about the wide social and political issues of the day than ever before. It is an assumption not only accepted by politicians and broadcasters, but the public itself believes that it gets more reliable information from the box than from other media such as newspaper, journals or radio.

Every survey shows that for most people television has become not only their primary source of information but their most trustworthy source. Because it is believed, it is also influential. A survey conducted by *The Times* amongst important people listed in *Who's Who* showed that the majority of a representative sample thought that the BBC was more influential in Britain than Parliament, the press, trade unions, the civil service, the monarchy and the Church.[11] If, then, television's influence is now recognised by all segments of the population — both the uninformed and the informed, the masses and the élite — as one of the most powerful in our society, is it not about time we enquired into the quality of that influence?

It is probably true that in terms of sheer volume the average viewer gets more information about current affairs from television than elsewhere. But how much of it does he retain, digest or understand so that he can use it to make meaningful decisions about what is best for himself or the community? Although the social scientists have been busy trying to assess how much of the information transmitted by the box penetrates the minds and consciousness of viewers, there has been relatively little investigation into the quality of that information. Is it more reliable, useful, fair and beneficial than information received from other media? Does it reinforce or undermine the values and goals of the educational systems of countries like Britain and America?

A survey conducted in 1971 by the broadcasting department of the University of California gives little support to the view that most people are better informed because of TV news. Some 2000 telephone calls were made in the San Francisco area immediately after the transmission of the evening news bulletin and viewers were asked to recall any of the items of news they had just heard. More than half of those who had heard or watched *all* of the news — one-third of those who had the news switched on hadn't listened to all of it — could not remember a *single* news story they had heard or seen. Similar surveys show that newspaper readers are not nearly so sievelike in their ability to retain the news aimed at them.

Confronted with the possibility that news might not produce the ratings that in entertainment-oriented television spell success, some producers have decided that what is needed is news with a sugar coating to make it more palatable. In Ammerica a number of local TV stations have discovered that if news is made silly and trivial enough, the bulletins will attract more viewers than they had before. Dressed up in funny costumes, a new breed of commentators uses the news as an excuse for gags, insults and puns. The format is called 'happy talk' and is meant to reassure the viewer that no matter how dire and depressing the news may be, it is nothing to worry about if it can be faced with a smile and a chuckle. Advertising the service, a Detroit station tempted viewers with this sort of come-on: 'So, good news or bad, laugh a little with your News-4 favourites. You'll feel better.'

According to *Time* magazine, a New York station began stories on the Middle East with leads like, 'Egypt and Israel continued to kick sand in each other's faces,' or 'The Israelis have as many reservations [about a truce continuation] as we have Indians.' Finding most of this happy-talk humour both witless and tasteless, *Time* commented: 'Whether or not the increasing levity in local news should make the nation feel better informed is another question. TV newscasts, after all, are the major source of news for most Americans. Locally produced news shows — 75 per cent of the total on the air — were never models of journalistic achievement. The average half-hour report allots only $16\frac{1}{2}$ minutes to news and editorials. Even without backchat or horseplay, the program is little more than a superficial headline service.'[12]

Should the British viewer feel that such an approach to the news would be unthinkable on British television, he might consider the direction that the BBC's *Nationwide* has taken in order to popularise a news and current affairs programme. Although the formula is not as blatantly irreverent as happy-talk shows, most of the items in the early days of this programme, which began in 1970, were of the quirky, idiosyncratic human interest type that often make a one-inch paragraph in a provincial newspaper.

At the height of the power workers' go-slow, when a shivering nation was in no mood for flippancy, viewers were told that the commentator was waiting for Mr. Chapple, the trade union leader, 'to come into the studio to see the light'. But before we could hear any information about the progress of negotiations, the programme's first item dealt with a man who had won an award for the best kept loo of 1970.

Of course, in a magazine show of this kind, it is essential that there be occasional pieces of light relief and human interest. But in *Nationwide* such stories determine the mood and feel of the programme. Because it juxtaposes serious comment with frivolity in such a way as to undervalue and discourage involvement in such comment, it is guilty of trivialising the news.

It is important to emphasise the fact that the major and important TV news services in Britain and America — national and networked news — do not shirk from transmitting ugly and unpleasant events when they occur. Indeed, both in Britain and America they have often been attacked for concentrating overmuch on the violent and horrifying happenings in places like Vietnam and Ulster. Instead of accepting TV news for what it is — a kind of pictorial shorthand illustrating through arbitrary pictures a synopsis of events of the day — viewers for the most part assume the summary to be the reality, the fragment to be the whole truth. Even for those who do pay attention, it is a source of disorganised, shallow, isolated, splintered, unco-ordinated bits of information. Unless the viewer goes somewhere else for a fuller account of what is being reported — a newspaper, a magazine, a book, a knowledgeable person — his mind will become a dustbin of diffuse data related to happenings without rational causes and events without logical conclusions. Since there is little evidence that television encourages recourse to supplementary sources of information — the overall total circulation of newspapers and magazines is shrinking rapidly — can we view with equanimity the prospects of a society where a substantial proportion of citizens make democratic decisions based primarily, if not solely, on the erratic, emotional, fragmented, dubious information received from the box?

It will be argued, of course, that the news is not the only source of information provided by television. There are documentaries, discussion and current affairs shows, and occasional programmes devoted to the arts, sciences, politics and finance.

In the first place, it would be interesting to discover how many ordinary viewers ever see any of this type of programme. Statistically, some of these programmes get ratings which suggest they are watched in Britain regularly by about 6 million viewers. Are we likely to find, as in the case of news bulletins, that a significant number of viewers remembered nothing at all of what they saw? Was there a difference in the quality of receptivity between those who know something about the subject and those who knew little about it? Were the latter more enlightened or more confused after the experience?

Like almost everything in television, the need to popularise or dramatise issues dominates the thinking and techniques of producers of current affairs programmes. Lady Wootton, writing about the BBC's duty to society, believed that it was the obsession 'with the standards and values of show business to which one must attribute the predilection for head-on collisions or dog fights in preference to constructive discussion from common premises; and it is this which engenders impatience with any kind of subtlety.'[13]

The impetus to turn every serious issue — industrial disputes, foreign affairs, capital punishment, housing, education, sexual deviation, drugs — into a 'good show' means that programmes are planned to ensure a dramatic confrontation between extreme points of view. Conflict television holds viewers; consensus television loses them. A true reflection of how problems are treated in a democratic society would reveal that most of them are resolved by a slow osmosis of like opinions. This process is rarely shown on the small screen. Instead, the polarised opposites are invited to take up belligerent stances in public, vowing to stand by their positions at all costs and making retreat from those positions even more difficult. By constantly reflecting social, political and industrial disputes in the guise of intransigent and stubborn conflicts, television too often distorts and misrepresents reality. It also encourages the protagonists to be more abrasive and uncompromising in their public relations postures than is either wise or profitable. The public are rarely offered more than half-truths about these situations.

During the 1972 miner's strike in Britain television gave the impression that the miners would never accept anything less than the full wage demands they were making. We were shown miners in social clubs, in studios, at the pitheads fiercely and unanimously asserting that compromise on their claims was unthinkable. Even after the Wilberforce findings, conceding most but not all the miners' demands, every collective group of miners on the box defiantly asserted they would not accept Wilberforce because it offered one pound less than what they had asked for. This display of unyielding intransigence gave the nation a most uneasy night because, if television were to be believed, the strike would go on in spite of a desperate shortage of electrical power. Yet this picture of unreasonable miners, determined to bring the country to its knees to get their way, was a totally fallacious reflection of the mood of the strikers. When a week later they were asked to vote on Wilberforce's recommendations they agreed by a majority of 27 to 1 to accept them. The box never for a moment hinted at the existence of such an overwhelming amount of moderate opinion in the miners' ranks.

There is a tendency amongst politicians and communicators to shrug off this dramatisation and polarisation of contemporary issues on television as a relatively harmless and irrelevant aspect of the political scene. But if the formation of public opinion is considered to be an important ingredient of democratic decision-making processes, politicians may find themselves hurried and harassed into taking decisions not because they think them right but because they feel they must obey the will of an electorate demanding extreme solutions due to the way some particular issue has been over-simplified, intensified, exacerbated, on the box.

We know, of course, that most adults will merely have their prejudices confirmed and reinforced by this sort of exchange of opinions. I have never yet heard a protagonist on any television show, no matter how long the debate, ever admit that he has changed his point of view or even had it shifted a fraction because of what he has heard someone on the other side say. Viewers are just as likely to cling to their convictions as the programme participants. The hope obviously is that people with no definite views on the matter will be provoked or stimulated into taking some positive stand. But there is little evidence that this occurs.

Even the much vaunted assurance that programmes on controversial issues provide a balanced picture of the opposing opinions needs some qualification in the light of British viewing habits. Because current affairs shows tend to start late in the evening, the argument in the early segment of the programme is likely to get a larger audience than those due to be heard later. Viewers switch off in mid-programme because they are easily bored by demanding debates and because they want to go to bed. In a David Frost programme on Ulster, for instance, the Catholics were given the first half of the show from 11.15 to 11.45 p.m. Since it was a Sunday night it can be assumed that by that hour a substantial section of viewers decided that the demands of work in the morning were more pressing than staying up until 12.30 a.m. to hear the Protestant side of the case. Thus for that substantial body of people who went to bed having listened only to the Catholics, the theoretical built-in balance of the programme was inoperative. Those viewers succeeded in being not only misinformed about the presence of moderate voices in Ulster, but they were also misinformed about the Protestant position because they never heard it.

While it is gratifying that a minority of 3 million or so are prepared to listen to serious issues seriously discussed at a very late hour (after all, this figure is over three times the combined circulations of *The Times* and *Guardian*), it is less gratifying that many millions became so bored or disinterested in these topics that they bluntly switched these programmes off before they were half over. No theatre would consider it had a successful play if half the audience had departed after the first interval; no publisher would boast about a book that half its readers never bothered to finish; no newspaper would think they had printed a useful article if over half its readers had read and absorbed only its first few paragraphs; no political meeting would assume it had been successful if a substantial number of its audience had left the village hall during the main speaker's speech. Television is unique in its ability to view with satisfaction a state of affairs that other responsible media would be unhappy about.

In writing about current affairs television, I have consistently spoken about its impact on 'most people'. There is a decided minority who do not look to the small screen for either news, information or any serious analysis or interpretation of current affairs. They may certainly watch it, but they have more faith in newspapers, journals, books or radio as sources of reliable and meaningful data about social and political issues. They are, for the most part, those with the highest level of education in the land.

Just how wide is the division between the educated and less educated in their assessment of television information was shown in a survey of American viewing habits conducted by Dr. Gary A. Steiner at the Bureau of Applied Social Research, Columbia University. Compared with radio, newspapers and journals, 30 per cent of the least educated thought television gave the 'most complete news coverage' compared with only 2 per cent of college graduates who thought so; 38 per cent of the least educated thought television 'presented things most intelligently' and only 2 per cent of college graduates thought so; 40 per cent of the least educated thought television was 'the most educational' medium while only 6 per cent of college graduates thought so.

'The higher-educated are much less inclined to praise TV generally, and much more likely to disavow its personal and social importance,' wrote Dr. Steiner. And commenting on another aspect of his wide-ranging survey, he had this to say: 'Education matters for critical tone, but not substantially until after high school. From then on, each successive group is less favourably disposed toward TV until those with education beyond college become the only viewing segment, in *any* such analysis, with a predominantly critical set of responses.'[14]

Since that survey was conducted in 1962 there has been little in the development of American television that has modified the intelligent man's scepticism about the medium. Although most intellectuals recognise its power and have some regard for its entertainment facilities, they have scant respect for its over-all level of information, education or culture. Voicing the concern and contempt of many intellectuals over the general performance of American television as a social force was Clive Barnes, the English-born drama critic of the *New York Times*. 'For the most part American television is the most dispiriting thing known to man' he wrote. 'It could, and I am serious about this, maim the intellectual and emotional responses of the nation.'[15]

The rejection of British television as a serious medium is not nearly so emphatic. The attitude of intellectuals to it is more one of indifference than scorn. Although commercial television is on the whole treated with disdain, there is still a lingering faith in the BBC's capacity to maintain some cultural standards and public-service traditions. The existence of BBC-2 offers some assurance that in the cultural fields of music and drama, at least, the headlong rush for popularity is not the predominant motive of the service. But BBC-1's eagerness to compete in the ratings race means the growing alienation of informed people from television as a medium for raising the level of debate about important social, scientific and political issues.

Commenting on ten programmes planned by the BBC under the title *The Gap*, to which he had been invited to contribute, Dr. David Martin, a Reader in Sociology at the London School of Economics, wrote: 'In each of these programmes, 15 people are to be offered an average of 1 minute 50 seconds each to opinionate on the armed forces, sex and the family, religion, education, drugs and so on. The young sociologist by whom I was approached concerning this series has assured me it is to attempt a much more profound probing of the issues than has been normal practice hitherto.'[16]

This dissatisfaction with the medium as a suitable arena for the dissemination or exchange of intelligent information was voiced by Professor Stafford Beer, writing in *The Listener* about the superficial manner in which television treats matters of science. 'If you have watched a serious scientific topic being discussed on *Late Night Line-Up*,' said Professor Beer, 'without a single scientist present, as happened when a programme called *2001 — An Earth Prophecy* was discussed, you will understand. It makes scientists want to kick in the screen; but, more important, it makes them vow not to risk their own professional careers in having dealings with a medium they increasingly regard as irresponsible . . . Whatever the reason, the mass media handle science at one remove — as it were, with a pair of sterilised tongs. The public may have snippets of science at the producer's discretion; the public may have glamorised science hosed at it. The public does not get the real thing.'[17]

The more people get their basic information and values from the small screen, the greater will be the pressure on decision-makers for quick, volatile, palatable solutions to complex issues. And the more suspicious will the majority become of those who recommend patience, restraint, delay and compromise. One can envisage, without being too outlandish, the emergence for a period of a sort of two-culture split in society with a minority clinging to patterns of thinking derived from the printed word and the majority demanding less circuitous, less determinedly rational, more immediate responses to the pressures of public opinion.

Just as there has always been a generation gap, so has there also been an intellectual gap. Amongst the poorly educated there has always been suspicion of the well-educated; amongst the ill-informed multitude there has always been resentment of an informed élite. 'The Athenians do not mind a man being clever,' said Plato, 'so long as he does not impart his cleverness to others.' The English, like the Athenians, are also not over-fond of politicians who are 'too clever' or public figures who are 'too clever by half'.

The conflict between the reasoning man and the instinctive man is an inevitable consequence of the duality of man's nature. It has been beneficial when the intuitive and less educated masses, conscious of their own self-interest, have recognised and checked the actions of leaders being driven into untenable positions by seeming reason and false logic. But there can be ominous repercussions when the intellectual gap is too wide. There are dangers that the minority with faith in rational argument will not only have their causes rejected by the majority, but will become increasingly subjected to suspicion and mistrust. Nazi Germany is a vivid illustration of what can happen to an advanced society when the populace becomes intolerant of men of reason and puts its trust and destiny in leaders and cults of instinct and emotion. Television, if it continues to act primarily as a disseminator and reflector of the shallow and escapist aspects of life, could become a significant factor in broadening the misunderstandings that exist between the intellectual and the common man.

It is important to stress again that there is no Machiavellian conspiracy on the part of broadcasters to provide the public with superficial, trivial or distorted impressions of news and current affairs.

The show business imperative encourages broadcasters to give news priority to the most exciting visual material; to demand the capsulisation of complex problems into ridiculously small time segments; to insist on debates being conducted in the atmosphere of a crowd scene rather than by a few informed and concerned protagonists; to present unbalanced interpretations of events by polarising discussion into extreme positions and neglecting the less dramatic consensus middle; to resort to such examples of news trivialiation as 'happy talk' shows in American and *Nationwide* in Britain.

The impetus towards treating current affairs in this manner will only diminish when television in Britain and America becomes a more mature and more consciously educative medium. No one suggests that it would be possible or even desirable, to provide current affairs programmes on the box with the volume of factual background and sophisticated analysis that is provided by the most serious papers in the land. But in a medium less dominated by entertainment priorities, a breed of broadcasters would be cultivated who were less concerned with ratings triumphs and more concerned with the quality of information they transmitted.

Considering, then, the medium's potentialities for deception and the difficulties of eliminating such misrepresentations, it is an astonishing reflection on the irresponsibility with which those in authority treat television that so little is done to educate people about the capabilities and intricacies of this powerful influence in their lives. There are no courses on television in the state school system, no place in the normal curriculum for anything that would help children understand the workings of the medium they watch more than they read books and absorb more deeply than anything they acquire from their teachers. 'Perhaps some day the appreciation of television — on however simple a level — will find its place in the school curriculum along with the appreciation of literature,' wrote Stuart Hood, a former BBC Controller of TV programmes. 'If children were able to discuss the difference between a good and bad Western, this would be pure gain. If they were led on to be discriminating viewers the benefits would be felt not only by the schools but by the television organisations. Generations are growing up which have not been taught how to discriminate as viewers.'[18]

It is not only television as an art form that has to be studied by children. Its structure as a system of communication and persuasion has to be grasped and understood. The telly generation receives, absorbs and interprets most of its informational data in quite a different manner from those whose information was acquired from the printed page. Not only does the child today receive his most vivid cultural and educational experiences from moving pictures, but he comes in contact with them many years before he starts to read. Just as anyone over 25 has been shielded from the full effects of the small screen because he came to it with a mind that was print-oriented in its formative years, so almost anyone under 15 comes to the experience of reading after his mind has been largely conditioned to receive information pictorially. The resistance to reading amongst TV children is far greater than it was amongst non-television generations.

Yet children are told practically nothing about the nature of this electronic mother that has reared so many of them. They are not taught in their most impressionable years where it comes from, how it works, what it does. They are given no knowledge which would equip them with the means of testing whether it was true or false, good or bad, reality or fantasy. They are left to grope towards their own understanding of this magic box and select from it the messages their young minds choose to retain as valid and admirable. Without guidance or training, they are expected to winnow out from the chaotic heap of visual experiences those that will be not only good for them but those that society would prefer them to select.

Clearly we are being both naïve and stupid when we assume that some innate sense of survival will enable the child to wander through the television maze without ever getting lost or hurt. We would never dream of letting a child cross a street on his own without first teaching him the rules of the road and the meaning of traffic signs. But we are totally indifferent to the many perils that face a child in his contacts with the small screen. What is needed is a recognition on the part of the educational establishment of this yawning gap in the knowledge of the young. As early as possible children must be taught the techniques of the camera, the logic of the editing process, the syntax of the montage, the grammar of the mosaic, the essence of the visual image. In the beginning, for most of them, was not the word, but the picture. Equipped and fortified with that sort of education, future generations will be able to confront the half-truths of the box with the same kind of understanding, awareness and scepticism that past generations have accorded the printed page.

CHAPTER TEN

The Electronic Catalyst

I had a call from a friend, highly intelligent, very down to earth, and with a great sense of humour. For rather sad personal reasons she had never married and had never seen a naked man. She had watched this programme (on marriage) the previous evening and had suddenly found herself confronted by a male nude on the screen in her living-room.
Mary Whitehouse in *Who Does She Think She Is?*

Children don't read Anne of Green Gables any more, they watch it on TV. The whole incentive to read has been replaced by the telly.
Terry Casey, General Secretary, National Association of Schoolmasters, *Daily Mail*, March 23rd, 1972

'I doubt if there are any rational people to whom the word "fuck" would be particularly diabolical, revolting or totally forbidden,' said the journalist and theatre critic Kenneth Tynan, on a late-night BBC satire show in November 1965.

It was the first time this particular four-letter expletive had been heard on British television. There were four motions of protest in the House of Commons. There were hysterical outraged articles in the press. There were demands that the BBC, Mr. Tynan and anyone else involved be prosecuted for obscenity. Nothing eventually happened. Somehow or other the nation managed to survive the shock.

The Corporation was as much taken by surprise by Mr. Tynan's blunt indelicacy as the viewers. The word had been used in the context of a serious discussion about censorship and in a live programme. Had the programme been taped beforehand, no doubt the remark would have been cut. Under the circumstances no one in the BBC could be accused of a deliberate affront to the sensibilities of the nation. As an incident, it is still recalled as one of the medium's most embarrassing moments.

The newspapers naturally had a field day at the expense of its media rival. Some thundered; some giggled. Arguing in the *Evening Standard* that the question was one of manners rather than morals, that four-letter words were the common communication coinage heard in any pub and at dinner parties in many respectable homes, that no one had ever been depraved or corrupted by expletives, and that the fuss was largely hypocritical, I had to be careful not to shock my own readers and used the asterisk device **** instead of the word 'fuck' throughout the article.

Explaining my linguistic reticence, I wrote: 'When I first began to write in the *Evening Standard* in 1948, my articles were pitted with euphemisms for taboo words. A prostitute had to be called a lady of the streets or of easy virtue. Adultery was referred to as a marital offence. Homosexuals were men of unnatural habits or vices.

'Now I can use words like whores, queer, tart, Lesbian, masturbation, fornication without compromising the *Standard*'s reputation as a family newspaper. I still cannot use **** or **** or ****. But I am sure the day will come.'

The gulf between Mr. Tynan's view of what rational people would consider acceptable language on television and what other people thought was permissible on the box, was illustrated in a broadcasting debate in the House of Commons only a few months before this startling linguistic breakthrough. Mr. William Shepherd, a Conservative M.P., had been attacking the BBC's Director-General, Sir Hugh Greene, for 'turning out filth at 9 o'clock'. When another M.P. pressed him to detail what he meant by 'filth', Mr. Shepherd described a programme in which a comedian, Lance Percival, dressed up as Father Christmas sang a song about children in which he referred to the children as 'little bleeders'. 'Surely,' protested Mr. Shepherd, ' "little horrors" would have been artistically a better phrase.'

Four years after Tynan's comment the dreaded word turned up on British television again. This time it was heard in a documentary about the treatment of mentally disturbed children at an institution in Canada called Warrendale. These children were such violent social misfits that no other institution could handle them. The camera, using cinéma vérité techniques, recorded the paroxysms of flailing, self-destructive rage some of these children exhibited and the efforts of the staff to control them by forcibly holding them down. During one of these hysterical outbursts a 10-year-old child constantly shrieked the word 'fuck'. Although this raw and disturbing documentary was at times almost unbearable to watch, the real concern about its suitability for television audiences was not its harrowing content but this objectionable expletive. In fact although *Warrendale* had been commissioned by the Canadian Broadcasting Corporation, that network after four months of deliberation had decided that they dare not show it. In America, too, it was not shown by any of the major networks in spite of the fact that it had won an American Film Critics Award as the best documentary of 1968. However, on an evening when most of the nation was engaged in watching a Eurovision Song Contest on the BBC, a few of the companies on the commercial channel took their courage in their hands and transmitted it. To protect themselves against charges of irresponsibility there was an introductory warning about the controversial nature of the film. Extra staff had been assigned to handle the flood of indignant telephone calls they expected because of the obscenities.

That night London Weekend TV had exactly 11 telephone calls about the programme — 7 from women congratulating the company for showing it, 2 enquiries and 2 complaining about the treatment methods. Not one caller objected to the obscenities. Harlech TV in Wales had a similar bland reaction. A week after the programme only 25 letters had been received about it. Most of them were congratulatory. No one complained about the obscenities.

As a demonstration of how much more liberal and tolerant the average viewer was about four-letter words than M.P.s and broadcasters believed, this was a most enlightening experience. Although no one would suggest that by 1969 the British public was ready to accept four-letter words as the common coinage of television programmes, it nevertheless proved that when such words were used in the cause of realism, the vast majority of viewers would consider them both necessary and appropriate. And when I discussed this programme in my *Evening Standard* column, it was not necessary for me to disguise from my readers the shocking reality of the word I was discussing. The paper this time printed the word 'fuck' instead of ****.

Now one must ask oneself why four-letter expletives that had rarely, if ever, been seen in serious or popular English newspapers could be printed in those papers in 1968 and 1969. By 1972 words like 'fart', 'shit' and 'fuck' could be found in respectable papers like the *Guardian* and the *Sunday Times* without a tremor of protest in the correspondence columns. What part, if any, did television play in this liberalisation of language?

Television is not only able to shape the attitudes of those who have been constantly subjected to it in their formative years, it can also exert its influence by changing other media which in turn affect the values and attitudes of society. It is in the exercise of this role as a catalyst for change in such media and art forms as newspapers, magazines, books, cinema, theatre, that I intend to discuss the impact of the small screen in this chapter. Where television does exert a discernible pressure on other modes of communication, causing them to alter or altering people's approach to them, I would claim that a peripheral TV factor is at work.

Whether the freeing of four-letter expletives from social censure will ultimately increase or decrease the sum total of human happiness is a nice question better left to semantic philosophers. That television plays some part in the process can hardly be doubted. Because television is so pervasive and ubiquitous, it can very quickly create a climate of acceptability amongst most people for language that had previously been socially frowned upon. Hearing Alf Garnett, the foul-mouthed Cockney hero of the BBC's comedy series, *Till Death Us Do Part*, week after week abusing 'kikes', 'niggers', and 'wogs' with volleys of 'bloodies' and 'damns' undoubtedly stimulated an imitative response on the part of viewers and other media. It is impractical to try to assess whether or not heard in this comic context the vituperative value of these abusive terms was defused. But undoubtedly it was difficult to maintain the same level of indignation about them when they were regularly heard, laughed at and enjoyed by the largest number of viewers for any programme on British television.

When in 1971, five years after *Till Death Us Do Part* was first seen on the box, CBS in America plucked up enough courage to put on an American version of the Garnett family in a series called *All in the Family*, the public responded with enthusiasm to the uninhibited language of a small-time bigot. 'Archie Bunker, the middle-American hero of "All in the Family", speaks what was utterly unspeakable on television before him,' wrote *Newsweek* on November 29th, 1971. 'He sees himself menaced by a rising tide of spades, spics, spooks, schwartzes, coons, coloreds, Chinks, chosen people, Commies and their Commie crapola, jungle bunnies, jigs, pinkos, pansies, hebes, yids, black beauties, bleeding hearts, tamale eaters, yentas, atheists, weirdos, dumb Polacks, dingbats, meatheads, fairies, fruits, fags and four-eyes. These are the words he uses, in a medium that usually minces words to the consistency of toddler food. He uses at least a few and sometimes a good many of them each Saturday evening, and some 35 million viewers lap it up. This puts the show near the top of the Nielsen-ratings, and its vast popularity adds fuel to the controversy over its vocabulary and philosophy.'

At first glance, it would seem to be somewhat contradictory to assign to a medium that 'usually minces words to the consistency of toddler food' the power to free newspapers from their constraints about the printing of four-letter expletives. The contradiction exists, of course, not in the potential power of television to influence attitudes to language but in the restraints that have been exercised on that power. The ease and speed with which television can create fads for words and phrases can be witnessed all the time in the readiness with which viewers pick up the slogans and jingles of TV commercials. British viewers may not know which precise brand of beer started it but they repeat parrot-like the expression 'I'm only here for the beer.' In America the comedy programme, *Laugh-In*, made 'Sock it to me!' and 'Ver ... ry interesting!' catch-words for the nation.

Perhaps instinctively aware of its quick and powerful impact upon linguistic responses, particularly amongst the young, the broadcasting hierarchy has been exceedingly cautious about permitting on the screen any words or phrases that might unduly offend a substantial proportion of viewers. In America, where the commercial ethos dictates a policy of offending nobody if at all possible, the taboos of linguistic orthodoxy have been strictly maintained. But in Britain, where the BBC under the questing regime of Sir Hugh Greene was bound by no such commercial strait-jacket, the language-prudery barrier was breached by such programmes as the satire shows, *Till Death Us Do Part* and *Steptoe and Son*. Although M.P.s, churchmen and groups like the National Viewers' and Listeners' Association led by Mrs. Mary Whitehouse attempted to stem this tide of linguistic permissiveness, they were defeated by the sheer popularity of these shows. The vast majority of viewers were clearly not offended by what they were seeing and if 'giving the public what it wanted' was to be the moral justification for broadcasting content, the British public clearly wanted a ration of vulgarity and obscenity. Who dared deny them their right to have it?

It is true that compared with the language found in novels or the *avant-garde* magazines and even a few films, the words heard on television in the mid-1960s were relatively mild and innocuous. What were a few 'bloodies' and 'farts' compared to the forbidden words tucked away in *Lady Chatterley's Lover* or *Ulysses* or *Last Exit to Brooklyn*? *Ulysses* was published in 1922 and the censor's ban lifted from it in America in 1933; the first unexpurgated edition of *Lady Chatterley's Lover* appeared in 1932. Whatever effects they may have had on freeing English literature, they certainly did not embolden newspapers to free their columns for taboo expletives even 35 years after these books were known to large groups of readers.

One would certainly not claim that a few spoken 'fucks' in a satire show or a TV documentary suddenly changed the nation's attitude to four-letter words. But whereas literature acts as a small poniard when it penetrates the protective fabric surrounding the cultural status quo, leaving a small opening which others enlarge, television acts as a spray of buckshot whenever it dares to challenge cultural barriers. In one night more people heard Mr. Tynan say 'fuck' in their homes than all the people who had read the word in *Ulysses* or *Lady Chatterley's Lover* in all the years since those books were published. In one night more people heard Alf Garnett say 'bloody' than all the people who had ever heard 'not bloody likely' in Shaw's *Pygmalion* in all the theatres in which the play had been produced since it was first written in 1912.

What the BBC was able to test — although not wittingly — was the level of public tolerance of proscribed language. It found it much higher than the orthodox guardians of public morality had been prepared to admit. Having established a climate of acceptability for certain words in a mass medium, the other mass media felt at liberty to move in the same direction. What minority media like books and *avant-garde* magazines could not accomplish in decades, television hastened in a few years. In America and Canada, where television has rarely breached the barriers of respectable language, the newspapers, too, have maintained a discreet reticence about dubious words. It will be interesting to see how long it takes for the vulgarities of *All in the Family* to creep into the columns of the respectable American press.

It is pertinent to note that while the American mass media — newspapers, radio and TV — still adopt this Puritan line about language, all around them the minority media and art forms — novels, magazines, the theatre, the Underground press — have pushed the threshold of permissive language to a point where it can hardly be said to be visible. Indeed, as far as words are concerned, America's minority print media have reached a stage of almost complete licence. It is difficult to envisage a successful prosecution in America for obscenity or pornography on the basis of words alone. The same can probably be said about Britain.

Thus in any analysis of how television affects other media, it is evident that two processes, sometimes contradictory, are taking place. The other media try to follow and exploit tastes and values stimulated by television; the other media try to cater for tastes and values that television neglects, rejects or shuns. It can be said that in many ways television is the large tail that wags the media dog. The contents of newspapers, films, magazines, books and plays — and the manner in which they were sold to the public in the late 1960s — have all been influenced in some minor or major degree by the existence of the small screen.

The way in which other media react to television can best be seen in their responses to television's treatment of sex. As we have seen, British television, for a few years during Sir Hugh Greene's regime, dared to go farther in the use of permissive language than nearly all British newspapers. This phase of outspokenness, although considerably curtailed, did not altogether disappear with Sir Hugh's departure as Director-General. Thus in a *Panorama* programme on February 2nd, 1970 the pros and cons of sex education in primary and secondary schools were aired. During the programme we heard a teacher discussing children's attitudes to sex in these terms. 'Schoolboys have at least 12 different names for penis,' he said. 'A winkle is a popular one. And we know that the testicles are called balls.'

Predictably the National Viewers' Association was offended by such talk at a peak viewing time on the BBC. Mrs. Whitehouse announced that she was seeking legal advice about taking action against the Postmaster General because the BBC was 'showing pornographic material under the guise of documentary programmes'. Again the average viewer appeared to be far less concerned about it than the morality pressure groups. The Corporation reported that it had only received a 'handful of calls' about a programme in which children were seen blithely and innocently discussing such topics as menstruations, erections, sperms and sheaths as openly as they would have enquired about the meaning of words like stalactite, longitude and hypotenuse. 'And not all of the telephone calls,' said a BBC spokesman, 'were complaints.'

While such frankness probably encouraged newspapers to follow suit, it cannot be said that British television very often displayed a serious, concerned or mature approach to sex. In spite of the assertions of morality groups, the overall record of British television on the transmission of provocative sexual displays or dubious sexual material is, as Noël Coward said of one of his plays, as clean as a whistle. There is a good deal of light-hearted smut in comedy shows like *Up Pompeii* with jokes about virgins and chastity belts, or *The Benny Hill Show* with laughs about queers and fly-buttons, but the great British public, judging by the viewing figures of these programmes, seems singularly unperturbed by farcical sex.

It was not this type of TV fare that roused the ire of the self-appointed guardians of the nation's morality. It was plays or documentaries with a committed or controversial or adventurous approach to sexual matters that stimulated the most vociferous protests. A BBC-2 series on *Casanova*, with its occasional displays of naked ladies, raised blood pressures, as did the brief sight of a full frontal naked model in a documentary about the artist, Modigliani. The BBC's *Wednesday Play*, which tried to examine in serious dramatic form subjects like abortion, prostitution, homosexuality, infidelity, was a constant target for abuse. Serious attempts to examine sexual education or censorship, because inevitably they demanded explicit illustrations of what the speakers were talking about, provoked angry complaints. There was too, an indignant letter to *The Times* from Lord Elton which said: 'Let it be recorded before this correspondence closes down that the Corporation contrived to include an attempted rape into (of all books!) *Tom Brown's Schooldays*.'[1]

Yet in spite of these few lurid examples of sexual boldness which could have depraved and corrupted nobody and which are dragged out to prove the BBC's determination to tread the primrose path of permissiveness, the total amount of time devoted to controversial sexual programmes is tiny. The commercial channel only rarely embarks on a questionable subject of this kind. And even at the height of Sir Hugh Greene's most provocative period, I doubt if anything like 1 or 2 per cent of the programmes could have stimulated the average viewer to anything more than a raised eyebrow. Yet, such is the residual impression left behind by these few incursions into daring programming, that tens of thousands of viewers can always be found to sign petitions accusing British television of purveying dirt and depravity. According to an Opinion Research Centre poll taken in 1967, there was a hard core of about one-third of viewers who were offended by the sex and swearing they found in TV plays. The greatest proportion of these were in the older age groups with over 76 per cent of those between 21 and 34 agreeing with the statement that 'there is very little which offends sensible people'.[2]

A study published by the Conservative Bow Group in 1971 admirably summed up British television's record on sexual permissiveness. 'There are for example those who believe that television is corrupting the moral fibre of the nation and encouraging permissiveness,' says this paper. 'They believe that when broadcasters claim to be reflecting moral trends, they are in fact steering and stimulating moral decline. In fact, compared with the cinema, books and magazines, television can scarcely be said to be powering the drive towards permissiveness. It is not proven that television is the corrupting influence alleged.'[3]

In America, in direct contrast to their approach to violence, the broadcasting executives treated sex as if they were afraid of offending those viewers who still believed in baby-carrying storks. The obliteration of anything specific on the subject was so complete that in a survey conducted in 1960 only 5 per cent out of over 2,000 viewers complained about sex or vulgarity in the medium. Even then the complaints were directed towards such innocuous items of titillation as 'scantily clad girls in dance shows' or 'sinful things like hugging and kissing'. When vulgar language was condemned, it never had a sexual connotation. Said one protesting parent in this survey: 'Remarks such as "You're a dirty, double-crossing rat." Can you believe my younger one called me that the other day? This is a sample of the language they heard on TV.'[4]

Until the mid-1960s the sexual purity of the American airwaves was so complete that according to *Time* magazine, TV cartoons showed cows without udders and not even a pause was pregnant. As usual, it was sex as a laughing matter that made the first significant dent in this prudery barrier. In 1967 *Laugh-In* demonstrated how popular a show could become by relying on a formula of quick-fire jokes and gags about sensitive subjects like race, religion, politics and sex. Trying to get jokes on the screen about the Pill or the Pope always involved a desperate tussle between the show's producers and NBC's censor. A joke that passed the censor was a news bulletin of the future: 'Vatican, 1988. The church today finally approved the use of the Pill. The announcement was made by Pope Le Roy . . . Junior. His father was not available for comment.' A joke that didn't get by the censor was a young girl saying, 'Don't talk to me about the Pill. It not only doesn't work but it keeps falling out.'

In the media league, television in Britain and America easily comes bottom in the permissive table. The most controversial sex programmes sound almost like Sunday school homilies compared with the erotic material purveyed by other media. Compare, for example, *Panorama*'s programme on sex education with the film, *Love Variations*, which had a cast of two demonstrating 69 positions for sexual intercourse interspersed with several doctors discussing different aspects of lovemaking. Compare the brief glimpses of nudity in the BBC's *Casanova* with the nudity in films like *Flesh* or *I am Curious, Yellow*. Compare the erotic incidents in the *Wednesday Play* with what one reads in novels like *Candy, Lolita, Couples* or *Portnoy's Complaint*. Compare the sex jokes in *Laugh-In* or *Up Pompeii* with the pornographic skits provided in the theatre by *Oh, Calcutta!* or *The Dirtiest Show in Town*.

Yet if television is directly a rather bland and innocuous stimulator of sexual appetites, its very existence has had considerable indirect influences on the permissive climate in Britain and America. Every other medium has in a sense been threatened by the development and speedy growth of television. The small screen not only competes with other media for the public's time and attention, but it also competes with them economically. In order to survive, other media have had to find audiences for something different from predictable television fare; exploit tastes and interests cultivated by the small screen; or provide a more heightened and more intense version of the kind of thing received from the box. Pornography and explicit sex are the commodities that television does not yet offer the public in sufficient doses to satiate it. In this field, the other media can still operate in the sure knowledge that their most powerful rival is not competing.

The medium that has with most fervour turned to sex for economic salvation has been the cinema. Social scientists, notoriously reluctant to commit themselves about anything, are at least agreed that the small screen has been a major factor in the disastrous decline in popularity of the large screen. In Britain in 1955, when commercial television first came on the air, there were 25 million weekly cinema admissions. By 1968 this figure had shrunk to less than 5 million weekly admissions. Almost half of the population in 1972 claims it 'never goes' to the cinema. 'Whilst most Britons read a daily paper and watch television every night, very few go to the cinema even weekly,' writes Winston Fletcher, analysing Britain's media pattern. 'Cinema admission figures show that probably fewer than 5 per cent of the population — i.e. those who claim to go "regularly" — can be going to the cinema every week.'[5] In America a similar precipitous decline in cinema attendances has taken place.

In order to keep afloat as a viable entertainment industry, the content of films has desperately tried to discover some formula that would be so different from television that people would leave their homes to watch it. Extravagant historical and biblical epics were produced which the modest television budget could not match. Then came the big screen Cinemascope. This was followed by the bigger screen Cinerama. Even three-dimensional films were tried and there was one attempt at a 'smellie'. None of these halted the decline in cinema-going. It was perhaps inevitable that explicit and pornographic sex would become one of the staple ingredients of film content. It was something the public could not get from their TV screens.

The causes for obsession with sex in Western societies during the late 1960s are both varied and complex. They include the breakdown in religious faith, the fragmentation of the family unit, the effectiveness of treatment for venereal disease, the invention of the contraceptive pill, the economic independence of women, the rejection of orthodox morals and values. Whether television had existed or not, the media would no doubt have reflected in some measure these changing attitudes to sexual behaviour. In an ultra-permissive society like Denmark, for example, where television is not important, it is unlikely that the pornography in other media was a defensive measure against the competition of the small screen.

But in countries like Britain and America, where for almost three centuries there has been a traditionally censorious approach to pornography or obscenity in public entertainment, it is startling how every medium, with the exception of radio and television, has in the years from 1965 to 1975 become preoccupied with the exploitation of sex in some form or another. The cinema, which has always had a very prim record on sex and has been supersensitive about alienating family audiences, had to risk the loss of such audiences in order to survive. A typical week in London's West End would show a large proportion of cinemas screening films like *I Am A Nymphomaniac*, *Sex Is My Game*, *Do You Believe In Swedish Sin?*, *The Yes Girls*, *Erotic Fantasies*, *Labyrinth of Sex*. Even such impressive films as *Women In Love* and *Midnight Cowboy* contained explicit sexual scenes which would have been unthinkable in films made by major American or British companies in the early 1960s. To suit the needs of the box-office there was a nude Lady Macbeth in Roman Polanski's version of *Macbeth*. With films like *Deep Throat* and *Last Tango In Paris* the cinema had pushed its erotic boundaries almost as far as they could go.

Just as sex became the commodity that audiences, particularly young audiences, could not get from the box, so ultra-violence was used by the cinema for box office appeal. Although in this respect, the overall message of television is that violence is moral and acceptable if done by good guys on behalf of good causes, the viewer is usually shielded from images of the consequences of physical violence. Here again there was an entertainment gap that could be filled by the cinema. The telly generations had for the formative years of their lives been pumped full of hygienised violence. When they went to the cinema — and became the only loyal audience the cinema had left — they were ripe for a richer and more intensive dose of violence than the box was giving them. Having acquired a taste for the stuff, they were ready to patronise the cinema if they were given higher and higher levels of what they had been regularly receiving in their own homes. Films like *Straw Dogs*, *The Dirty Dozen*, *Clockwork Orange*, *The Devils*, revelled in the most sickening displays of rape, brutality, physical torture and details of burnt, torn and crushed bodies. Like everything else in the cinema, this may be a cycle which will eventually pass as audiences turn to something else for excitement. But what will remain behind is a standard of visual portrayal of sex and violence which will have become accepted as a norm for the medium. It is more than a reasonable guess that television played a significant role in stimulating or provoking the cinema to achieve such norms.

An interesting and thoroughly unexpected illustration of the manner in which the cinema, particularly in Britain, is clinging on to the coat-tails of television is the sudden eruption late in the early 1970s of films whose theme and characters are exact replicas of popular series on television. Instead of growing tired of programmes like *Till Death Us Do Part, On The Buses, Up Pompeii, Steptoe and Son*, audiences clearly cannot get enough of them. Films based upon these series have proved that the British public, at least, is even prepared to pay for an extra dose of the same thing they can get free on the small box. Some of these films have been the biggest box office successes in Britain and if the trend continues, the once-vaunted superiority of the cinema over television as a source of creative visual ideas will be more difficult to sustain. If the limited amount of facilities for making films in Britain is to be used for regurgitating the most popular fare of the box, the artistic and imaginative potential of the cinema is bound in the process to be dwarfed and diminished.

When it comes to trying to assess what impact television has had on newspapers, the picture is much more confusing. 'Reading through the forty-odd studies on the effect of television viewing on the press is enough to cause the student of the media to lose faith in social research techniques, not to mention faith in his own intellectual ability to draw together what would appear to be bewildering contradictory evidence,' writes James Curran in *Media Sociology*. 'The findings of these studies are so totally inconsistent that it would seem to be impossible to generalise about the variables influencing TV audience reaction to the press, let alone arrive at a firm conclusion about the overall effect of television on newspaper use.'[6]

It is not my intention to tread heavily where social scientists move only with caution. Although Mr. Curran, in spite of his initial doubts, concludes that television's impact on the press has been exaggerated and that 'the newspaper has an independent life and distinctive appeal of its own', it is a finding that can at best be tentative. By 1968, when Mr. Curran's survey ended, the first telly generation had only just begun to buy newspapers. What impact its attitude to print would eventually have, and what changes it would demand of newspapers, could not be known until that generation had become the predominant buyers of papers. That would not occur until sometime in the late 1970s

Nevertheless there are some trends that are worth discussing. All surveys agree that in Britain and America there has been a drastic decline in newspaper circulation, *per capita*, that coincides with the growth of television. In Britain that decline has been spectacular. In 1968, says Mr. Curran, there were an estimated 762·8 million fewer national newspapers bought than in 1951. But he is not prepared to blame most of this on television, even though other experts do. He suggests that this decline in newspaper readership could be due to an expansion in recreational activities (every survey shows that television is easily the most popular and time-consuming leisure activity in Britain) or to a deterioration in the quality of the press (though most people would argue that the British press has improved in the late 1960s). Mr. Curran's most telling argument that the press has not been seriously affected by television is that although total circulation has gone down from 1950 to 1968 by about 15 per cent, the actual number of *pages* sold has doubled. This is because all newspapers are thicker than they used to be. This increase in pagination, of course, is largely due to the increased space taken up by advertising — display and small ads — but there has also been an increase in the amount of editorial material. Whether this establishes that people are reading more in newspapers is most doubtful. I would doubt that *one* paper containing 48 pages would stimulate more reading than *two* papers of 24 pages each. There's a nice question for some social science study.

If one has to make a choice between conflicting surveys, I would think that common sense would come down on the side of those that believe that declining circulations of newspapers are not merely coincidental with the rise of television viewing but that the latter is a direct cause of a large share of that decline.

But whether or not people read more pages than they used to, there can be no doubt that their choice of newspaper reading material has been seriously curtailed. In New York City most major newspapers have folded since the war, including the *Daily Mirror* and the serious *Herald Tribune*. National newspapers in Britain that have closed since 1945 include the *News Chronicle*, the *Sketch*, *Reynolds Press*, the *Sunday Dispatch*, the *Empire News*, and the *Sunday Chronicle*. Only one new paper, the *Sunday Telegraph* has been started to compensate for this wholesale newspaper decimation. Wherever television functions as a serious competitor for advertising revenue, the newspaper industry is in a bad way.

It is unquestionably the struggle for advertising, rather than readers, that kills newspapers and magazines. When the *News Chronicle* died it was still selling 1,162,194 copies per day. The *Empire News* had a circulation of 2,084,397 when it had to give up the ghost. This narrowing of choice so that fewer alternative political attitudes and opinions can be reflected in the press can, in the long run, have considerable repercussions on the ability of democracies to function. After all, a democracy presumes that minorities have the right and capacity within the political structure to one day become majorities. But if the number of newspapers continues to shrink, and television denies to minorities the right to be effectively heard, the frustrations that can be built up in the body politic are self-evident. It is no consolation for the millions of Liberal supporters who read the *News Chronicle* that they can now read more pages of newsprint in the columns of the Labour *Daily Mirror* or the Conservative *Daily Express*.

Since 1968 there are quite apparent signs that newspaper content is increasingly shaping itself to adjust to the demands of a telly society. We have already indicated that the greater permissiveness in language may have taken its cue from a freeing of language on television. Similarly, television has affected the make-up and design of newspapers and magazines. For decades journals and periodicals would continue to offer the same look to their readers. But in the past few years there has been a constant tinkering and manipulation of layout and type faces as papers try to excite and stimulate the eye with their stories and pictures. The *Guardian*, with its large pictures and almost jazzy presentation, has in the last few years become almost unrecognisable from the staid, dour *Manchester Guardian* of the past.

Only *The Times* seems to have retreated from a bolder, looser, more pictorial make-up into a tighter concentration on more words per column-inch. And even that policy has come about as a direct reaction to the competition of television. 'The great weakness of television,' said its editor, William Rees-

Mogg, 'is the brevity of its current affairs and news coverage ... the brief vivid snapshot, the actual sight of the people involved, the headline news or the inconclusive five minute discussion, often make television coverage an aperitif for newspaper coverage in greater depth.'[7] It was clearly this line of thinking that moved *The Times* to a policy of more wordage per page so that it could take advantage of television's intrinsic inability to provide adequate treatment of the news.

The vast expense of colour printing, which most newspapers have undertaken in the late 1960s, has also been a direct answer to the arrival of colour television. Although the minority channel, BBC-2, was able to transmit colour in 1967, it was not until November 1969, that colour came to BBC-1 and the commercial network. Once advertisers began to recognise the pulling power of colour TV commercials, the newspapers were forced to provide the same sort of service. By 1972 most newspapers were printing a certain proportion of their pages in colour. As technological advances make this process more efficient and cheaper, colour will take over more areas of paper space. One can envisage eventually all-colour papers. The timing and speed of this innovation can be directly attributed to the impact of television.

Although the material provided by the press will remain basically the same — hard news, human interest stories, sports, cartoons, current affairs features, gossip, comment, photographs — the treatment of these ingredients is changing because of television. The quality papers like the *Sunday Times* regularly produce in-depth studies of situations like the American elections, Ulster, Bangladesh, running into tens of thousands of words. Some of these features by their Insight team are so long and so comprehensive that they have been turned into highly successful paperback books. The other quality newspapers have also started to print these long, behind-the-scenes investigations which are believed to attract serious readers because this sort of detailed analysis is rarely seen on the box.

The popular British papers have, like the cinema, embarked on a formula which, on the one hand, tries to give the reader what he can't get on the box and, on the other hand, acts as a sort of fan magazine for the characters, programmes and performers that appear on television. The most successful newspaper in 1971 in Britain, in terms of circulation, was *The Sun*. Taking over an ailing newspaper which traditional newspaper proprietors had written off as a doomed property, the new owners concentrated their efforts on sex features and a plentiful supply of bare-bosomed beauties (neither of which the small screen supplied in large doses) and television supplements of gossip and pictures which ranged in size from four pages on weekdays to eight pages for weekend viewing. By 1971 *The Sun*, after only two years' operation, had almost trebled its circulation in a period of declining newspaper circulations. The other popular papers got the message and have started to provide the same sort of material. It should also be noted that *The Sun* picked up a large share of its readers from Britain's first telly generation. It would need very large blinkers to contend in 1975 that the British press had not been significantly affected in appearance, approach and content by the competitive pressures of television.

Television, too, has had a crippling effect on popular magazines in Britain and America. In Britain until 1954 magazines enjoyed a constantly rising share of the total advertising revenue. But with the advent of commercial television, this advertising slice diminished rapidly. Magazines like *Picture Post, Everybody's, Illustrated*, were forced to close. In America some of the most famous magazines in the country and with circulations numbering many millions — *Saturday Evening Post, Colliers, Look, Life* — were crushed in the fierce fight for advertising.

Again it was by offering what the small screen did not generally provide that magazines succeeded in holding on to readers. Television, oddly enough, has never discovered a successful formula for a woman's programme which could offer the blend of home hints, knitting patterns, recipes, beauty advice, fashion pictures, advice to the socially worried and lovelorn, romantic short stories, that make up the bulk of material in women's magazines. On the whole, therefore, journals like *Woman, Vogue, Woman's Weekly, Honey*, have survived in the telly age. But they, too, are undergoing a transformation as television makes more and more inroads on the total national advertising revenue. The trend towards frank and outspoken articles on sex — how to rouse your man, advice on contraceptives, the problem of frigidity — in women's magazines reached a publishing climax in 1972 with the advent into Britain of *Cosmopolitan* whose declared policy of sexual aggressiveness and awareness included the promise of a double-page spread in colour of a male frontal nude. Already a highly successful magazine, it looked as if *Cosmopolitan* had reached another willing market in Britain when its first edition of 300,000 copies was sold out just two days after publication. Of course, the ability of magazines like *Playboy* and *Penthouse* to flourish in the telly age because of their titillating fare has long been known. The demand for *Cosmopolitan* indicates that the appetite for permissive reading and pictorial matter — which the box does little to satiate — is increasingly shared by both sexes.

Since the theatre is very much a minority art form, it has not been too adversely affected by the popularity of television. Although most of Britain's big variety theatres have closed, the music hall tradition still flourishes in large drinking clubs — particularly in the North of England. The big increase in tourism during the late 1960s has tended to obscure the size of Britain's theatre-going public since London's West End now counts upon visiting foreigners for a major share of its financial support.

Yet in an oblique way, television has been partly responsible for a Governmental decision which has had considerable impact on the kind of plays the public can now see in Britain. In 1968 the Lord Chamberlain's responsibility for the censoring of plays was abolished. This decision has left the theatres free to show anything they like subject only to the normal laws of libel, blasphemy and obscenity. Although numerous attempts had been made by such formidable figures as Bernard Shaw and John Galsworthy to remove theatre censorship, they had always failed. Pornography and indecency were not the only subjects that the Lord Chamberlain prohibited on the stage. His *fiat* enabled him to prevent the depiction of any living person on the stage and to reject anything he considered deleterious to the nation's morals or political sensibilities. He could ban anything from the angle at which a plank was carried in a comic sketch to the production of a play about Winston Churchill. But his strictures and judgments

303

appeared more and more untenable and ludicrous in view of what the public could see uncensored in their living-rooms. While the Lord Chamberlain had doubts about Sartre's *Huis Clos*, the BBC had no hesitation about transmitting it. While the Lord Chamberlain prohibited skits about Jacqueline Kennedy or rude references to God, the BBC satire shows were providing blistering and mocking denunciations of living Cabinet Ministers and biting and vulgar sketches about religion.

It was clearly a preposterous situation to have the Lord Chamberlain preventing a few thousand theatre-goers from seeing exactly the same type of material that was being watched by many millions on television. Even Parliament recognised the incongruity of this state of affairs and finally in 1968 deprived the Lord Chamberlain of his censorship function. The very next day *Hair* (which the Lord Chamberlain would never have permitted) turned up in the West End and not only ran for over five years but was in 1972 invited to put on part of the show in St. Paul's Cathedral. Plays which would not conceivably have had a chance of being licensed under the Lord Chamberlain, and which have since had runs in London, include *The Soldiers, Oh, Calcutta!, The Dirtiest Show In Town* and *Let My People Come*. The *avant-garde* drama has demonstrated practically every phase of physical and sexual activity in its gropings towards a freer and more meaningful contemporary theatre. For this freedom from censorship and blossoming of a more adventurous and experimental spirit in the theatre, television must undoubtedly get some of the credit.

The early optimism that television, by stimulating curiosity and interest in a large number of activities not normally seen by viewers, would encourage people to read books about those interests and thus spread the reading habit has recently suffered some decisive checks. Although it is true that the number of book titles published annually in Britain and America has continued to rise during the television era, it is probable that this proliferation of books owes as much to the general affluence of society and to the escalating sums of state money spent on educational books as it does to any real increase in the population's desire to read.

As any publisher knows, the market for hardback novels is

shrinking at a rapid pace and the overall demand for fiction — paperback and hardback — is declining. With many publishers refusing to publish any new novels, the prospect of unknown writers seeing their work in print is not great. 'Unless a novel is either outstanding or very filthy,' a prominent British agent told me, 'I haven't a hope in hell of selling it.' It is interesting to note again how books, like the cinema, magazines, papers and the theatre, have turned to the one staple ingredient that television does not generously provide — sex — for economic viability.

If the prospect for literary fiction is gloomy when the majority of book-buyers still belong to the non-telly generations, the prognoses for some future revival of interest in books are hardly reassuring. In February 1972 the National Foundation for Educational Research published the results of a test designed to judge the general cultural knowledge of British trainee teachers. They were asked to name, amongst other relatively simple questions, the authors of *War and Peace, Mein Kampf, 1984, Brave New World, Crime and Punishment, Peter Pan, Under Milk Wood, The Hound of the Baskervilles, The Decline and Fall of the Roman Empire, Dr. Zhivago.* More than half the trainee teachers got 80 per cent of the answers wrong. When the *Daily Mail* tested these findings by selecting four typical student teachers of their own, aged between 19 and 22, they were only able to answer 25 per cent of these questions.[8]

Asked to comment upon this appallingly low level of knowledge about some of the most famous books in Western culture, a spokesman for the National Union of Teachers had this to say: 'Youngsters are better informed today but the kind of general knowledge they have is different from that gained by their examiners 25 years ago. They tend to read fewer books than their predecessors but they go to more films and see more television and gain a wide range of a different type of general knowledge from these sources.'[9]

Although one cannot make too many deductions from a single survey, the response of these young people conforms to the general picture of a declining interest in literature. Since this test was taken amongst potential teachers whose views and tastes would ultimately be communicated to their pupils, it does not indicate that future generations are likely to be imbued with any zeal or passion for books by educational guardians brought up in the telly age.

A further blow to any complacency about the reading habits of telly-oriented children came in March 1972, with a report by the National Foundation for Educational Research. It revealed that instead of a rising curve of reading efficiency amongst young children, reading skills had been on a descending curve since 1964. In spite of the huge sums of money spent on better schools, higher paid teachers, more efficient teaching methods, schools in Britain were turning out marginally more illiterates in 1971 than they were in 1964. The 11-year-old of 1971 was four months behind his 1964 equivalent in reading ability. Seven out of ten children at the age of 15 did worse in reading than the previous generation ten years ago. For the first time since records were started 25 years ago, reading standards had dropped.

The immediate result of this report was a heated argument amongst educationalists about the efficiency of modern methods of teaching reading. So alarming and dispiriting was this evidence of an educational set-back that the Minister responsible for education, Mrs. Margaret Thatcher, announced an investigation by a committee of experts into the problems of reading in primary schools. Although officialdom said little about the relationship between the rise of television and this state of affairs, there were a number of informed people who did.

Said Nicholas Bagnall, educational correspondent of the *Sunday Telegraph*: 'How many children who, before the mid-'sixties, would have gone to bed with a story read from a book now get their soporific from the television screen? How many who in earlier days would have grown up seeing their parents reading, even if the reading matter was only newspapers or magazines, now merely see them watching? If anyone is to look closely into the reasons for this apparent decline in reading standards, the first thing to be done, perhaps, is a careful survey of parents' reading and viewing habits.'[10]

Supporting the findings of the 1972 reports of the National Foundation for Educational research was a survey published by the University of Sheffield in 1974. It found a definite correlation between reading and TV — the more that children watched television, the less they were likely to read.

The deterrent impact upon reading and literacy skills of television was also noted in other countries besides Britain. In 1974 the University of California reported with some alarm that half of their latest intake — and they came from the top 12 per cent of high school graduates — were semi-illiterate. No less than 52 per cent of these students needed remedial instruction in basic English. And the University laid the blame for this startling drop in reading standards squarely on television.

And in Germany a survey by the West German Book Association in 1974 showed that one-third of all West Germans had not read a book in the previous 12 months. In spite of a considerable rise in leisure time during the seven years since their last survey, the hours spent reading books had gone down by some 4 per cent. Time spent watching television had risen from 25 hours weekly, in 1967 to 31 hours in 1974. Books for entertainment had particularly suffered; educational books had just held their own. Being well-read, which previously had been rated highly by Germans as a desirable social quality, was no longer so.

More complacent about the fall in reading standards in Britain was the Bullock report on reading which was a direct result of the 1972 findings by the National Foundation of Reading. In a cumbersome report of over 600 pages, involving no less than 330 conclusions and recommendations, it said that although there was no evidence of a general decline in reading amongst children, it was clear that standards had been falling in slum areas and among the children of semi-skilled and unskilled workers.

Its express consideration of the impact of television in this area was superficial and based upon generalisations rather than any specially commissioned research data. Having found that children spend an average of 25 hours weekly in front of television — about the same as they spend in a classroom — they concluded that long hours watching TV could be detrimental to reading skills but need not necessarily be so. If parents supervised a child's TV watching and if children watched the better programmes, the deleterious possibilities of television could be nullified. Since all the evidence shows that most parents have only a cursory control over their children's viewing habits and that children prefer cheap undemanding programmes to so-called good ones, the Bullock findings cannot be said to offer much enlightenment about this particular aspect of children's literacy. Of course, any society, if it is prepared to exert the necessary effort and spend the necessary money, can maintain a reasonable standard of reading skills amongst its people. What the Bullock report has singularly failed to answer is whether the existence of television in its present form in Britain — with its special addictive appeal to children — has made the task of maintaining reading standards more difficult and more costly.

Whatever else television may be doing, it does not seem on this evidence to be furthering the literary aspirations of a society whose main cultural experiences have been derived from the printed word.

Thus almost every other medium has been subtly or overtly forced to adjust its content and direction because of the very existence of television. Again, as I have continued to stress in this book, it would be impossible to make any positive value judgments about the ultimate effect of these changes in media upon society. It could be argued, for example, that the competition of television has forced the cinema to make fewer films but better and more imaginative ones; that it has brought about more lively and more readable and more colourful newspapers; that it has helped the theatre by contributing to an atmosphere that ended censorship. It may even be contended that societies stimulated and provoked by visual stimuli and less reliant on the logical constraints of the printed word could in the long run prove to be happier and more humane than those that have existed since Gutenberg invented moving type.

Time alone will test these arguments. But it would seem to be unarguable that there is a peripheral TV factor operating significantly on the most important cultural and communications structures in Western societies like Britain and America. Recognition of its existence and deciding whether that influence should be curbed or encouraged is a task that confronts ruling bodies and establishments if they wish to maintain any control or understanding of the shape and direction their societies are taking.

CHAPTER ELEVEN

The Best Television in the World?

*The quality in human nature on which we must pin
our hopes is its proven adaptability.*
        Arnold Toynbee, *Cities on the Move*

*Without at all being a do-gooder, a broadcaster is in all
his decisions involved with the moral life of his society,
with its patterns of value, with the stresses and changes
those patterns are undergoing.*
        Richard Hoggart, Reith Lectures, 1971

Broadcasters, like prophets, are usually without honour in their
own country. Few voices are confidently raised in praise of
their own national television service. It is a medium that intellectuals have written off, academics shrug off, politicians dither
about and the masses accept. After 25 years of existence, the
predominant mood of those concerned with its future is resignation. 'Contempt for the general public is built into employ-
ment in the American media of mass communication and soon
translates itself into self-contempt,' wrote Diana Trilling of her
country's television. 'To work for television, in particular,
implies that one has turned one's back on the values most
prized by education. One has become, if not a huckster oneself,
then his henchman.'[1]

Newsweek, noting the BBC's 50th anniversary year, claimed
that in 1972 most discriminating viewers in America would
enthusiastically agree that British television was the best in the
world. This was because they had been seeing on their own
screens such successful BBC shows as *The Six Wives of Henry
VIII, The Forsyte Saga, Civilization, Elizabeth R, The Search
for the Nile* and two popular comedy shows, *All in the Family*
and *Sandford and Son* which were American versions of the

Corporation's *Till Death Us Do Part* and *Steptoe and Son*. Yet *Newsweek* had to admit that its complimentary assessment of the BBC was not shared by 'thoughtful' British viewers. 'For the surprising fact is that the government-owned BBC is currently under unprecedented siege from both within and without its august sanctum,' it wrote. 'The BBC stands accused of both arrogance and timidity in its news coverage, of discouraging enterprise among its younger producers and of mining the historical-epic format to the point of downright obsession.'[2]

The radio and TV editor of *Variety*, Les Brown, also posed the question of the respective merits of national television systems. 'Now what do you suppose is the finest, best or greatest TV system in the world?' he said. 'I didn't know, so I asked several well-travelled people, and the answer always came out the same. Without hesitation they answered "West Germany". The reason, they said, is that broadcast values there are relatively pure. Programs go on the air not because they will attract large audiences or make a lot of money but because they *ought* to go on the air. And I'm told, the professionals at the two German networks strive continually to improve upon their craft, to venture further with program concepts, cultural content and ideas as well as with technology and production techniques.'[3]

Yet when I spoke to a number of knowledgeable West Germans they derided the idea that their television was either very good or in any way exceptional. Similarly the most severe criticism I have heard about Swedish, Dutch, Italian and French television has come from Swedish, Dutch, Italian and French broadcasters or journalists. Judging from their output, it is not likely that 'thoughtful' viewers in East European countries are any more enchanted about their programmes than are 'thoughtful' viewers in the West. Writing from Moscow in *The Times*, David Bonavia had this to say about Russian television: 'Addiction to television is less common here than in the West, because the programmes are frankly less enticing. A lecturer in broadcasting at Moscow University was called on recently to defend the medium after a woman had declared in the press that she had never been happier than since the set broke down, though she had once thought she could not do without it.'[4]

What is there, then, about this twentieth-century medium

that provokes universally such a sense of disillusionment and resignation amongst discriminating and concerned people? I suspect that this feeling of disappointment stems from a suspicion about the influence of television and a recognition that its real potential for further cultural and moral values has hardly been scratched. Surely something so powerful should be better!

Yet while governments pay constant lip-service to the concept of 'good' television, its quality always has a lower priority in their minds than other aspects of the medium. In totalitarian or monolithic societies the need for television to act as a conditioning or educative force for the prevailing ideology is more important than the 'quality' of programmes. In so-called free societies questions of financing the medium, the satisfaction of commercial interests, the need to appease political parties and pressure groups, are felt by all governments to be more important than 'quality'.

Operating under such constraints, television is never free. In totalitarian states its chains are forged out of strict doctrinaire demands; in democracies it is hobbled by state licensing and financing regulations and the need for advertising revenue. As yet, governments have been free to handle television exactly as they please. No public anywhere has yet recognised television as a serious social issue demanding undue passion, interest or concern. There are unlikely to be massive demonstrations about it; its shape or structure has never been a major election issue; its handling has never threatened or toppled any government.

On the contrary, the masses have been singularly docile about whatever diet of television they have been offered. Minorities may grumble and a few politicians mutter but, except for isolated programmes, the public on the whole tolerantly accepts what the small screen provides. In Hungary at peak-time on a Saturday night viewers are offered a 1½-hour portrait of the artistic director of the State Folk Ensemble. A Russian peak-time show lasting 1½ hours is billed as 'a meeting between Moscow workers and artists'. In Britain four times a week in the early prime-time hours the commercial channel provides an unimaginative, predictable, badly written soap opera called *Crossroads*. These programmes reflect in their respective ways the general tone of these television services. They

311

are received and watched without any undue complaints from the bulk of viewers in these countries.

Where viewers have a choice, they unhesitatingly choose lighter fare over more demanding programmes. Where, as in America, the choice can be between five or six types of light entertainment throughout the entire evening, public preference can be very fickle. But while the popularity and ratings of individual programmes may rise or fall, the actual act of viewing remains relatively constant. In many homes in Britain and America the set is switched on like an electric light and remains on throughout the evening. In Britain if three serious programmes were to confront each other on the main channels, the total number of viewers tuned in to them would not be far less than if two popular and one serious programme were in competition. The viewing see-saw may change but the total volume of viewers does not alter very much. Of course, some major popular event like a Royal Variety Show, the Eurovision Song Contest or a World Cup Final could jolt the total viewing into an above-average figure but generally the peak-time audience, give or take a few percentage points, remains remarkably static.

To illustrate the point, let us look at the ratings in the London area for the first week in April 1972. On Monday at 8 p.m. a serious current affairs show (*World in Action*) on ITV, opposite another serious current affairs show (*Panorama*) on BBC-1, with a popular film on BBC-2, produced ratings of 38 for ITV, 14 for BBC-1 and 17 for BBC-2. Total viewing figures: 69. On Thursday of the same week at 9.30 p.m. a serious current affairs programme (*This Week*) on ITV, opposite a serious play on BBC-1, with a popular variety show on BBC-2, produced ratings of 26 for ITV, 24 for BBC-1 and 21 for BBC-2. Total viewing figures: 71. A half hour earlier when commercial television has a popular show, BBC-2's ratings were only 3. But the total viewing figures were 74. Thus it can be seen how the minority channel, BBC-2, which usually averages a weekly 5 rating, attracts unusually high ratings only when the other major channels go serious. These figures show that within a few percentage points viewers cling loyally to the box — whatever happens to be on.

It is evident, then, that for most people the act of watching the box has become a habit rather than a conscious discriminatory act. There is growing evidence, too, that it is becoming for many people an addiction. It was noted in the early days of British television when the BBC discontinued transmitting in the early evening to enable mothers to put children to bed without the competitive attractions of television, that sets remained switched on during this 'toddler's truce' even though the only thing to see was a slow-turning water-wheel.

Confirmation of the addictive nature of television came from an experiment conducted in 1971 in West Germany by the Munich Society for Rational Psychology. The society asked 184 habitual viewers to give up television for a year. As an inducement, married couples were paid four pounds a week — single people half that sum — if they stopped watching. Within three weeks one man was back on the box; within five months all had returned to it. Commented the German psychologists: 'We did not expect that all participants would stick to our rules for a whole year, but that nobody was able to abstain for six months from viewing television defies all our forecasts.'

The report also showed that with television out of the way, people returned to more active and wider social activities. Their visits to the cinema increased threefold; they saw friends and relatives twice as often; they spent twice as much time reading and playing games. A significant result, in terms of what TV can do to the family structure, was that 93 per cent of the sample said they were more concerned than they had been before about what their children were doing.

But deprivation of the box also increased tension in the home; there was more quarrelling and physical aggression. Sexual activities also changed. Husbands had more extra-marital affairs; performed less frequently and less satisfactorily in bed. When they returned to the small screen, sexual habits went back to normal, although for a short time orgasms and masturbation practices increased. 'Men and girls appearing on TV stimulate viewers erotically,' says the report. 'They tend to forget or suppress their personal problems and embrace each other under the influence of television regardless of whether they are watching late news or listening to a weekend sermon.'[5] The psychologist, Henner Ertel, did not assume, however, from this limited experiment that television was either a tranquillizer or an aphrodisiac. 'With people who watch regularly,' he said, 'many behaviour patterns become so closely related to TV that they are negatively influenced if one takes the set away. The problem is that of addiction.'[6]

A similar noticeable change in social activities was seen when Britain — probably one of the heaviest TV addicted societies in the world — had to go on a three-day working week in 1973-74 due to the oil shortage combined with a coal miners' strike. During this economic dislocation all television was shut down by 10.30 p.m. for about three months. The deprivation of television immediately resulted in an increase in the sale of paperback books, a rise in cinema-going, a greater demand for chess-sets and games like Monopoly, an increase in the sale of cotton, wool and knitting patterns. No doubt if anyone had seriously investigated the matter, it could have been shown that this dark period also saw a heightening of visits and social intercourse between families and friends as well as an increase in conversation between children and parents in the family circle.

If, then, TV societies are creating large numbers of tube addicts — large enough to make up a substantial share of the nation — it would appear that any government's television policy in such societies would have to consider and resolve two major problems. First, should TV addiction be encouraged or discouraged? Is a society healthier if most people prefer to get most of their vicarious emotional and cultural experiences from the box rather than from books, the cinema, the theatre, etc.? Is a society saner and sounder if people watch more and do less?

Secondly, if viewers become addicted it appears that they will watch almost anything that is shown to them, even serious or boring programmes, rather than switch the set off. Does this not indicate that the desire of the public for entertainment programmes has been exaggerated? Does it not suggest that a state television policy which insisted on a more serious programme diet during peak-time hours would not annoy or outrage the telly public? Might it, at worst, merely cause people to switch off their sets and thus take them a tiny step towards breaking their habit or addiction? And would this necessarily be a bad thing?

Any determined Government policy to wean away people

from reliance on the telly would naturally affront advertisers whose aim is to get more people watching the box more of the time. Since television is a very expensive service, many states turn to advertising revenue to help defray some of its costs. But a great many countries — Belgium, Denmark, Norway, Sweden, the East European states — have no advertising on the small screen and finance it by licence fees, a tax on sets, or direct state grants. Many European countries limit the amount of advertising, the income from which is usually siphoned into the national exchequer. In Western Germany, where the service is financed by licence fee, advertising revenue goes into a fund for the encouragement of the arts and other leisure activities. Oddly enough only a very few countries have systems which permit private commercial stations, financed by advertising, to operate in competition with a state TV system. These are Britain, Canada, Japan, New Zealand and Australia. America is the only nation in the world that has no state TV channel although a limited educational network gets federal funds, and, with that exception, has its entire TV system dependent on advertising money.

With such a diversity in the financial structuring of national systems — even amongst free societies — the question that obviously must be asked is which methods produce the 'best' television? As has been noted, the 'best' as assessed by discriminating viewers, is usually somebody else's television, and depends, of course, upon what is meant by 'best'. If the prime purpose of television is to earn money then American television is clearly the 'best' in the world. 'Ours is by far the most productive television system in the world — in terms of product made and marketed — and without doubt it is the most profitable,' wrote Les Brown in *Variety*. 'We do know better than anyone how to make mass appeal shows for the lowest common denominator. And this year our industry will sell more than 90 million dollars worth of product abroad. We are where the money is, but those who would define that as "finest broadcasting in the world" show where their values are.'[7]

If the prime purpose of television is to indoctrinate viewers with ideological principles then it might be argued that Chinese television after the Cultural Revolution is the 'best' in the world. Before the Cultural Revolution, under Liu Shao-chi,

315

Chinese television transmitted shows of general interest, aesthetic appeal and entertainment. These latter were known as 'laughing parties'. But the Revolution gave a harder purpose to the box. 'What is television?' said a Peking TV administrator. 'It is education. We have newsreels, documentaries, forums and revolutionary model opera, ballets and orchestral music. They all teach. So did "laughing parties". They taught. "Be easy going: don't be intense. Relax a bit." We educate the people to make great efforts in studying the works of Marx, Engels, Lenin and Mao Tse-tung, to remould their world outlook, to encourage them to make their contribution to society, and help them to do their vocational work well.'[8]

If the prime purpose of television is to provide relaxation and entertainment, with a small stiffening of informational programmes which do not seriously challenge the status quo, and cultural programmes which do not make too many mental or emotional demands on viewers, then it could be argued that British television is the 'best' in the world. But if the purpose of a television service is to recognise that there are moral and cultural goals towards which every society must, no matter how gropingly and how imprecisely, strive, and that its duty is to help in the struggle to achieve those goals, then British television is far from the 'best' in the world. It stands on the sidelines of that struggle; it is rarely in the heart of the mêlée.

When people, particularly foreigners, talk about the performance of British television they tend to think of the BBC. But over half the viewing time in Britain is spent watching the commercial channel, not the BBC. The programmes that bombard most viewers minds most of the time are not the BBC's *Civilization* or *Panorama* or *Play of the Month,* but ITV's *Coronation Street, Callan* or *Hawaii Five-O.* Ninety per cent of the commercial network's schedule at peak time is devoted to entertainment. Although commercial companies contend that they produce almost as many hours of serious programming as of light entertainment and sport, if not more, the volume of viewers that watch these generally off-peak programmes is a tiny fraction of those that watch the peak-time programmes. In the case of children, the imbalance between the hours occupied by watching entertainment rather than informational or educational programmes is even greater.

Ever since the arrival of commercial television and the BBC's decision to compete with ITV in showing at peak times amusing and frivolous programmes, with a special emphasis on sport, the tilt towards a national service primarily dedicated to an entertainment ethos has been dramatic. The argument that television functions in this way because it is merely reflecting life was neatly dismissed by Richard Hoggart in his 1971 Reith Lectures when he said that this kind of reflector usually means 'someone in power's idea of what the culture should look like'. It might also be asked how a service that confesses that most of its material is escapist can also claim that it is mirroring society. Something that escapes from life can hardly be a mirror of it. The contention that what is being provided is 'what the public wants' is not only objectively unprovable, but as the TV addiction patterns demonstrate, the public is fast reaching a point where it will watch anything it is given. The fact that in Britain party political broadcasts — probably the most boring fare regularly seen on the box — which must be shown on all channels simultaneously causes no significant switch off or drift away from the set, proves how nonsensical is the parroted shibboleth that television will only be popular if it serves up 'what the public wants'.

Sir Hugh Greene called 'giving the public what it wants' a loaded phrase. 'This phrase is linked with "democracy" and with "trusting the people" — the simple faith, preached by many men who are not at all simple, that what most people want all people should have,' he said. 'To use the word "freedom" in this connection is an abuse of language. What we are in fact concerned with at this point is tyranny — the tyranny of the ratings or the mind machines ... Does democracy really triumph if we merely give some mild pleasure or a soporific to people too indifferent to switch the programme off? Are we not doing more for democracy if we sometimes, even quite often, give great pleasure to a few people even at the cost of provoking many into switching off?'[9]

But countries who rely upon advertising revenue to finance a large share of their television services obviously cannot advocate policies aimed at breaking the TV habit or designed to limit seriously the goals of advertisers who want their commercials to be seen by the largest number of viewers. Once the volume of viewers becomes the major success criterion of a television service, it is bound to become primarily an entertainment medium.

There are only a handful of countries in the world that consider entertainment to be the dominant purpose of television — America, Britain, Canada, Australia and Japan are the most significant. The vast majority of countries maintain a much more equitable balance between entertainment, education and information in their overall output. Their ability to use television more seriously than just for 'laughing parties' is based upon their readiness to forgo advertising revenues as a major source of financing. Thus West Germany allows 30 minutes of advertising per day, Holland 24 minutes, Finland 20 minutes, Italy 17 minutes, France 8 minutes. Many countries have no advertising at all. Britain, by comparison, permits one hour of advertising daily — twice to three times as much as most European countries. Countries like America and Canada have much more advertising than Britain. The relationship between the volume of advertising and the volume of entertainment is clear. Television in America and Canada is more entertainment-oriented than it is in Britain. Television in Britain is more entertainment-oriented than it is in any other European country.

If the reader concedes that television is a major conditioning and environmental factor in people's lives, he may still conclude that television's influence has not been particularly baleful or that alternatively its benefits have balanced its evils. Having discussed the possible consequences of TV violence on children, Dr. Hilde Himmelweit in her 1970 Japan Prize Lecture summed up the moral equation in these terms: 'What I am stressing here are two things: first that television unintentionally provides a one-sided view and, second, that this view derives from the news as much as from fictional programmes. These effects (the deficits of the television age) must be placed alongside its equally powerful benefits, namely its capacity to enrich the child's view of life through science, drama, art, music and sport.'

What we must ask ourselves is not only whether television frustrates a society's goals but whether it can ever be enlisted to further them. If television is expected primarily to amuse or provide an escape from reality it is obvious that it can do little to bring viewers an awareness of reality. But if it helps guide viewers, and particularly the young, into paths deemed false or dangerous by society should that society remain indifferent to those consequences?

In outlining the manner in which television acts as a positive, probable or peripheral TV factor in countries like America and Britain where most people use television chiefly as an escapist medium, it is pertinent how the years 1964 to 1968 turned up again and again as the critical years when certain social trends began to heighten and intensify in an abnormal manner. In those years we saw an unusual escalation of violence amongst the young, a blossoming of the hippie movement with its rejection of conventional mores and standards, an unprecedented revulsion against parental and establishment authority, a startling rise in drug taking, a stand-still in reading standards and a diminution of interest in literacy. And, of course, 1964 to 1968 were the years when the first telly generations the world had ever seen moved into adolescence and early maturity.

Countries that did not have entertainment-oriented television or had little television — Russia, West Germany, Holland, France, Norway, Switzerland — did not experience these developments amongst the young to anything like the same degree.

It is important to remember when discussing how television can best be used to enhance the life-style of a society that it is the totality of the medium that matters. Trying to hitch various kinds of programmes to specific social reactions is bound to be a fruitless and frustrating exercise. After many years of studying the impact of violence, the social scientists have grudgingly accepted that there is some causal relationship between the vast volume of TV violence and the stimulation of aggressive tendencies amongst the young. But the TV mosaic stimulates violence not only by directly portraying it on the screen but by transmitting a coarse, selfish and shallow vision of life.

Only a tiny segment of this kind of television encourages the young to be socially aware, to be co-operative and responsible, to be community conscious, to value the truth, to despise cruelty, to cultivate a sense of duty, to be charitable, to be selfless, to be kind. Most of it is indifferent or neutral about social values, inculcates little sense of communal duty or responsibility, promotes the acquisition of goods as a criterion of success, glamorises the trivial and superficial, justifies violence as a means to moral and legal ends, encourages an escapist approach to reality and concern, builds up false expectations, stimulates an undue craving for material rewards. Broadcasters do not transmit these values deliberately or callously; they are the accidental by-products of the system. But the pro-social messages are heavily out-weighed by the anti-social messages.

Impressive and authoritative support for the view that television is one of the dominant factors in the development of the contemporary American child comes from the social scientist, Urie Bronfenbrenner, who frequently advises the American Government on matters affecting national policy on children. In his book *Two Worlds of Childhood*, Mr. Bronfenbrenner reports on the results of an intensive, eight-year comparative study of the behaviour patterns and social attitudes of American and Russian children. The book has been described by academic authorities as 'one of the most important books of this generation' and 'one of the most important books in the field of child rearing to have been published in the last quarter century'.

Dr. Bronfenbrenner's findings make disturbing reading in the West. His surveys show that American children are more likely to be cruel, inconsiderate or dishonest, that fewer of them are polite, orderly, kind or helpful, that many are selfish and few have any real sense of responsibility compared to Soviet children who develop a concern for others and a feeling of community at an early age. The reasons for this increasing anti-social behaviour of American children, according to Bronfenbrenner, are that increasing urbanisation and other social changes have diminished the role of the family as a socialising agent. Economic and technological progress has decreased the opportunity for contact between children and parents. American parents do not spend as much time with their children as they used to, or as much time as do parents in Russia and other European countries. 'If a child is not with his parents or other adults, where does he spend his time?' asks Bronfenbrenner. 'There are two answers to this question. First and foremost, he is with other children — in school, after school, over weekends, and on holidays ... But there is a second context in which American children spend much of their time. And again they are propelled there in part by parental pressure. They watch television.'[10]

Bronfenbrenner then goes on to examine the vast amount of time children spend in front of TV sets and the various studies that have been done assessing the relationship between observed violence in TV programmes and subsequent aggressive behaviour. His conclusions? 'The implications of these research findings for the impact of television on its viewers are obvious,' he writes. 'Given the salience of violence in commercial television, including cartoons especially intended for children, there is every reason to believe that this mass medium is playing a significant role in generating and maintaining a high level of violence in American society, including the nation's children and youth.'[11]

Bronfenbrenner points out that the institutions in America that were traditionally responsible for character education no longer effectively perform that task. The role of the Church has withered. The family is no longer in a position to exercise its responsibilities. The school is 'debarred by tradition, lack of experience, and preoccupation with subject matter from concerning itself in any major way with the child's development as a person.' Where then does the child acquire most of his moral and cultural attitudes and precepts? 'The vacuum, moral and emotional, created by this state of affairs is then filled — by default — on the one hand by the television screen with its daily message of commercialism and violence, and on the other by the socially isolated, age-graded peer group, with its impulsive search for thrills and its limited capacities as a humanising agent.'

For the British reader who may be comforting himself that Dr. Bronfenbrenner's findings are peculiarly American, and have no relevance to the state of affairs in Britain, there is a sting in the tail. 'It is noteworthy that, of all the countries in which my colleagues and I are working, now numbering half a dozen both in West and East, the only one which exceeds the United States in the willingness of children to engage in antisocial behaviour is the nation closest to us in our Anglo-Saxon traditions of individualism. The country is England, the home of the Mods and the Rockers, the Beatles, the Rolling Stones, and our principal competitor in tabloid sensationalism, juvenile delinquency, and violence. The difference between England and America in our results is not great, but it is statistically reliable.'[12]

Since both America and Britain have similar approaches to television entertainment, since television of that kind plays a significant role in causing anti-social behaviour amongst children in America, it should come as a surprise to no one that British children are moving in the same bewildering and frightening direction.

What then is to be done about the ravenous eye? Should we avert our gaze from its malevolent glare and pretend that it is changing nothing? Or should we pay heed to the warnings of people like Dr. Bronfenbrenner, Margaret Mead, Walter Lippmann, Arthur Schlesinger Jr., Malcolm Muggeridge, Clive Barnes, the late Lord Reith and many others who have from time to time expressed serious concern about the kind of television to which children are being subjected in Britain and America?

Until we reach a total television society in which almost every individual has been a telly baby suckled on the electronic nipple in its earliest years, we will not know what the ultimate consequences of the box will be on any society. It is predictable that for the next twenty years or so, when the first telly generation will be middle-aged, there will be a continual rise in the kind of attitudes and behaviour patterns television hopes to encourage and stimulate. It might well be that, barring some new revolutionary media technology, a plateau of violence, authority rejection, social irresponsibility, narcotic escapism, will be reached which society can accept as normal and tolerable. It will certainly be more violent, paranoid and disordered than the way life was organized before the middle 1950s, but other living conditions may provide compensations for such a mode of existence. It may be a price society is willing to pay for the benefits of entertainment-oriented, free enterprise television.

For those who do not view such a prospect with equanimity, who believe that the cost of escapist television is becoming too

322

expensive in social terms, there are only two alternative solutions. Either society must try to discourage addiction to the box or television must take a different direction. Since it is unlikely that any British or American government would contemplate subjecting viewers to some sort of mass aversion therapy in an effort to break the telly habit — indeed indications are that most governments plan more television for its people rather than less — the only course left is a shift towards more responsible and more socially aware television.

The mere suggestion that television should have some positive part to play in the deliberate cultivation of social and moral standards causes some politicians, academics and intellectuals to raise their hands in horror at the prospect of state control or censorship. They cling hard to the illusion that the kind of television we have in America and Britain is the result of the free play of individual freedom and communal preferences. It is, of course, nothing of the kind. The kind of television that dominates American screens, and to a lesser extent British ones, has been dictated by the demands and pressures of commercial interests whose one interest in the medium is to tempt the largest number of potential viewers to see their goods advertised. It is their tastes and their influence that indirectly determines the output of most television organisations as surely as if there were some sort of governmental committee laying down specific broadcasting criteria. It is not a question of a choice between free television and regulated television. It is a question of who should have the job of regulating it — commercial interests or the national interest. What is good for General Motors and Unilever is not necessarily good for society.

'The real question seems to be: Who makes the decisions, to distribute or to ban?' wrote Professor Raymond Williams, discussing the question of the content of media. 'On what grounds are these made or publicly justified? It may be very difficult to find the best possible system, either in institutions or in values, but, as Carlyle said, "If you ask which is the worst, I answer, this which we now have, that chaos should sit umpire in it; this is the worst." For we have evidently not made up our minds between the competing cries, "freedom to publish", "duty to be responsible", "what's wanted should be provided", "perversion or confusion of our values". Until we are clear about this, and have some real principles and procedures, which we are prepared to recognise over the whole field, the chaos, and any possible damage, will continue.'[13]

As far as television is concerned are we not in America in a position, and approaching it in Britain, where 'chaos does sit umpire' in the medium. And is not that the worst? When Reith ran British broadcasting there were no outraged cries that the medium was in the grip of some vicious form of censorship or state control. On the contrary, British radio was hailed throughout the 1920s and 1930s as the 'best' in the world — and with far fewer reservations than when British television is described as 'the least worst television in the world'. Reithian broadcasting by contemporary standards appears to be too worthy, too dedicated, too restrictive. But it was sustained by an unfettered conviction that broadcasting was inevitably a moral, spiritual, ethical and cultural force in the land. Commercial television, and the BBC that has largely adopted the same creed in the late 1960s, has no such conviction and consciously seeks to avoid any responsibility for guiding or leading society. Unfortunately, by the very act of denying a moral centre or purpose in its activities, it persuades a lot of people, particularly the young, that society itself has no moral centre or purpose. When television escapes from social commitment, it teaches its children that there is no such thing as moral commitment or that it is not worth having. It becomes the Pied Piper leading society nowhere and away from somewhere.

What hope is there that in America or Britain the technological resources of the electronic media can ever be used to reflect and disseminate a more worthwhile and truer interpretation of social values and aspirations than the hollow and distorted picture that it now presents? Some optimists see in pay TV, cable TV, cassettes and other technological developments a way of giving the people something better to watch and thus weaning them from the trivia offered most of the time by the broadcasting organisations. But economically such a widening of choice by the cheap availability of visual cassettes is many decades away. Pay TV and cable TV, as we have seen in most of the early forays into this field, are more likely eventually to cater to the taste being cultivated by popular TV than to try seriously to achieve economic viability by producing something more demanding to be relished by minorities. At best, if they do survive, it will still be only the minority that benefits or is enlightened by its services. The vast majority will still prefer what they can get free during peak-time hours.

In America one sees no real recognition by the power structure or the political hierarchy that television in its present form needs any changing. Theoretically there is available a Federal body — the Federal Communications Commission — that could by edicts or decrees insist upon a more responsible form of broadcasting. But the American conviction that ultimate reliance on the profit motive can never have morally deleterious results and a constitutional tradition that constraints on freedom of speech are evil, makes the Commission's task of setting standards an almost impossible one.

Although there are literally hundreds of TV stations in America recognised by responsible citizens as falling well short of providing even the barest form of public service, the chances of their losing their licences are practically nil. Although TV stations can be bullied or intimidated by politicians into keeping clear of involved or controversial programming, there seems no way in which they can be persuaded or urged to put on better programmes. The excuse that serious programmes would harm their profits is always accepted as incontrovertible, ethical justification for not transmitting them.

Although numerous Senate investigations have urged the networks to make some response to the build-up of evidence that their programmes contribute to violence in America, they have continued to raise stone-walling arguments against the evidence and made only the most minimal adjustments in their fare. After the almost overwhelming findings of the Surgeon General's report in 1972 revealing a conclusive causal connection between television and aggressive behaviour amongst both normal and abnormal American children, industry spokesmen promised the Pastore Senate Committee that they would make adjustments in their schedules in the light of these latest findings.

'It soon became obvious that the days when an industry spokesman could argue before a Congressional committee that the impact of televised violence isn't really known are over,' said *Variety* on March 29th, 1972, reporting the agreement of TV executives to tone down their density of violent programming. Yet the very next week, *Variety* reporting the release of next season's network autumn schedules under the headline 'Plenty Action, Despite Pastore' had this to say: 'Percentage-wise, the schedules work out to 98 per cent entertainment and the remainder topical. Balance? Of the surprises, perhaps the biggest is that the violence hearings conducted by Sen. John O. Pastore did not result in any substantial cutback of violence-prone shows, although it is to be supposed that the networks will urge producers to mute the mayhem and eliminate violence for its own sake.'

As for the Public Broadcasting Service, which with the aid of federal funds was to provide some more mature and responsible broadcasting on non-commercial channels, it has not only failed to woo any substantial number of viewers to its programmes but has also been subjected to Governmental pressure from the Nixon Administration to keep out of news and public affairs. 'A public television system that is prohibited from examining the people's concern by law, or administrative edict, or plain cowardice, is a system without brains or heart,' said Elie Abel, Dean of Columbia University's graduate school of journalism, complaining about this effort by the White House's Office of Telecommunications Policy to neutralise and castrate the significance of public-service broadcasting.

But like the BBC-2 in Britain, this kind of minority ghetto channel will matter little in shaping the nation's morals and values which will still be imbibed from the frivolous and escapist output of the major channels. It seems that in the foreseeable future nothing much can be done to shift the American television system from its present reliance on commercial criteria as the basis for its broadcasting philosophy.

The random and ramshackle philosophical foundations of American television were well described by Charles Reich. 'Technology gives us television,' he said, 'and the imperative of technology, unguided by other values, insists that we produce it and use it without attempting to consider what it should and should not be used for, what harm it might do, what controls are essential to its use. When private manipulation is added to the equation, it produces programmes expressly designed to win huge audiences so that mass-produced products can be sold, even if this means a degradation of popular taste and consciousness. It is the worst of all possible worlds: uncontrolled technology and uncontrolled profiteering, combined into a force that is both immensely powerful and utterly irresponsible.'[14]

In view of the intractable and immovable nature of America's entertainment-oriented television system, one tends to sympathise with the 'Final Solution' suggested by the American journalist, Charles Sopkin. He had locked himself into his New York flat with five TV sets during the week of April 22nd, 1967 and watched for an entire week the comprehensive output of American TV from 7 a.m. to 3 a.m. the next morning every day. Twenty hours a day he did nothing but watch television. He recorded his marathon, mind-boggling experience in a book called *Seven Glorious Days, Seven Fun-Filled Nights*. His conclusions? 'Well, what can one say? That the networks are trying? They obviously aren't ... I naïvely expected that the ratio would run three to one in favour of trash. It turned out to be closer to a hundred to one ... I will freely confess that, immediately after my week-long ordeal, I thought that the only way to solve TV's problems was, literally, murder — i.e. send in squads of machine-gunners and summarily execute every executive at every network and start from scratch.'[15]

In Britain, fortunately, there is still some hope that present trends can be reversed. Not only has the tradition of Reithian broadcasting sunk some deep roots in the national consciousness but there is a growing uneasiness amongst articulate minorities and a few politicians about the path that British television has been taking. The volume of this concern was amply demonstrated when protests at the prospect of the commercial network being handed another channel caused the Government in 1972 to postpone a decision which many of the TV entrepreneurs thought was in the bag. Since the licence tenure of both the BBC and ITV runs out in 1979 there is an opportunity to wipe the slate clean and examine fresh ideas about the structure of British broadcasting. But since tradition and vested interests usually conspire against radical changes in important institutions on the British scene, it is not likely that in 1979 there will be any drastic upheaval in television's shape of things.

There is, however, one concrete national asset — the fourth channel — which must be handed out. The uses to which it should be put afford an opportunity for a great debate not only on who should be given this asset but also on the overall question of whether television has been serving the national interest as effectively as it might. The two major post-war investigations into British broadcasting — Beveridge in 1949 and Pilkington in 1960 — could only speculate in a vague philosophical way about the impact of television on society. Their views that it was an important socialising factor were instinctive and unprovable. And because they believed that the medium had some significant power for good or ill, both committees viewed commercial broadcasting with a wary eye. Beveridge recommended that there should be no commercial television; Pilkington wanted to revise the structure so that commercial interests would have much less influence on broadcasting policy. Governments of the day paid no attention to their suspicions about commercial television and strengthened rather than weakened its power to affect the quality of total output.

The Labour Government in 1974 set up another broadcasting committee under Lord Annan to examine the social and technological problems of the medium. Judging from the past, particularly since the Conservatives have declared no interest in the finding of such a committee, its labours may eventually turn out to be as abortive as those of Beveridge and Pilkington. It is just possible that public opinion, slightly more concerned about television than it used to be, may force the Government of the day to pay more heed to such a committee's proposals.

Any governmental enquiry with an eye to the future will have to consider what effect commercial television has had on the public service ethos of the BBC. It will also have to consider whether the drift of British broadcasting away from an educative and informative function towards popular entertainment has been harmful or beneficial. They will have on hand to help make that judgment the first telly generation. If, as people like Dr. Bronfenbrenner and others contend, commercial television with its emphasis on crass, superficial and violent values is helping to produce a deterioration in the moral and ethical attitudes of those exposed to it when young, then such an enquiry will have to face the choice of denying such effects are taking place or doing something about changing the nature of British television.

If it is decided that British television should become more responsible and should be more conscious of the national interest, it will have to curtail to some extent its entertainment bias. This cannot be done by insisting that, for example, the fourth channel become the equivalent of BBC-2. That would merely further fragment minority viewing. It must be recognised that so long as any single channel is permitted to concentrate almost exclusively at peak time on undemanding programming, it will attract to it the vast majority of viewers. Any effort to raise the over-all quality of what most people see can only succeed if all channels operate under the same sort of rules and regulations about the content of their programmes. For example, if it were thought that the nation would be better served if peak-time programming gave only 65 per cent of its hours to light entertainment and sport while the remaining 35 per cent went to other things — as Pilkington suggested — then all channels would have to operate under such restrictions if the country were going to reap any benefit out of such a formula.

If the commercial interests complained that such a diet of serious programming at peak-time would seriously affect their economic viability then the Government would have to make some other financial concession to ensure them a reasonable profit. But the question of how to pay for television should never have a higher priority in any government's mind than what to do with television. To date, British governments have tended to give the financial considerations of running television too much weight and the social considerations too little. The health of the nation should always be of more concern than the health of the telly companies.

Just as the BBC was under Left-wing pressure during Labour's period of office so it was under Right-wing sniping when the Conservatives were returned to power in 1970. Its attempts to cover the Ulster situation and an unsatisfactory series on the British Empire resulted in a spate of accusations about socially disruptive elements in the Corporation deliberately setting out to belittle the national heritage and undermine the status quo. Its Right-wing opponents were howling for its blood and suggesting either rigorous state control of the BBC or a disestablishment process which would break up the organisation into smaller units and thereby deprive it of its stature as the electronic voice of the nation.

The astonishing aspect of this constant abuse of the BBC was that it was taking place when the Corporation was being far less adventurous, more compromising, less controversial, more escapist, less involved than it ever was under the liberal and controversial regime of the Director General, Sir Hugh Greene in the period between 1960–69. While on the one hand it was being attacked for disrupting traditional values, on the other it was being abused for having surrendered itself to the ratings race and for being as frivolous and uncommitted as its commercial rival. Outside its walls, the BBC was being criticised for irresponsibility over serious matters; inside its walls, sections of its staff were publishing pamphlets attacking it for selling out its ideals and bowing too easily to political pressure. To all these criticisms, the BBC was staunchly maintaining that since the country was deeply divided, it was doing its job by reflecting those divisions. The truth was that BBC television was hardly reflecting the fragmentations in society at all since it was devoting most of its time to producing popular fare and sport. Having largely abandoned the public-service tradition which under Reith had given it such strength, it could rally few supporters to its cause. Since it confessed to be much the same as commercial television, providing the same service and the same philosophy, there was no compelling reason why the state should grant it any special privileges or status. If the BBC was ready to become just a larger commercial channel, why should it be given the right simply to be larger than its rivals? A determined effort to be different from the commercial channel, with public-service being its main concern rather than entertainment, would be the only justifiable basis for treating the BBC as something unique and special.

Growing complaints about television obviously reflected the recognition of its power in the land. Inevitably those who complained felt that the broadcasting organisations were too secretive and too cavalier in their treatment of criticisms. Should there not be some court of appeal to which an aggrieved person could go if dissatisfied with the way in which the BBC or the

IBA had handled his grievance? There was much agitation for the setting up of a Broadcasting Council which would independently judge such criticisms. But the broadcasting authorities saw in such a council a threat of censorship and political control.

But what was evident was that few of the ideas about what should happen to television in the future dealt with the fundamental, disturbing question of the medium's very existence. What was the mere act of watching on this scale doing to society? And how could the medium best be used to further the national interest — if anyone knew what the national interest was? When the BBC had total monopoly of the air waves, it was possible for someone like Reith to reconcile everything the Corporation was doing as being involved with the public interest. The public interest came first and viewers second. When, however, the BBC had to consider its competitive position *vis-à-vis* the commercial channel, its priorities were changed. First came the BBC, next came the viewer, and third came the public interest. What the BBC was mainly doing was reacting to the IBA in the struggle for viewers. If, to maintain superiority in that struggle, the public interest had to be neglected that was just too bad. This did not mean that the BBC deliberately produced programmes *against* the public weal; it just did not produce many programmes *for* the public weal. With each broadcasting organisation primarily concerned with its own profits, prestige and popularity, there was no body in the land charged with judging the over-all performance of British television and with assessing whether or not the total mosaic was advancing the goals of British society. It is in this capacity, as a protector of the public interest rather than as a complaints tribunal, that I think a National Broadcasting Council would make a significant contribution to the raising of television standards in Britain.

Some of the duties such a Council could perform would be:

(a) The laying down of regulations about content balance that every channel would have to abide by, particularly during peak-time hours.

(b) The means by which more access to television could be

given to groups and interests that now have practically none. The mere act of insisting on a reduction in the volume of entertainment programmes would automatically free the air for wider participation in the medium.

(c) The question of how much advertising revenue should be permitted to flow into the medium if other media like newspapers are threatened by such a diversion of advertising money. The argument that the press should not be given any special protection and that papers that cannot survive the heat of the competition with television should be allowed to die is, of course, a specious one. Commercial television and newspapers do not compete on equal terms. The state has ensured that all the odds are staked in favour of commercial TV. Not only has the IBA a monopoly position which permits no other rivals to be set up against it — unlike newspapers which have to face fierce competition constantly — but the commercial companies are guaranteed a fair return on their capital outlay by the state and need never fear bankruptcy. Indeed, any time they get into a financial jam — as they did in 1970 — they can count on the State bailing them out, filling their coffers for them and putting them back in profitable business. Newspapers have no such fairy godmother waving a state wand over them whenever they face financial disaster.

(d) The hearing of complaints as a final court of appeal.

(e) Investigating the over-all question of hours, the volume of television, and whether or not it would be in the national interest to try and break the public addiction to it. Perhaps an occasional holiday on the box would do not harm. In Hungary there is no television at all on Mondays, except for special events. Would there be any merit in a TV moratorium from time to time that encouraged viewers to find something else to do — read, talk to their children, visit friends, go to a pub or the cinema, take a walk, play games, experience a bit of life away from the mesmeric glare of the ravenous eye?

(f) The study of technological developments such as cassettes, cable TV, pay TV.

(g) The commissioning of research on the influence of television on such matters as violence, anti-authority attitudes, family relations, drug taking, gambling.

(h) The encouragement of the study of television in schools and the setting up of courses on the significance of broadcasting, other media and communications in general.

(i) The organisation of training schools for students setting out to make television a career.[16]

Such a Broadcasting Council would, of course, have to be guaranteed independence from political control. And it would need strong enough teeth to make its ruling effective. Sitting as a custodian of the national interest over four separate TV authorities (three if it is decided the BBC should not be split up), it would be able to replace the dictates of commercialism and the censorship potential of 'giving the public what it wants' with a more civilised and mature supervision of the medium's power and potential. With this kind of enlightened regulation of television, the viewer might discover in the boundless cornucopia of this wondrous medium, riches, joy, excitement, beauty and stimulation that have hitherto been denied him.

Above all, we might be able to recognise television as a positive force in the cultural and communal socialisation of children rather than merely a negative or neutral force. To Plato's question, posed 2,000 years before television, we would have a sure and unequivocal reply.

'And shall we just carelessly allow children to hear any casual tales which may be devised by casual persons,' he asked, 'and to receive into their minds ideas for the most part the very opposite of those which we should wish them to have when they are grown up?'

We would be able to say no.

Notes

Chapter One

1. William A. Belson, Address to Royal Society of Arts, August 22nd, 1968.
2. *Spectator*, October 25th, 1968.

Chapter Two

1. James Halloran (ed.) *The Effects of Television* (London 1970), p. 12.
2. *Report of the Pilkington Committee on Broadcasting, 1960* (H.M. Stationery Office, London 1962), p. 15.
3. Arnold Arnold, *Violence And Your Child* (Chicago 1969), p. 129.
4. *Planning For Leisure* (H.M. Stationery Office, London 1969).
5. *Evening Standard*, October 25th, 1968.
6. Quoted in Arnold, op. cit., pp. 111–12.
7. Jonathan Miller, *McLuhan* (London 1971).
8. Joan Bakewell and Nicholas Garnham, *The New Priesthood* (London 1970), p. 131.
9. *Late Night Line-Up*, BBC-2, April 21st, 1971.
10. J. D. Halloran, R. L. Brown and D. C. Chaney, *Television and Delinquency* (Leicester 1970), p. 67.
11. William A. Belson, *The Impact of Television* (London 1967), p. 212.
12. Quoted by Halloran, Brown, Chaney, op. cit., p. 43.
13. Arnold, op. cit., p. 31.
14. Halloran, Brown, Chaney, op. cit., p. 120.
15. Bradley S. Greenberg, *Mass Media Behaviour and Attitudes of the Urban Poor:* Testimony to President's Commission on Violence, 1968.
16. Arnold, *op. cit.*, p. 114.
17. J. G. Blumler and D. McQuail, *Television in Politics* (London 1968), pp. 43–4.
18. Herbert Marcuse, *One Dimensional Man* (London 1968), p. 24.
19. Ibid., pp. 192–3.

335

Chapter Three

1. Halloran, Brown, Chaney, op. cit., p. 67.

Chapter Four

1. Robert MacNeil, *The People Machine* (London 1970), p. 147.
2. Quoted by MacNeil, ibid., p. 149.
3. *Daily Mail*, December 2nd, 1963.
4. Kurt and Gladys Engel Lang, *Politics and Television* (Chicago 1968).
5. MacNeil, op. cit. p. 296.
6. Ibid., p. 309.
7. *Variety*, February 4th, 1970.
8. *Newsweek*, November 24th, 1969.
9. *Sunday Times*, April 5th, 1970.
10. MacNeil, op. cit., p. 307.
11. K. Lang and G. Lang, op. cit., pp. 306–7.
12. *Observer,* July 5th, 1970.
13. David Butler and Michael Pinto-Duschinsky, *The British General Election of 1970* (London 1971), p. xiv.
14. *New Society,* June 6th, 1968.
15. Butler and Pinto-Duschinsky, op. cit., p. xiv.
16. Harold Wilson, *The Labour Government, 1964–1970* (London 1971), pp. 463–6.
17. *The Times*, June 1st, 1970.
18. Chris Welles, 'The Sociology of Dumb', *Esquire*, May 1971.
19. *Evening Standard*, January 6th, 1968.
20. Vance Packard, *The Hidden Persuaders* (London 1962), p. 164.
21. Joe McGinniss, *The Selling of the President* (London 1970).
22. Ibid., p. 188.
23. Ibid., p. 103.
24. Ibid., pp. 137–8.
25. *Sunday Express*, August 8th, 1971.
26. *Newsweek*, October 19th, 1970.
27. *TV Guide*, October 22nd, 1966.
28. See Robert MacNeil, op. cit., pp. 194–6 for similar views.
29. Butler and Pinto-Duschinsky, op. cit., p. 211.
30. Ibid., p. 229.
31. *Guardian*, March 8th, 1971.
32. *Guardian*, July 15th, 1971.
33. *Guardian,* June 19th, 1971.
34. *The Times*, June 19th, 1971.

Chapter Five

1. *The Times*, October 26th, 1968.
2. *Sunday Mirror*, September 5th, 1971.
3. *Sunday Express*, April 4th, 1965.
4. John Eppstein, *Has The Catholic Church Gone Mad?* (London 1971), p. 79.
5. Independent Television Authority, *Religion in Britain and Northern Ireland* (London 1970), p. 13.
6. Duncan Williams, *Trousered Apes* (London 1971), p. 38.
7. *Religion in Britain and Northern Ireland*, op. cit., p. 50.
8. *The Times*, June 23rd, 1969.
9. *New Statesman*, May 28th, 1971.
10. Interview with Ian Waller, *Sunday Telegraph*, May 30th, 1971.
11. *The Times*, July 18th, 1968.
12. *News of the World*, November 16th, 1969.

Chapter Six

1. Quoted by Arnold, op. cit., p. 124.
2. Personal interview, January 1969.
3. Personal interview, January 1969.
4. Personal interviews with Reuven Frank and Richard Salant, January 1969.
5. *Sunday Times*, September 8th, 1968.
6. Television Research Committee, *Second Progress Report and Recommendations* (Leicester 1969), p. 38.
7. Arnold, op. cit., pp. 130–31.
8. Ibid., p. 130.
9. Eda J. Leshan, *The Conspiracy Against Childhood* (New York 1967), p. 284.
10. *The Times*, October 19th, 1971.
11. Arnold, op. cit., p. 131.
12. Raymond Williams, *Communications* (London 1968), p. 104.
13. Ramsey Clark, *Crime in America* (London 1971), p. 45.
14. *Report of the Committee on Broadcasting* (Ottawa 1965), p. 23.
15. *Sunday Times*, November 7th, 1971.
16. Halloran, Brown, Chaney, op. cit., p. 171.
17. Ibid., p. 124.
18. *ITV 1970* (London 1970), pp. 22–3.
19. *The Times*, April 23rd 1968.
20. G. M. Trevelyan, *History of England* (London 1926), p. 273.
21. *Variety*, June 2nd, 1971.

22. Alistair Cooke, summary of the Report, *Guardian*, November 25th, 1969.
23. *Daily Mail*, December 18th, 1969.
24. *Daily Mail*, August 25th, 1971.
25. *Daily Mail*, February 6th, 1970.
26. *Daily Express*, March 15th, 1971.
27. *Daily Mail*, June 23rd, 1971.
28. Quoted by Denis McQuail, *Towards a Sociology of Mass Communications* (London 1969), p. 46.
29. Halloran, Brown, Chaney, op. cit., p. 58.
30. Quoted by McQuail, op. cit., p. 50.
31. Halloran, Brown, Chaney, op. cit., p. 67.
32. Quoted by Pamela Hansford Johnson, *Encounter*, February 1970.
33. Quoted by Arnold, op. cit., p. 121.
34. Hilde T. Himmelweit, A. M. Oppenheim, Pamela Vince, *Television and the Child* (London 1958), p. 56.
35. Arnold, op. cit., pp. 116–17.
36. Fredric Wertham in O. N. Larsen (ed.), *Violence and the Mass Media* (New York 1968), p. 39.
37. Halloran, Brown, Chaney, op. cit., pp. 51–2.
38. Quoted by R. Williams, op. cit., pp. 106–7.
39. *Sunday Times*, June 9th, 1968.
40. Halloran, Brown, Chaney, op. cit., p. 170.
41. *Newsweek*, March 6th, 1972.
42. *Variety*, March 29th, 1972.
43. Clark, op. cit., p. 45ff.
44. *FBI Crime Report, 1969* (U.S. Government Printing Office, Washington 1970) p. 32.
45. Clark, op. cit., p. 54.
46. Ibid., p. 17.
47. *The Times*, April 25th, 1968.

Chapter Seven

1. D. Williams, op. cit., p. 110ff.
2. Theodore Roszak, *The Making of a Counter Culture* (London 1971), p. 2.
3. Richard Neville, *Play Power* (London 1970), pp. 18–19.
4. Charles Reich, *The Greening of America* (London 1970), p. 160.
5. Bakewell and Garnham, op. cit., p. 72.
6. Reich, op. cit., p. 251.
7. Ibid., p. 150.
8. Quoted by Roszak, op. cit., p. 58.
9. Ibid., pp. 60–61.

10. S. M. Lipset and E. C. Ladd Jr., 'College Generations and Their Politics', *New Society*, October 7th, 1971.
11. Roszak, op. cit., pp. 74–5.
12. Neville, op. cit., p. 175.
13. MacNeil, op. cit., p. 78.
14. Neville, op. cit., p. 157.

Chapter Eight

1. *The Non-Medical Use of Drugs*, Interim Report of the Canadian Commission of Inquiry (London 1970), p. 219.
2. Ibid., p. 109.
3. *The Use of Cannabis*, World Health Organisation, Technical Report Series N. 478 (Geneva 1971), p. 11.
4. *Time*, March 16th, 1970.
5. Norman E. Zinberg, *Why Now? Drug Use as a Response to Social and Technological Change*, Address to International Association for Cultural Freedom, Aspen, Colorado, August 29th, 1970.
6. Lewis Yablonsky, *The Hippie Trip* (New York 1968), p. 348.
7. Ibid., p. 120.
8. Ibid., p. 161.
9. Canadian Drug Commission, op. cit., pp. 221, 236.
10. Zinberg, op. cit.
11. Yablonsky, op. cit., p. 319.
12. World Health Organisation, op. cit., pp. 16–21.
13. S. I. Hayakawa, Address to American Psychological Association, San Francisco, September 2nd, 1968.

Chapter Nine

1. Sir John Lawrence, *The Times*, January 31st, 1972.
2. Bakewell and Garnham, op. cit., p. 171.
3. Ibid., p. 173.
4. Ibid., p. 174.
5. *Sunday Times*, January 30th, 1972.
6. *Sunday Times*, February 6th, 1972.
7. *Sunday Times*, January 30th, 1972.
8. *Time*, March 4th, 1972.
9. *Sunday Express*, February 27th, 1972.
10. MacNeil, op. cit., p. 73.
11. *The Times*, October 1st, 1971.
12. *Time*, February 8th, 1971.
13. Barbara Wootton, *The Listener*, July 22nd, 1965.
14. Steiner, op. cit., pp. 32–9.
15. *The Times*, May 8th, 1971.

16. *The Times*, June 26th, 1971.
17. Stafford Beer, *The Listener*, February, 25th, 1971.
18. Stuart Hood, *A Survey of Television* (London 1967), p. 167.

Chapter Ten

1. *The Times*, December 18th, 1971.
2. *Evening Standard*, June 20th, 1967.
3. Terence Kelly *et al.*, *To Guide Not Gag*, Bow Group pamphlet (London 1971), p. 1.
4. Steiner, op. cit., pp. 91–3.
5. Jeremy Tunstall (ed.), *Media Sociology* (London 1970), p. 90.
6. Ibid., p. 104.
7. Quoted by Jeremy Isaacs, 'Television Journalism', *Encounter*, March 1968.
8. *Daily Mail*, February 22nd, 1972.
9. *Daily Telegraph*, February 21st, 1972.
10. *Sunday Telegraph*, March 26th, 1972.

Chapter Eleven

1. *The Listener*, February 22nd, 1968.
2. *Newsweek*, March 20th, 1972.
3. *Variety*, March 4th, 1970.
4. *The Times*, January 27th, 1972.
5. *Daily Telegraph*, March 24th, 1972.
6. *Time*, April 10th, 1972.
7. *Variety*, March 4th, 1970.
8. Roger Howard, 'Chinese Message', *New Society*, November 18th, 1971.
9. Greene, op. cit., pp. 73–6.
10. Urie Bronfenbrenner, *Two Worlds of Childhood* (London 1971), pp. 95–102.
11. Ibid., p. 114.
12. Ibid., p. 116.
13. R. Williams, op. cit., p. 109.
14. Reich, op. cit., p. 81.
15. Charles Sopkin, *Seven Glorious Days, Seven Fun-Filled Nights* (New York 1968).
16. A Broadcasting Council along similar lines was recommended by the Conservative Bow Group in *To Guide Not Gag*, op. cit.

Index

ABC (American Broadcasting Corporation), 175, 206, 215; News, 165

ACTT, see Association of Cinematograph and Allied Technicians.

Abrams, Dr. Mark, 201–3

Adam Smith, 128

advertising periods in various countries, 318

Agnew, Vice-President Spiro, 22, 73–4, 108, 115–16, 239

All in the Family (CBS), 289, 291, 309

America (*see also* United States): research in, 19–20; broadcasters in, 23; impact of TV on living habits, 23; history of TV in, 29–30; viewing hours, 32–3; main purpose of TV in, 37–40; Presidential broadcasts on TV, 51; political effects of TV in, 52–5 *passim*; violence in, before 1960s, and after, 190–92; other explanations of crime in, 214–15

American: attitudes to 'respectable' language, 289–91; broadcasting, attempts to browbeat, 115–16; Broadcasting Corporation, see ABC; children's development dominated by TV, 320; elections in 1970s: TV campaigns, 106–9; political candidates and paid TV commercials, 103–4, 107–8; Presidential access to, and use of, TV, 72–3, 75–6

American Presidential elections: (1956), 103–4; (1960), 107; (1964), 53; (1968), 53, 102–3; (1972), 90–92, 268–69

American: school integration crisis, 77–78; TV practically all commercially run, 315; TV's attitude to sex, 294–5; TV networks attacked by Vice-President Agnew, 22, 73–5, 115–16; TV's 'random and ramshackle philosophical foundations', 326–7

Amery, Julian, 156

Angry Brigade, 235

Arnold, Arnold, 21, 31, 173–4, 200

Association of Cinematograph and Allied Technicians (ACTT), 143

audiences, peak-time (BBC-1 and ITV), size of, 40–41

Australia, 212

authorities, institutional, and TV, 121–60

BBC (British Broadcasting Corporation): Governors of, 22, 119; broadcasters, 24, 39; Third Programme (radio), 24; competing with ITV for audiences, 39–40; policy, 40, 41; and President Kennedy's assassination, 56–8; Harold Wilson on TV, 81–3; satire shows (1967), 84; Richard Crossman, 101; obsession with sport, 111; British general elections: (1966), 116; (1970), 117; harassed by the Left, 117; and by the Right, 117; *Yesterday's Men* and British Labour Party, 118–20; and *Sunday Break*, 126; and trade union movement, 142–3; news bulletins, 143; violence on, 180 (*see also* violence); most popular programmes of, 180–81; children's film competition (1971), 194; its monopoly, and chief purpose (1954–56), 200; Reithian, 199, 207–8, 324, 327, 330; and May uprisings in France (1968), 238; and Ulster, 278; reaction of educated people to, 279–81; and four-letter words, *q.v.*, 285, 290; Eurovision Song Contest, 287, 312; Fiftieth Anniversary, 309; 'under siege', 310; licence expires in 1979, 327; public service, ethos of, 328; and political parties in power, 329; criticism and defence of, 329–30

BBC-1, 40, 180, 280; and World Cup and general election (1970), 111; Church services on Sunday mornings, 127

BBC-2, 40, 280, 326, 329

Baldwin, T. F., 216

Barnes, Clive, 279, 322

Bay of Pigs, 78

Beatles, the, 83

beatniks, 226, 233, 235

341

Belson, Dr. William, 16
Benn, Anthony Wedgwood, 110, 147
Beveridge Commission and Report (1949), 328
Biafra, 166
Blue Peter, 41, 46
Blumler and McQuail study (1964), 35
Bonavia, David, 310
books and reading habits, influence of TV on, 304–7
Bow Group (Conservative) study (1971), 293–4
Brandon, Henry, 75
Brandt, Chancellor Willy, 92
Britain: American and British drama series shown in, 180–81; violence in, during 1960s, 192–215; fear of molestation in, 194; environmental factors in, 215; drug taking in, 244; juvenile anti-social behaviour in, 321–2
British Broadcasting Corporation, *see* BBC
British Election of 1970, The (Butler and Pinto-Duschinsky), 85, 87
British Empire, The, 262, 329
British general elections: (1964), 35; (1966), 116; (1970), 53, 85–7, 96, 110–11
British Prime Minister, Ministers and Opposition: access to TV, 73, 76–7
British TV: chief purpose of, 10, 41; in 1960 and after, 324; still hopes for, 327
broadcasters: excuses for programmes, 21; and research, 23, 215; and the medium, 24–25, 27; American and British, 39; 'without honour ...', 309
broadcasting, Reithian concept of, 22, 199, 207, 324, 327, 330
Brogan, Professor Sir Denis 59–60, 91
Bronfenbrenner, Dr. Urie, 320–22, 328
Brown, George (*now* Lord George-Brown), 55–6, 59–64, 92, 99
Brown, Les, 310, 315
Butler, David, 85, 87

CBS (Columbia Broadcasting System), 75, 161, 166, 175, 215, 240; Reports, 50; and Congress and its Pentagon documentary, 115–16; and Chicago marijuana party, faked (1968), 266; crews on Tawi River, 268
Cambridge (England) hotel riot, 235
Canada: and American programmes, 179; crime in, *see* crime rates; drug taking in, 243–4, 248; environmental factors, 214–15; national elections (1972), 89–90; and 'respectable'

language, 287, 291; TV in, 179–80, 210–15 *passim*, 219; and violence, 180
Canadian Drug Commission Inquiry and Report (1970), 243–4, 249
Casanova, 293, 295
catharsis, as defence of violence on TV, 197–8
Cavett, Dick, 98; Show, 98, 101
Cawston, Richard, 136–40 *passim*
censorship and/or control of TV, 26, 331–3
Charles, Prince (Prince of Wales): Investiture (1969), 134–5; and David Frost on TV, 136, 140
Chicago, 234; conspiracy trial, 240; Democratic Convention (1968) riots, 165
children: age groups, 28–31, 32–3; American, Russian and British compared, 320–22; and TV, 14, 19, 23, 28–32 *passim*, 231–3, 282–4, 319–22, 333; anti-religious attitude of, 131–2; behaviour of, 31; environmental influences on, 27–9, 33–6; late viewers, 41; special programmes for, 41
'Children's Hour', 41
China and Chinese, 260; Red Guard, 222, 224; President Nixon's visit (1972), 268–71; Cultural Revolution, 315–16; TV in, 315–16
Christian Science Monitor: report on violence in TV programmes, 175
Christianity and TV (*see also* Church), 126–33, 126n
Church, the, and TV, 126–33, 126n, 141, 158–9
Churchill, Sir Winston, 51, 53–5, 70, 96, 124
cinema, the: attendances at, 295–6; and sex, 294–7; and violence, 297; copying TV programmes, 298
Clark, Ramsey (former United States Attorney General), 98, 177, 209–10, 213; on causes of crime, 213
Cleveland (Ohio) riots (1967), 265
Cohn-Bendit, Daniel, 227, 238
colour TV, 301
Columbia Broadcasting System, *see* CBS
Columbia University: Bureau of Applied Social Research, 279; Graduate school of journalism, 326
commercial executives: American, 23; British, 23–4
commercials, 213, 238, 315–17, 317–18; environmental norm of, 251, 252
Common Market, the (EEC), 112
Communism, 28, 37, 39, 130

342

343

345

Also by **MILTON SHULMAN**

DEFEAT IN THE WEST

'Not many books written in the heat of action survive into the cool of history but there is one that does. ... The author's sound judgment and narrative style make it still the best and most vivid account of the German collapse'

Professor Hugh Trevor-Roper, *The Sunday Times*

'An absorbing history of the war in the west as it looked to the German army.'

William L. Shirer, author of
The Rise and Fall of the Third Reich

'Of permanent value to historians and of absorbing interest to anyone ... deserves to be a thoroughly popular book.'

The Observer

CORONET BOOKS

NON-FICTION IN CORONET

☐ 18176 1 | **MILTON SHULMAN**
Defeat in the West | 50p

☐ 18995 9 | **NESTA WYN ELLIS**
Dear Elector: The Truth about MPs | 50p

☐ 18770 0 | **PETER GROSVENOR** and
JAMES McMILLAN
The British Genius (illustrated) | 60p

☐ 15089 0 | **ROBIN MOORE**
The French Connection | 35p

☐ 18631 3 | **PETER NORDEN**
Madam Kitty | 50p

☐ 18284 9 | **ANTHONY SAMPSON**
The Sovereign State | 50p

☐ 18833 2 | **LYALL WATSON**
Supernature | 50p

☐ 19682 3 | **CARL SAGAN**
The Cosmic Connection
(Large format, illustrated) | 85p

All these books are available at your local bookshop or newsagent, or can be ordered direct from the publisher. Just tick the titles you want and fill in the form below.

CORONET BOOKS, P.O. Box 11, Falmouth, Cornwall.

Please send cheque or postal order, and allow the following for postage and packing:

UK AND EIRE – 15p for the first book plus 5p per copy for each additional book ordered to a maximum charge of 50p.

OVERSEAS CUSTOMERS AND B.F.P.O. – please allow 20p for the first book and 10p per copy for each additional book.

Name ....

Address ....

....